#42
1st

(1224) 744300

AMERICAN

in the Rough

* * * * *

The Autobiography of
W. M. (BILL) COFFMAN

Simon and Schuster  New York, 1955

FIRST PRINTING

LIBRARY OF CONGRESS CATALOG CARD NUMBER: 55-10058
DEWEY DECIMAL CLASSIFICATION NUMBER: 92
MANUFACTURED IN THE UNITED STATES OF AMERICA
BY H. WOLFF BOOK MFG. CO., INC., NEW YORK

FOREWORD

Dɪᴅ ʏᴏᴜ ᴇᴠᴇʀ dream of running away from home as a kid and riding the rails to the topless towers of New York? Did you ever dream of coming through, miraculously unscathed, such adventures as fights in a Bowery saloon or the ordeal of being shanghaied onto a British sailing ship for a trip around the Horn?

Or what about dreaming yourself into the Barbary Coast when it was barbarous, and into Goldfield and Reno when rough and tumble men would bet on anything, including their lives?

I'm sure you've dreamed all these things, plus associating yourself in slumber with such historic catastrophes as the San Francisco earthquake and fire, and all sorts of great moments in sports.

Well, I have bad news for you.

It wasn't you. You weren't there.

It was Bill Coffman.

Bill has had more lives than the Bengal Lancer. It's a long, long jump from the role of singing waiter in a New York honky-tonk to benefactor of hosts of crippled children. It's a trek of awe-inspiring scope, too, from a cell he shared with murderers to his offices as Park Commissioner of San Francisco and as a top executive in the Underwood Corporation. Bill has made a piker out of Horatio Alger.

I first came across Bill Coffman in the course of an angry research into the question of what happens to the money collected at "bowl" football games. His East-West Shrine Football Game,

ix

which produces about a quarter of a million dollars a year for the Shriners Hospitals for Crippled Children, restored my faith in the institution of post-season football and, indeed, in the heart of man. If there were more Bill Coffmans in sports, we'd have no need of commissions, investigations and cops. I need not confine it to sports. If there were more Bill Coffmans in our world, the same benefits would accrue.

Bill waited a long time to write a book. He must have been tempted to do so many times, especially in later years when there were so many magazine pieces and columns written about him. *American in the Rough* is a full-blooded job that must have been hard to put together. A book is as hard to build as a bridge. But it is typical of my friend Bill Coffman that now the book is here, and a delighted public is buying it, he is turning over all his royalties to the cause for which he lives—the cause of crippled children.

God bless him.

BOB CONSIDINE

* I *

* 1 *

IT WAS midnight of July 10, 1900, when I slipped out of the house and made my way to the near-by freight yards. Keeping a wary eye on brakemen coupling freight cars being shunted back and forth, I watched my chance, climbed into an empty boxcar and slid the door shut behind me.

After long hours of waiting, broken by jarring shocks as groups of cars came crashing together, the long train was finally made up, and after much huffing and puffing by the clumsy engine we were on our way. Where to—I neither knew nor cared.

Using my folded coat for a pillow, I lay on my back and let my thoughts run over the troubled past and the uncertainties of the future. I wondered if this could be the same boy who at thirteen had so blithely run away from home because of a fancied grievance, only to be intercepted and returned safely home by an indulgent father.

No, this was no week-end adventure, but a sober facing of a new kind of world, and I was equipped with only a few bits of silver and the clothes on my back. Leaving the only home open to me, with every prospect of never returning, I realized the differences from that other boy of four short years ago. There would be no father to come and fetch me home, no mother to make my excuses. This time I was on my own.

Bouncing on the hard floor of the swaying freight car, only dimly conscious of the hum of iron wheels on bumpy rails, I realized that each passing mile was taking me farther from the little town of Portsmouth, Virginia, city of my birth—and, yes, from the few people on earth who cared what might become of

3

me. Soon they would awaken to the shock of my desertion. I could only hope they would realize, as I did, that to remain would only add to their already heavy burden.

My thoughts drifted back to a short and not always happy childhood, marked by the loss of a loving mother when I was barely fourteen and my remaining parent two years later.

My father, Robert Andrew Coffman, was a second son, born to the Reverend Andrew Jackson Coffman and Maria Jane Daniels in the Shenandoah Valley of Virginia on January 17, 1855.

The reverend preached his first sermons in Luray, Virginia, and on occasion was one of the clan known in pre-Civil War days as a circuit rider, or traveling parson. His pastorate was a somewhat inaccessible section in the Blue Ridge Mountains, and there he spent most of his life traveling from one farmhouse to another, dispensing religion, officiating at the departure of a loved one or uniting two souls in wedlock, according to the needs of the occasion.

Despite long and frequent absences from home, he managed to accumulate a progeny of eleven children, four boys and seven girls. These were Sarah; Artil, a son; daughters Lola and Lucy; my father, Robert Andrew; three more daughters, Lilly, Annie and Kate; Lindsay, a third son; another daughter, Lena; and a fourth son, Willie, who passed away early.

Unlike the seven sisters, all of whom wandered far afield, the three brothers elected to settle down in Nansemond County, Virginia. Though separated by only a few miles, they led widely dissimilar lives. Artil, the eldest, who was called "Oddie," became an itinerant fisherman, living partly from the bounty of his fish nets, crab traps, and oyster beds and partly by his wits, of which he had a plentiful supply. He probably never had fifty dollars at any one time in his long and humdrum life, but he managed to live more than seventy years, ate and slept well and died happy, though penniless.

Fifteen miles from Uncle Oddie's shack was one of the finest farms in Virginia. It was owned by the youngest brother, Lindsay, and his wife, Nora.

Early in life Lindsay, with a partner, took over a section of good farm land on a sharecropping basis and in a few years was able to buy out his partner. In due time he purchased the original property and continued to add to the acreage and improve his holdings, until by the early nineties he was considered one of the most prosperous farmers in Nansemond County.

Unlike his older brother, Uncle Lindsay was a handsome, distinguished-looking man and the accepted leader in every community effort. A director of Portsmouth's principal bank, he frequently guaranteed the farm loans of his neighbors. He built the Community Church with his own funds, paid one half of the minister's salary and provided his horse and buggy. He was not a particularly religious man, but Nora, his wife, knew the real value of a church foundation in a full and contented life.

While Oddie fished and Lindsay farmed, my father Robert chose a different career. Gravitating to the town of Portsmouth, he served his four-year apprenticeship and became a master machinist in the navy yard where many of the nation's largest naval vessels were built.

At the age of twenty-six he married Ida Florence Bond, a delicate, frail girl just a few months younger than himself. She was quiet, retiring in manner, and, from my earliest recollection until the day of her death when I was fourteen, I do not recall ever hearing her voice raised in anger, no matter what the provocation.

We lived in a rather nice house, old but comfortable, and it was there her seven children were born. The first was Robert Andrew, Junior, nicknamed "Moncey." I came along on June 27, 1883, and, for some reason known only to my mother, was christened William Milo. While I did not exactly repudiate this lush name, I did manage to soft-pedal the use of it in later life.

Next came my first sister, Ella May, who arrived less than three years after me and was followed at regular two-year intervals by Laura Dudley, Williamson Bond, Charles Grantham, and finally Ida Louise. Ella May lived only two years.

This series of seven arrivals within thirteen years had its good and its bad features. Baby carriages, teething rings, toy trains, and knit goods were put back into use progressively, to say nothing of passing along a Buster Brown suit from number-one boy all the way down to number-four boy. Although admittedly tough on boys number two, three, and four, it certainly proved practical in our family, though I may be a bit prejudiced, having been in the number-two spot.

Because my mother was definitely not the robust type, but always patient and uncomplaining, each successive confinement took its toll from her health. Before the last child was born, when she was barely forty, a hacking cough and kindred symtoms left little doubt that her health was slowly failing.

Our household included an Aunt Cyrena inherited from some source whose origin has become obscured over the years. Presumed to have been born in 1816, she was in her middle seventies when I first became conscious of her existence around the house. Instead of being helpful in rearing half a dozen youngsters, she was just an added burden to my mother.

There was also old "Uncle Joe" Gibson, a Negro of doubtful age who clumped around the house on a homemade peg leg. His skin was wrinkled. He had a thick crop of kinky white hair and he looked as old as Methuselah. He owned an old fiddle which he loved to play as often and as long as he was allowed to. Uncle Joe had been a slave before the Civil War. When emancipated, he seemed unable to adjust himself to the life of a free man. He attached himself to Father, did odd jobs around the house, and was treated as a member of the family until the day came when he hung up his old fiddle and passed on.

American in the Rough

I detested school and played hooky at every opportunity, which meant whenever the sun shone brightly and the birds sang in the trees. I developed a violent allergy to study of any kind with one exception. I loved to read, provided the subject and the author were of my own choosing. Every nickel or dime I could raise was invested in the exploits of Nick Carter, Frank Merriwell, Diamond Dick, Old King Brady, and the James boys. These exciting booklets were on the newsstands each week, and it became almost a religion with me never to skip an issue for fear I might miss some exciting episode.

Playing truant from school in those days was not difficult in the easygoing South. I learned to imitate Mother's writing and wrote my own excuses to explain frequent absences from classes. When this practice caught up with me, I stolidly took my lickings and sought other ways to outwit both parents and school authorities.

Once, after drawing a month's suspension, I intercepted the school principal's notice mailed to my home. Then I continued to leave early each morning, books and lunch in hand, spent the day at my hideaway and nonchalantly returned home each afternoon at the usual hour. Each night I pretended to study diligently and, when finally caught, kept the usual rendezvous with Father in the woodshed.

During the numerous absences from school, my hide-out was an old abandoned tabernacle. With several delinquents of my own age, we rigged up the trappings of an indoor circus in the barnlike building and risked our necks balancing on horizontal bars and swinging precariously from the rafters, like the man on the flying trapeze.

High up in the rafters, reached only by a ladder of cleats nailed to the wall, we built a small room from parts of packing cases. In this room we indulged in our social activities, mostly reading the latest dime novels hot from the newsstands while munching crackers and other delicacies procured from the corner grocery and charged against the family account unbeknown to my mother.

Not that I did not pay dearly for these special privileges when found out. Besides numerous scoldings and whippings, the penalty included failure to pass school examinations, which meant starting the new term with boys much younger than I. This may have hurt my pride but not enough to cause a change in my habits.

My three brothers were well aware of my many falls from grace but they were not influenced by the bad example I set, which was fortunate, because my worried parents had enough trouble trying to keep me on a fairly straight and narrow path. Some of the townsfolk were apt to refer to me as merely mischievous; others flatly predicted that "the Coffman boy was born to be hanged."

My harassed parents always looked forward with relief to the long summer vacations which my brother and I divided equally between Uncle Oddie's ramshackle place on Pig Point and Uncle Lindsay's fine farm at Hodges Ferry.

Life at Hodges Ferry had all of the grandeur of the Old South. Here was the fine house, always crowded with interesting and exciting guests from faraway places like Baltimore and Atlanta. Here were horses to ride and colored children to order around, and here also were the long wharves and the sloops piled high with watermelons and cantaloupes. And best of all was the swimming and rowing, the riding and feasting and lazing in hammocks swung between great shade trees.

Of course, it was not all play and no work, but even so, the few hours' work each day was both pleasant and profitable. Shortly after daylight hundreds of colored farmhands, including little fellows barely able to walk, would spread themselves over acres of strawberry beds still wet with dew, filling quart-size baskets with luscious berries. Stationed at a central point under a canvas awning, it was my duty to redeem these baskets by handing out tickets valued at two cents each. Other attendants nailed the baskets into crates, which in turn were hauled down to the wharf in time to reach the markets twenty-four hours later. Hampers of peas and string beans were likewise picked and turned in for tickets valued at eight and ten cents each. When tickets were redeemed on Saturday night, some of the Negroes cashed in hundreds, while others were empty-handed and must stretch their credit until Monday's harvest provided the wherewithal to start another crap game. For my services Uncle Lindsay gave me two dollars each week, which added up to a nice sum to spend on my return to town.

Independence Day was always the occasion for a big patriotic celebration. The crack Virginia Grays and the Portsmouth Rifles polished their buckles and swords, shouldered their muskets and proudly paraded down High Street. The great day always wound up with an awe-inspiring display of fireworks.

Just after celebrating my thirteenth birthday, the folks insisted that my brother and I go to the Hodges Ferry farm to remain through July. I wanted to remain in town until the Independence Day celebration was over, but was overruled by Father.

I asked permission to drive into town with Uncle Lindsay, but was refused. After dark I stowed away on one of his schooners due in Norfolk the next day. When I was missed next morning, there was a lot of excitement and several Negroes were put to work dragging the river for the body. Uncle Lindsay drove into town to report my disappearance. I remained in Norfolk until dusk, then took the ferry across the river to Portsmouth to see the fireworks display, being careful to keep out of sight in case my brothers and sisters chanced to be around.

At midnight, just as the last rockets were shrieking into the heavens, I noticed a large pile of furniture in front of a second-hand store. Consumed with the patriotic fervor of the moment,

9

I was weak enough to touch a match to the canvas cover. The pile burst into flames, and soon the horse-drawn fire engines came plunging to the rescue, but too late to allow any salvage, while a badly frightened boy hurried home to sob out his story.

My distracted parents were undecided whether to rejoice over the repentant sinner or to weep over his dubious future. After sleeping on the dilemma, Father settled with the merchant and that night marched me to the police station. There, Father and the judge decided upon an experiment intended to shock me into mending my ways. They placed me in a jail cell next to an old fellow serving time for vagrancy. The idea was to impress upon me, a youngster of thirteen, what a terrible thing it was to be put in jail. After a while I was just beginning to feel sorry for the old fellow when he bestirred himself, walked over to a shelf and fished out two hen's eggs. These he broke into a tin drinking cup and held it over the gas jet, frying the eggs, which he proceeded to eat with gusto, remarking casually about necessity being the mother of invention.

When Father and the judge returned expecting to find me pale and shivering from the horror of a prison cell, I forgot why I had been left there and launched into a graphic description of a man cooking eggs in his humble prison cell. It was plain that the intended lesson had been entirely lost on the culprit. Father escorted me home and direct to the woodshed, where he whaled the living daylights out of me.

* 2 *

THE WHIPPING had come so long after my crime that I never forgot it and spent many hours in my hideaway high in the rafters of the old tabernacle building, brooding over my alleged persecution. I decided to end it by running away from home.

As a companion to share my new plans I selected a local

boy who, like myself, was "always being picked on at home." Harry was a year older and much larger than I but he lacked initiative. He also lacked funds. I had saved nearly fifteen dollars for just such an emergency.

For some time I had been intrigued by a fancy pearl-handled revolver and a keen-edged stiletto on display in a pawnbroker's window, but, being small for my thirteen years, I had hesitated about trying to negotiate a deal.

Harry had no difficulty in purchasing the articles for six dollars. I gave him the knife and retained the gun.

Three nights after the bonfire episode, we crept into the "blind baggage" of a departing passenger train, just behind the coal-burning engine. We huddled above the couplings partially hidden from sight. It was a local train and at every stop we would shrink back into the darkness. Red-hot cinders cascaded on us. Our faces became black and scorched from soot and smoke.

At times we went quite fast when going down hill but when climbing even a slight grade we just poked along, losing all track of time.

When signs of daylight appeared, we hopped off, thinking it best to keep out of sight until dark. We felt sure we must be hundreds of miles from home. When we passed a man who appeared to be mildly interested in our movements, I inquired the way to the town hotel. The man said he was going that way and we might follow him.

Soon we came upon a small squat building with bars on the windows. Our guide took out an ominous-looking bunch of keys, fitted one in the lock and a moment later I was in the "hoosegow" for the second time in a week.

We looked so young and innocent that he neglected to search us, so immediately after we were left alone, I detached the arsenal from my person. Cutting a hole in the bottom of the mattress, I stuffed the weapons inside, almost weeping in my disappointment. Harry took it stolidly. He wanted to go home and didn't care what happened to our hard-got armament.

Our cell window was just above street level, so it was not long before the village boys discovered that the town jail held a couple of new exhibits and we became the center of much curiosity. We also learned we were in the town of Suffolk, only thirty miles from the home we thought we had left far behind in our dark and bitter past.

Later, before the justice of the peace, I refused to talk, but Harry, badly frightened, broke down and told our story. The sheriff, one Mat Kilby, turned out to be a distant relative of my father. Our parents were notified and Harry was placed on a train for home. Father requested that I be held until he could come for me Saturday night.

The sheriff took me to his own home and locked me in a spare bedroom until Father arrived.

As the folks had not seen each other for some time, the gathering at the home of the sheriff became a gala affair. They even trotted me out and gave me a place at the table. To my surprise, not one word was said concerning my escapade.

There would be no more whippings. I felt rather foolish and, for a time at least, became less of a problem to my parents. I even discovered that I had a conscience, attended school regularly and managed to pass my examinations, though I was still far behind other boys of my age.

At summer vacation time, however, Uncle Lindsay let it be known that he was skeptical of my reformation, so I was shipped to Uncle Oddie at Pig Point, where I ran into more trouble, though not of my own making.

One afternoon after disposing of my last bunch of fish while old Pansy jogged along dreaming of the oat bin, a Negro stepped out of the woods and grabbed the bridle. After robbing me of the day's receipts the highwayman disappeared in the deep woods. Although terrified by the experience I turned Pansy around, drove back to Huntersville and reported the robbery to the town constable.

Before nightfall the man was in custody, and two days later had been sentenced to six months in jail. The justice advised Uncle Oddie to send me home for fear the Negroes might harm me out of revenge. I had no such fear of the Negroes, many of them friends and customers, but the justice insisted, so back to Portsmouth I went.

At home I found Mother ill in bed. Her lungs were deeply congested and it was plain that the end was near. She continued to fade each day until there seemed to be little left except her thin, lovely face set in a halo of thick brown hair. When the end came, she roused herself enough to take one long look at her six children surrounding the bed, closed her eyes in a tired way and sank back against her pillows. She had taken leave of us with as little trouble as she had given anyone during her short life on earth.

For all the loving care and comfort she had given to her little world, she had received scant pay. In forty-two years she had burned herself out, asking nothing in return. That was September 4, 1897, a date which marked the deterioration of a grief-stricken father and the half-orphaned family whose only real tie had been that self-effacing mother.

Mother's sister, my Aunt Lina Gaskins, undertook to hold the family together. A colored woman was hired as cook and housekeeper, sleeping in the house overnight, and under this arrangement we managed after a fashion. Work in the navy yard was curtailed, Father was laid off and remained unemployed for many months. Then, when it seemed that we were scraping the very bottom of the barrel and facing really hard times, our humdrum way of life was interrupted.

On May 15, 1898, the battleship *Maine* was sunk and America was at war. Father was called back to work, and we were able to pay off some of our accumulated debts. For a while Portsmouth and Norfolk became beehives of war activity. Thousands of troops from the Deep South detrained in Portsmouth, were poured aboard transports bound for Cuba. Then, as suddenly as it had begun, the shooting was over and the streets were filled with troops heading for home.

By midsummer the navy yard had completed its wartime chores and once again Father, with thousands of others, was laid off. As a machinist, first-class, his wage was $3.04 a day. On this he had managed to support a family of eight in comparative comfort. Now, after months of unemployment, we found ourselves in straitened circumstances.

I had managed to attain another grade in grammar school. However, despite my sixteen years, I was only in the seventh grade. I never got any farther. I found myself a job in the local knitting mill sorting cotton. The wage was seventy-five cents a day. Later I learned to operate a set of spindles where the raw cotton was converted into yarn and then fed through the knitting machines, coming out in endless rolls of cloth.

Then came the second tragedy in two years. In November of 1899 Father became seriously ill and passed away. Disturbed in the middle of the night by his heavy breathing, we found him unconscious and called the family doctor. He passed away without recognizing his children gathered around the bedside.

The passing of Mother two years before had created the problem of keeping six half-orphaned children together under one roof. With Father's death, that problem ceased to exist. The children were merely divided up and parceled out like so many pieces of merchandise.

Louise, aged five, and Charlie, aged seven, were taken by a farmer and his wife. Louise, like her mother, was very frail and after a long illness passed away in her early twenties. Laura, aged eleven, went to live with a family in Newport News, and eventually married and settled down there.

Bond, aged nine, was taken by Aunt Lina, who later moved to Newport News. Today he holds a responsible position with the Newport News Shipbuilding Company. Moncey, then eighteen and quite ill at the time, lived for a while at Hodges Ferry. Later, however, he returned to live with Aunt Lina. He passed away in the late fall of 1900 while under her tender care.

As for me, the problem child, Aunt Lina fell heir to me as well.

I owe much to this dear aunt of mine. She was deeply religious and the one person to whom I always turned when my youthful indiscretions threatened to overwhelm me. Her husband, John Gaskins, also worked in the navy yard. Since he had learned no trade, his wage as a day laborer was only $1.76 a day. On this they raised a family of three children, and when the time came they did not hesitate to assume the burden of Bond and me and, later, Moncey during his last illness.

For six months all went well. Then, a few days after my seventeenth birthday, I took the day off without permission and lost my job at the mill. I decided to sever all home ties and make my own way in the world.

In a short note to Aunt Lina, I thanked her for all she had done for me and solemnly promised to write her from wherever I might be in the years to come. Now I was really on my way, destination unknown.

Thoughts of a troubled boyhood, and loved ones being left behind with every turn of the wheels, were punctured now and then by jarring, shuddering stops as the long train came to rest on some siding while a hurrying passenger train went shrieking past in the darkness.

Occasionally light from a brakeman's lantern flashed into my side-door Pullman, but I was not disturbed until noon the next day when a grizzled hobo climbed in to share my commodious quarters. About dusk we remained so long on a siding that I ventured out and found myself on the outskirts of Charlotte, North Carolina, so I went foraging for dinner.

I knocked on the back door of a house and, when confronted by a buxom lady, timidly offered to chop wood for a bite to eat. Evidently surprised by my youthful appearance, the lady gave me a cold potato and a bit of bread and meat, at the same time asking me who I was and how such a small boy happened to be away from home. I hurried back to the tracks and hung around several hours until the next freight train stopped, then swung into an empty car.

Twenty-four hours later I hopped off at Greenwood, South Carolina, and into the waiting arms of a railroad detective, who said he had been waiting for me for two days and if I would now just tell him my name and where I was from, everything would be just fine.

After gulping a couple of times I decided to tell my right name; he immediately said it was a lie but that he knew who I was anyhow and would wire my parents to come for me. After failing to convince him that it was a case of mistaken identity, he locked me in a hotel room, where I gobbled up a meal at his expense. The next morning when I had eaten a good breakfast, also on the house, a man and a woman looked me over with a pained expression on their faces and sadly admitted I was not their little boy.

I secretly wished I was, as by now I had lost much of my confidence and was quite frightened. The disappointed cop then took me before the justice of the peace, who gave me twelve hours to get out of town. I got.

* 3 *

THREE DAYS LATER I rolled into my first big city, Atlanta, Georgia. I had been on the road one week and, while my meals were back-door handouts, I was enough of an amateur hobo to give value received by doing such chores as wood chopping and washing dishes. My youthful appearance made it easy to forage for food, but this also caused sympathetic mothers frequently to report me to the police.

The July nights were warm. With my folded coat for a pillow, I slept in empty freight cars or under any convenient shelter, constantly watchful for railroad police and small-town cops.

After writing my first letter to Aunt Lina, I leisurely toured Atlanta. One landmark that intrigued me was a large Civil War cannon placed at the intersection of two important streets. A slot large enough to receive a silver dollar gaped invitingly a few inches from the sealed end of the cannon. When the sun was right, the silver coins could be seen nestling just below the opening. There was little left of my original two dollars. This unique savings bank offered an opportunity to rebuild my finances. I waited until traffic dwindled and then went to work with specially turned pieces of wire.

Sometimes I would coax a coin up to the slot and then "ker-plunk." I fished away, nonchalantly leaning over the gun barrel as if Civil War objects fascinated me. Presently a cop came up and whispered, "Let me help you, Sonny."

I fled in confusion.

Not so funny was my next adventure in Atlanta. On the outskirts of all large cities, particularly railroad centers, are the "hobo jungles," a common gathering place for those perpetual wanderers who consider it beneath their dignity to stoop to toil. Near a creek or water tank, under convenient shade trees, tired members of the hobo clan rest during the warm daylight hours and build up enough energy to forage for food after nightfall. In patched hand-me-downs, with hands and faces grimy and skins actually scaly, they are rarely successful in obtaining handouts from cynical housewives, who sometimes insist on having wood chopped.

The specialty of these old-timers is to graft themselves to some youngster, using him to forage for food while they direct the campaign from the safety zone of the hobo jungle camp. I drifted into one of these camps and was accepted with patronizing indulgence. Still wearing knee pants and looking like a fourteen-year-old, I was too good a provider to overlook. It was not long before a couple of villainous-looking denizens attached themselves to me with compliments and friendly pats on the back.

My timid knock on the back door of a prosperous-looking house was generally answered by a belligerent-looking lady with a broom, for protection against the usual type of hobo. After the first glare she would unbend slightly and ask, "What is a child like you doing away from home?" A few carefully rehearsed answers generally brought a bag of leftovers that ultimately found their way into the community of hoboes, in a pot of mulligan stew. Because of my innocent appearance I would often be invited into the kitchen for a hot meal. When this happened too many times in one night, it put quite a strain on my youthful waistline. My only recourse was to divert the attention of my benefactor while stuffing bread, potatoes and meat into my pockets. Stew, or wet hash from leftovers, was a favorite dish with Southern housewives. When this was ladled out in relays, my stomach rebelled, and the problem of carrying away food was taxing.

In the jungle camp late one night two grizzled tramps, who

had begun to dominate all my actions, suggested a stroll. I tried to beg off, but they prodded me along and I was too frightened to rebel.

We walked for more than an hour before reaching a section of Atlanta far out on Peachtree Street. The houses were aristocratic, surrounded by well-kept lawns. I was badly scared, but with a man on either side of me there was nothing I could do but trot along—and pray.

We stopped at the rear of a fine home. One man climbed a fence, the other hoisted me over, then followed. The three of us crouched in the darkness. The slightest whisper was thunder in my ears. Each time I tried to swallow, a hard lump came into my throat and seemed to choke me. Just above our heads a small window was open.

Instructing me to unbolt the back door from the inside, they removed my shoes and shoved me through the window, head first, holding onto my feet while I hung upside down inside the house. My outstretched hands located the floor, and I eased myself down into a sort of pantry. With my heart pounding, I tried to stand erect and found my legs so shaky they almost folded under me. Slowly opening the pantry door, and with ears strained to catch the slightest sound, I felt my way toward the back door to let my companions in.

Suddenly I turned and began making my way toward the front of the house. Blindly I groped my way through the gray dark, guessing at each obstacle that loomed in my path, sensing, rather than hearing, the signs and sounds of human beings around me, above me, restless in sleep perhaps, waiting . . . A creaking floorboard, a breathless pause, every nerve edgy. At last I felt the old-fashioned lock of the front door, turned a key and fled silently out into Peachtree Street.

Several blocks from the scene, I stopped running, removed my stockings and in bare feet walked furtively to the railroad yards.

Before daybreak I was in a freight car slowly moving south. Two days later I hopped off at Macon, Georgia. There I worked in a knitting mill for a few weeks, just long enough to buy shoes and a few other items before shoving off for Savannah.

En route, while luxuriously stretched out on the top of a refrigerator car, I saw the brakeman approaching from a distance. I dropped into the empty ice compartment and pulled the cover into place. Later, when I pushed at the cover to peek out, I realized that the catch had snapped. I was locked in.

Hunched up in the small compartment, I removed a shoe and whenever I thought I heard footsteps I pounded hard on the cover, but the hours passed and nothing happened. After crouching there for endless ages of sweating discomfort I risked all of my strength on one last heave. The lid flew up and over the side. No doubt the "brakie" had caught a glimpse of me and had battened down the hatch.

By contrast with the hustle and bustle of Atlanta, Savannah was as familiar as my old town of Portsmouth. Masts of great square-rigged sailing ships towered high, and the docks were lined with rusting, clumsy-looking tramp steamers. I walked across the gangway of a big Norwegian windjammer and wandered around at will, while longshoremen worked at the winches. There was a lighter alongside from which sailors had been painting the ship. I climbed down the rope ladder, removed my coat and shirt and then reclined on my back, gawking up at the complicated rigging, and dreamed of myself among those ropes and spars.

The sun was hot. The dirty river looked cool. I removed the rest of my clothes and dove into the fast-moving current of the Savannah River. Soon I was scraping barnacles from the bottom of a large ship with my bare back. End over end, the swirling current carried me the full length of the ship ahead. I gulped muddy water by the gallon until I hit some projection with a mighty wallop and blissfully passed out.

Two Negroes in a rowboat saw my body pop out from under the ship's hull and gave chase, picking me up two city blocks from my starting point. They worked some of the water out of my system, then handed me over to dock workers who took me to the emergency hospital where the draining process was continued until my stomach gave out only a hollow sound.

The next stop was the Savannah jail. Charge: bathing in the river against a city ordinance. Sentence: get out of town within twenty-four hours. Taking advantage of the twenty-four hours' grace, I tried the water front again and applied to the captain of a three-masted American schooner for a job, giving as reference my experience on Uncle Lindsay's river schooners. He had a full crew but agreed to let me work my passage to Philadelphia, which meant washing dishes and waiting on table in the cabin.

The *Millie R. Bohannan* made a fast trip of seven days to Philadelphia. When not working in the galley or cabin, I mingled with the crew night and day, eagerly learning everything I could about the working of a ship. When I went ashore in Philadelphia the captain gave me one dollar.

The first day I spent twenty cents for food and twenty-five cents for a bed. The second day I cut the food budget to fifteen cents, spent another quarter for a bed and started the third day with ten cents for dinner and a nickel for emergencies. I walked all over town in three days, but nobody wanted to hire me at any price. On the fourth day, after aimlessly wandering around for hours, I found myself in a residential section where there were rows of houses set slightly back from the sidewalk, each fronted by a short flight of stairs ending in a "stoop." On these stoops, family groups sat in clusters. I had walked miles since morning and was not only tired and hungry but terribly homesick for the first time since leaving Portsmouth.

I had noticed that Northern boys of my age wore long trousers. I felt all alone in my short knee pants. I became self-conscious and imagined that people were staring and jeering at my appearance. A friendly voice called to me from one of the stoops, "Where on earth did you come from, Sonny?"

I forgot to be offended. Here was a friendly voice, and I replied that I was from Georgia. In a few minutes I was the center of a family group who wanted to know how I came to be so far away from home, how old I was, and where did I get that funny accent.

The man with the friendly voice was Mr. J. Schonder, owner of the Lester Milk Co., and various ice-cream stores, the largest of which was right around the corner. We adjourned to the latter, found a big table and there, surrounded by Mr. Schonder and his wife, their son, daughter and two nieces, I tried to answer their questions. Finally the old man exploded that it was a shame that a little fellow like me had no home, so he, Mr. Schonder, would give me a home and a job as well.

After filling up on ice cream, I went home with them. Then Mr. Schonder showed me to a spare bedroom and told me to consider myself one of the family. The next morning I was rigged up in a pair of young Schonder's long trousers and put to work in the milk bottling plant at the rear of the house.

As my first job, I picked up the bottles from a tank of soapy water, pushed them over a whirling electric brush, rinsed them in clear water and dropped them in racks to drain. Later I learned to operate one of the huge vats that moved slowly over long rows of bottles, filling twelve dozen at one time by the mere turn of a lever. Then the racks of filled bottles were placed in tanks of water for sterilizing, after which they were capped and ready for delivery.

At first I drank large quantities of rich cream scooped from the top of forty-quart cans but was cured of the habit when my face and body broke out in pimples. The sudden change of diet was just too rich for my thinned-out blood. I shared the family

Moncey (Robert, Jr.), Mother, Laura,
Father and Bill Coffman (at the age
of 5)

A young singer of illustrated songs, W.
Milo Coffman of the London Burlesquers, Chicago, 1901

Cork, Ireland.
March 10th/11 03.

Dear Aunt Lina:-
    I know you all are anxious
about me by this time. We arrived in
Falmouth England on March 3rd/11 after
a 143 day passage from San Francisco.
  Before I go any further, please excuse all
mistakes, I am writing under dificullies
There are sixteen sailors here in the Forecastle
and every one is trying to talk at once.
  I rec'd your letter a few days ago, and
you can imagine how glad I was to hear
from you, although the letter was posted
more than three months ago.
  Every one has been in a state of suspence
the last few days before arriving in Port
  Almost all the sailors were expecting letters
and there were many disapointments when
the mail arrived from Queenstown.
  I will never forget the day. Late

The author's letter of March 10, 1903, to Aunt Lina Gaskins from Cork, Ireland, describing his first voyage around Cape Horn. (This is page 1 of a twelve-page letter.)

British three-masted bark, *Belfast*, under full sail

The calling card of Miss Nellie Norman

Miss NELLIE NORMAN

Will be pleased to see any of her old

Seafaring Friends at

O'Connell's Hotel, Bolton St., Newcastle.

The *Watson A. West,* four-masted schooner, in which the author circumnavigated the globe 1904-05, starting from Aberdeen, Washington

John McGee, of Dublin, and the author — shipmates on the *J.H. Barrow,* three-masted schooner, 1903

British four-masted bark, the *Celticburn,* under jibs and topsails

"Frenchie" of the *Celticburn,* dressed for shore leave

The *Lyman D. Foster*, four-masted schooner

Bill Coffman's certificate of discharge from the *Lyman D. Foster*. Capt. Dan "Crazy" Killman corrected these discharge papers after a fist fight off Cape Flattery

Count Felix von Luckner

The *Seeadler*

The *A. B. Johnson*, later sunk by Count von Luckner's *Seeadler* in the South Pacific, as noted by the Count in his inscription, "I sunk this ship!"

The San Francisco Earthquake
and fire as I saw it. April 18-06.

William Milo Coffman
San Francisco Cal.
October 20-1906.

At a quarter past five on the morning of April 18th/06. I was suddenly awakened by a terrific shaking. The movement was not a heaving, but a quick shaking back and forth; the windows were rattling and it created a terrific din. Upon awaking, my first impress. was, that I was at sea, as the sensation was exactly the same as I have experienced aboard a sailing ship when the ship was in stay. and all of the sails were shaking. In another instant I realized what it was, as I had often heard of the earthquake here in 1868.

As I sprang from the bed, the plastering began to fall. I hurriedly dressed and ran out upon the sidewalk. Tehama, a very narrow street, was crowded with excited people. The greater part of whom were dressed, just as they had sprang out of bed.

Our house was a two story brick build- ing, that had survived the earthquake of 1868, but now it was cracked and seamed and looked as though another slight sh...

The first page of young Bill's 33-page on-the-spot story of the San Francisco earthquake

Vallejo Calif.
Apl. 18. 06
To whom it may concern
This gentleman is willing to
do any duty assigned to him

J.I. Madison
Mayor of Vallejo

A hastily written permit issued to Coffman to re-enter the burning city of San Francisco, signed by the mayor of Vallejo

San Francisco in ruins after the 1906 earthquake

Certificate of membership and statement of account, signed by Andy Furuseth, one of the outstanding crusaders for better living conditions among seamen

Rules for the Sailors' Union of the Pacific

Certificate of Membership.

No. *943*

NAME *W. Milo Coffman*

When properly signed by the Secretary and sealed with the Seal of the Union, THIS CERTIFICATE is evidence of the fact that the bearer, if corresponding to the description annexed, is a FULL MEMBER of the SAILORS' UNION OF THE PACIFIC, and entitled to due faith, confidence, credit and assistance from all members and all or any of the Workingmen of the World.

And if the statement of account hereafter annexed shall show that his dues are PAID UP, or that he is not more than Three Months in arrears, then said member is in GOOD STANDING. If he is six months or more in arrears, then he stands SUSPENDED, only to be reinstated upon proper payment.

(Seal)

A Furuseth
Secretary.

RULES GOVERNING
Interchange of Membership Cards

EDERATED SEAMEN'S UNION OF AUSTRALASIA

AND

AILORS' UNION OF THE PACIFIC.

Adopted December 19, 1892.

1. Any financial member of either Union who ports himself before departure shall be accepted membership upon payment of contributions for rrent month in which he reports himself on her side.
2. Any financial member who does not report mself before departure shall pay half arrears either side.
3. Any member leaving either side, and un-ancial, shall pay all arrears to the Branch in hich he reports, and for denying membership r the purpose of evading payment of arrears all, upon being detected, be dealt with by the anch

19___

STATEMENT OF ACCOUNT.

Month Paid for	Dues	When Paid Assessments	Remarks
January	A, FEB 28 1909		
February	A, FEB 28 1909		
March	A, FEB 28 1909		
April	A, FEB 28 1909		
May			
June			
July			
August			
September			
October			
November			
December			

The barkentine *Wrestler* races a scow schooner in San Francisco Bay

Coffman's ship's discharge from the *Wrestler*

To whom it May concern this is
to certify that Mr W. H. Coffman has
been with Me as 2nd Mate on Bktn "Wrestler"
of San Francisco from Dec 7 1908 to Feb 26 1909
and have proven to be capable in performing such duty also been sober and civil
in his ways and can therefore cheerfully
recommend him to anyone who
may need his services

Portland Ory. Feb 27 1909

P. H. Bjarnstrom
Master of Bktn "Wrestler"

Bill Coffman as YMCA swimming instructor, 1912

The Sutro Baths, 1910

Duke Kahanamoku, former world's swimming champion (fifth from left), and teammates of the Hui Nalu Club, Honolulu. The team was in training for the National Championships at the Sutro Baths, July 4, 1913

Notre Dame's Johnny Lujack receives the William M. Coffman annual award from Jack McDonald, sports editor, *San Francisco Call-Bulletin,* and president of the Northern California Football Writers' Association, as the outstanding player in the East-West game

ISLAM TEMPLE 1954 FOOTBALL COMMITTEE
650 GEARY STREET   SAN FRANCISCO
TO BANK OF AMERICA N.T.& S.A. 11-177
    POWELL STREET BRANCH   February 10, 1955

VCHR 200-A   CHECK 200
NO.   NO.

...Y TWO HUNDRED FORTY THOUSAND THREE HUNDRED THIRTY-SEVEN and 96/100 $240337.96

THE   BOARD OF TRUSTEES   ISLAM TEMPLE 1954 FOOTBALL COMMITTEE
DER   East-West Football Funds
                   San Francisco, California   Perce E. Allen   Wm Coffman
                                                        POTENTATE   MANAGING DIRECTOR

                          Chairman Hospital Board   Herman Wearn
                                                        GENERAL CHAIRMAN   RECORDER

CHECK IS IN FULL PAYMENT OF ITEMS SHOWN ON ATTACHED REMITTANCE
OF WHICH PAYEE ACKNOWLEDGES BY ENDORSEMENT ON BACK HEREOF.

The check for the 30th anniversary East-West game, turning over almost a quarter of a million dollars in proceeds to the Shriners Hospitals

William Leiser, sports editor of the *San Francisco Chronicle* and past president of the Football Writers of America, presents the award for Football's Man of the Year, 1946, to Bill Coffman

The San Francisco branch of the Shriners Hospitals for Crippled Children

The 30th anniversary East-West game, January 1, 1955

Chicago, Ill.

Portland, Ore.

St. Paul–Minneapolis, Minn.

Lexington, Ky.

"The World's Greatest Philanthropy"—

Greenville, S. C.

Philadelphia, Pa.

Salt Lake City, Utah

Los Angeles, Calif.

St. Louis, Mo.

Springfield, Mass.

Shreveport, La.

Spokane, Wash.

Shriners Hospitals for Crippled Children

Honolulu, T. H.

Winnipeg, Canada

Mexico City, Mexico

Montreal, Canada

Coffman Island, Echo Lake, California

The author as he appears today

table and was treated exactly like Mr. Schonder's own son, who had just entered the University of Pennsylvania. My work in the plant started at six in the morning and was generally over by one o'clock, after which I worked in the ice-cream store afternoons, *except* on baseball days.

Mr. Schonder was a baseball fan and liked company. On days when the Phillies were in town, the two of us would spend the afternoons in the ball park, rooting for the home team, especially when the rival Pittsburgh Pirates were the opponents and then we could root our hardest for Mr. Schonder's favorites, Nap Lajoie and Ed Delahanty, who played against Pittsburgh's great Honus Wagner.

This pleasant Philadelphia interlude did not last very long. With the wonders of New York so close, I decided to move on. My benefactors had taken me in wholeheartedly, and had even talked of adoption and made plans to continue my neglected education, but they could not change my decision. I had saved my earnings and after paying ten dollars for a new suit, shoes and a cap, I still had more than forty dollars left. Bidding good-by to my good friends, I proudly purchased a ticket to New York. For the first time in my life I rode the cushions in style.

Leaving the ferry at the foot of Cortlandt Street, I started the long walk up Broadway, pausing now and then to gawk at the world's tallest buildings. In one hand I held a guidebook and map of the city, and with the other I carried a small bag, one of those telescope affairs costing fifty cents. My suit was of light green and reflected my general appearance. Blissfully unaware of amused glances from passers-by, I continued as far as Park Row, a familiar name resurrected from the limbo of my dime-novel days. Out came the map again and when I found that only a few short blocks led directly to the Bowery, I underwent a struggle before deciding to stick with Broadway while it was still daylight, leaving the Bowery to be explored after nightfall.

I reached Union Square just as thousands of luminous white lights burst upon my startled vision, above saloons, restaurants and amusement arcades.

Despite the passage of time and the brilliant spectacle of Times Square, Broadway and Forty-second Street of later years, I still recall the gay Rialto of Fourteenth Street in the year 1900, including some of the shows that were playing on that first visit. Chauncey Olcott in *Come in Out of the Rain*, at the Fourteenth Street Theater; Denman Thompson in *The Old Homestead*, at the Academy of Music; Tony Pastor's, with the elderly Tony making one of his last appearances in his own theater; and James O'Neill in *Count of Monte Cristo*.

Next to Pastor's was Tammany Hall, and directly opposite was Tom Sharkey's gaudy saloon, where the old warrior himself could be seen in person presiding behind his highly polished mahogany bar.

A few doors away was Huber's Museum of circus freaks, the Eden Musée of wax figures and near by a mammoth arcade, housing juke boxes, electric banjos and hand-cranked moving-picture machines.

Crowds surged along the sidewalks from curb to curb. Pitchmen, panhandlers and fakirs, young hustlers and older ones pretending to be young, oggling and giving the eye to passers-by.

Lugging my small bag, I elbowed my way through the crowds, stopping now and then to gaze at some new wonder. On Broadway just off Fourteenth Street the marquee lights of a large theater announced Terrible Terry McGovern in *The Bowery after Dark*. Paying ten cents, I climbed flights of stairs high up into the gallery, shoved my bag under the seat and settled down to enjoy my first Broadway show. Later I paid thirty-five cents for a small room and went to bed to dream of the big city and fabulous sights yet to be seen.

I spent the next afternoon gaping at a conglomeration of human freaks and monstrosities who spent the winter months between circus seasons at Huber's Museum. Snake charmers, sword swallowers, flame eaters, glass blowers, giants and midgets, armless wonders and legless women, India-rubber men, fat ladies and living skeletons, fish-faced men and dog-faced boys, bearded ladies and Circassian beauties.

After Huber's, I took in the Eden Musée. Here were rows of lifelike figures, including a choice assortment of thugs and murderers, past and present. I was not at all surprised to come upon two old dime-novel favorites of mine, Frank and Jesse James, whose exploits had so intrigued me only a short time ago. It was late when I turned south on Fourth Avenue and headed for the great adventure.

The real Bowery of that day began just below Houston Street and continued ten to twelve blocks as far as Chatham Square, where it split into New Bowery leading into Broadway. I felt I had actually "arrived" when I came face to face with gaudy posters and a glaring electric sign reading McGurk's. I thought of looking in but drew back when a tough-looking gent near the entrance gave me a baleful glare. Shivering slightly, I moved on. My youthful appearance was anything but a badge of welcome in the Bowery dives. Every few minutes the elevated train thundered along overhead, showering hot cinders and soot to the streets below.

I trudged on past Delancey, Broome, and Hester streets, my hand in my trousers pocket clutching my purse, trying to look casual. Panhandlers popped out from dark entranceways whining for a dime; streetwalkers, sometimes young but mostly old, edged alongside, slipping their arm through mine. I shook off all approaches and continued on with an occasional nervous glance over my shoulders, keeping beyond easy reach of the furtive, weasel-eyed figures lurking in almost every doorway. And I was not drawing on my imagination when I sensed that most of my fellow travelers were undoubtedly thieves, pick-pockets, pimps, dope fiends and broken-nosed thugs who would like nothing better than to get me in a dark hallway for a matter of minutes. In my new outfit I looked prosperous, and green, and not a day older than fifteen, and here I was at midnight in one of the toughest spots in the New York of 1900.

Crossing the street near Chatham Square, I found myself in front of a large, well-illuminated building, the Atlantic Garden music hall. Feeling a bit panicky, I entered without hesitation, walked down the main aisle and took a seat at a table near the large stage on which several ladies in abbreviated costumes were performing. I had barely settled myself at the table when a hand descended on my coat collar from behind, another grasped the seat of my trousers, and then, to my mortification, I was marched straight down the aisle, through the swinging doors, and rudely thrust into the night.

My sudden ejection attracted several watery-eyed bums who attempted to brush me off while trying to frisk my pockets, but I disengaged myself and hurried on. Apparently I was consid-ered too young and inexperienced to indulge in such frivolities as burlesque shows and beer drinking.

Passing Steve Brodie's saloon near Grand Street, I recog-nized the name as another of my heroes who had attained fame years before by supposedly jumping from the Brooklyn Bridge. I was tempted to try my luck again, but my experience in the Atlantic Garden was too recent to overlook.

Next door to Brodie's saloon a crowd was being entertained by a public performance of tattooing. Behind a display window the artist sat embroidering a beautiful butterfly on the hairy chest of a Navy man. After watching for a while, fascinated by the martyred expression on the face of the young sailor, I, too, became a willing victim.

Selecting the design of a hefty female in tights, I shelled out several of my precious dollars in return for which the artist mercilessly jabbed needles into my quivering flesh, wiping away the oozing blood from time to time with a dirty, inky rag. I almost fainted when the electric needle bit into my skinny breastbone with a drumming sound that was actually audible. Having paid for the torture in advance and being conscious of the admiring audience outside the window, I determined to stick it out if it killed me.

By the time I reached my room on Fourteenth Street the flesh had swollen badly, and I narrowly escaped blood poisoning.

* 4 *

AT GENERAL DELIVERY next day I found a letter from Aunt Lina. Brother Moncey was ill, not expected to live, and he wished to see me. Could I possibly come home?

I had less than forty dollars, but a round trip, second-class, could be made on an Old Dominion Line steamer for seven dollars. Twenty-four hours later I disembarked at Norfolk, took a ferry to Portsmouth and soon was clasped tightly to my Aunt Lina's motherly bosom. After greetings, and with a desperate attempt to avoid tears, the folks gathered around and listened while I told the story of my wanderings—with certain reservations.

Two days later, on November 3, 1900, Moncey passed away. I was thankful for having arrived in time to spend the last days with him.

And now I was the head of the family, although only a few months past seventeen. Aunt Lina begged me to remain in Portsmouth, but I explained that I had a fine job waiting for me in New York and must return soon.

Of course no job was waiting for me and only a few dollars were left in my purse, but in the four short months since leaving the old home town, my knee-length pants had been replaced by a neat suit with long trousers. I felt more sophisticated and grown up, especially in the presence of boys I formerly ran around with. I had regaled them with some fancy tales, and now with funds running low it was no part of my plan to disillusion them by taking a hundrum job at home.

With my little telescope bag in hand I walked up the gangplank nonchalantly waving good-by to my good old aunt for the last time, and to my brothers and sisters, whom I would not see again for many years.

When the steamer docked at a North River pier in New York the next morning, a light snow was falling. Walking across town to Broadway, I asked directions from a policeman and was guided to the Mills Hotel at 36 Bleecker Street. The Mills was known as the "poor man's hotel" where one could have a good clean room for twenty-five cents a night and equally reasonable meals.

With the prayers of my old aunt still ringing in my ears, I determined to find myself a job in New York while I still had enough money to support myself and while my scanty wardrobe was presentable enough to impress favorably a prospective employer. But good resolutions have a way of dissolving under the influence of bright lights and temptation. Each day I postponed until tomorrow the hunt for a job and each day my capital diminished until I realized on the tenth day that less than ten dollars remained between me and an uncertain future.

The Bowery scene at the turn of the century was something to behold and to remember. It was rowdy, lusty and exciting. Whether in daylight or darkness, both sides of that wide thoroughfare comprising the short distance between Houston Street on the north and Chatham Square on the south fairly teemed with a moving, unwashed stream of semi-humanity, whose appearance, demeanor and apparent objectives in life baffled description.

They spilled over into Chinatown's Pell, Mott and Doyers streets and Little Italy and into the crowded tenements over toward the East River. Bums eddied in and out of pawnshops, poolrooms, and beer halls. They eased themselves into dim hallways, waiting to spot a lurching drunk. Pickpockets plied their trade and easygoing ladies did the same. Street fakirs showed their tricks and their wares, and barkers reminded one that the show going on inside cost a dime, ten cents.

I investigated such wonders as the Globe Museum near Houston Street. Its vast interior, called the Theatorium, was crammed not only with curiosities of every description but human oddities as well. Here was the phrenologist who could examine the bumps on my cranium and tell me of the tremendous influence each and every one would exert on my veiled future. In the Theatorium the unique feature was the size of the fee. This inconsequential detail depended entirely upon the apparent prosperity of the seeker of knowledge. If the professor murmured "One dollar" or perhaps "Five," it would be well to gulp and pay. That is, if you valued your classic profile. Either the professor received his fee or the conscientious objector left the premises with a brand-new physiognomy. After a quick appraisal of my as yet unshaven cheeks and my new store clothes, I was assessed three dollars. I reluctantly obliged, while resolving to profit by the lesson.

There were also anatomical museums where one could gorge himself examining the horrible effects of social diseases as exemplified by the casts and wax figures. I parted with a dollar to view a phony mermaid through a peephole.

After that, I became cagey and tried to act less like a country bumpkin. A seat in the gallery at Miner's, the Windsor, the People's or the Thalia cost only a dime. My evening at the Thalia was not worth even the dime; I found after comfortably seating myself that the entire performance was in Yiddish.

My favorite theater was Miner's near Delancey Street. The show was divided into two parts, vaudeville acts and melodrama. On Friday nights there was a third section, amateur night. This started at midnight. The hook was used so frequently that only about half of the ten acts were allowed to finish. When the last act was over, the amateurs were lined up before the audience, and a five-dollar gold piece was dangled over the head of each in turn. The applause, represented by whistles, yells, stomping and hand clapping, determined the winner. Each act allowed to finish received one dollar, which in many cases meant the first bed and hot meal in several days.

Of all the dives, the one that intrigued me most was a red brick building on the east side of the Bowery near Houston Street run by one John McGurk and known as Suicide Hall. Like the Atlantic Garden, its large interior held dozens of tables, an elevated stage, and on each side private boxes half hidden by curtains. On the stage was the usual bawdy show. Singing waiters entertained between acts while serving steins of beer for a nickel. Between the serving and the singing the waiters also bounced undesirable patrons.

Masculine patrons used the front entrance, but the "girls," as they were courteously called, entered through a convenient alleyway, with the understanding that they were to place their charms at the disposal of the patrons as a consideration for admission to the hall. And should a gentleman desire to spread himself to the extent of buying a bottle of wine for the lady, curtained-off boudoirs were available at a slight premium, depending upon the degree of intoxication of the paying guest. Many of these carefree ladies had seen better days, having already been thrown out of the toughest joints on the Bowery even though the standards of the other dives were not unusually high.

As long as they observed the house rules at McGurk's, the

ladies were tolerated, but at times they were unappreciative, messing things up by choosing the place of business of their benefactor as a nice homey spot to end it all. It was said that the previous year, 1899, thirteen women attempted to take their lives at 295 Bowery, of whom only seven recovered. In almost every instance the same method was used: carbolic acid poured into a glass of whisky and gulped down before the watchful waiters could interfere.

It was also said that waiters were provided with chloral hydrate to be used as knockout drops. As the real use of the sedative was intended to render patrons unconscious for plucking, they were under very definite instructions to limit the dose to something less than fatal. The boss was very touchy on this point, being afraid the joint might get a bad name. In no case did the police find the body of the victim on the premises. It was always discovered in the alley near by.

Night after night I sauntered by McGurk's, anxious to see what went on inside but wary about entering because of my unfortunate experience in the Atlantic Garden. I had discarded my boyish-looking cap in favor of a hat which made me look a little older, especially when pulled down over my eyes. Timing my entrance so that I walked in behind another party, I eased over to an inconspicuous table, and when the waiter approached to take my order for a beer, I had made myself look taller by sitting on one foot drawn up beneath me. He accepted the order without question and soon I was blowing the foam from a large stein of beer and enjoying the show. I felt important.

When the show was over and the bright lights flashed on, the waiters began mopping the tables and looking questionably at the customers for orders. When one started in my direction, I made a sudden exit, expecting any minute to be propelled toward the door by a helping hand or a foot from behind.

31

∗ 5 ∗

I SUDDENLY REALIZED that my few remaining dollars would soon be gone, and I must find work. By then it was nearly the middle of November. The weather turned cold, with a heavy fall of snow.

Tramping the streets of the lower East Side, day after day, I was grateful for a few hours of work when I could find it, which was seldom. Toward the end of the month, unable to afford the luxury of a permanent lodging, I disposed of my belongings, including the little telescope bag, for a few dimes. And then, when the dimes were gone, I was really on the town, without even a change of socks.

The first night after giving up my room at the Mills, I paid fifteen cents for a cot in one of the better flophouses on the Bowery near Canal Street. There was one thin blanket but no sheets, and my cot was directly under a window where I could reach out and almost touch the flying elevated as it thundered by every few minutes during the night. At seven in the morning we were hustled out on the street.

Two days later came my first Thanksgiving without a home, but at least I would eat well as a guest of the Bowery Mission where, following a custom of years, a free turkey dinner was served to all comers. The doors would open at noon, but hours earlier the line before 227 Bowery began to lengthen until it extended completely around the block. Cops strutted back and forth using their clubs to jab the impatient ones into place as the hungry and homeless slowly shuffled along, each step carrying them nearer to the first good hot meal in weeks.

After hours in line I wondered if the food would hold out until my turn came. The food did hold out and the helpings were generous. When darkness fell, the line was still moving slowly into the mission. Probably many were coming up for a second helping. If so, who could blame them? Thanksgiving came only one bellyful in three hundred and sixty-five hungry days.

With my stomach comfortably full, I was faced with the grave decision of disposing of the last two dimes that stood between me and tomorrow. I could walk the streets and save the twenty cents for another day, or I could spend fifteen cents for a cot and let tomorrow take care of itself. I chose the cot.

Next morning I found a place where they served one egg, a slice of bread and a cup of coffee for five cents. True, the egg was just short of disintegration, but I was in the same condition.

I have no difficulty, after more than fifty years, in remembering vividly the happenings of that Thanksgiving night of 1900. Utterly broke, without even the seven cents that would have provided a three-by-six-foot space on the floor of the cheapest flophouse, I kept moving until the streets were nearly deserted, then curled myself up in a darkened hallway with newspapers for a covering.

Awakened by the rapping of a policeman's night stick against the thin soles of my shoes, I was bundled into a patrol wagon. There were other riders and I thought we were on our way to jail, but instead we were delivered to the Municipal Lodging House, referred to by fellow lodgers as the City Dump.

Following instructions, we removed every stitch of clothing, formed a line, stepped under a shower-contraption and vigorously scrubbed head and body with strong soap and water. Next, each was handed a long cotton nightshirt and assigned to a cot with two clean sheets and a blanket.

At six in the morning I was handed a bag containing my clothes and given a hunk of dry bread and a cup of coffee in return for one hour of wood chopping. The night's sleep between clean white sheets had been wonderful, but when I dumped my clothes out of the small bag into which the whole mess had been crammed and fumigated overnight, I felt like the outcast that I had really become. What had been a fairly decent suit of clothes now had a thousand wrinkles and smelled strongly of sulphur. I felt ashamed and self-conscious, but when I hesitated, a cop told me to get moving, so I shuffled back to the only refuge I knew, the slums of the East Side, carefully dodging police on the way.

After wandering around all day with even my fellow bums giving me an extra look, I decided I might as well get another night's sleep and coffee, so I turned up again at the City Dump. I went through the delousing process all over again and slept fine but, after receiving my bread and coffee, was told to get out and not return.

A cold, drizzling rain was falling, and soon I was soaked through. As I sloshed my way toward the only part of town where my kind was tolerated, I could feel my sleeves and trouser legs crawling upward. My eight-dollar suit was not the unshrinkable kind.

When I finally dried out, I was a sight to behold. My trouser legs were four inches short. The coat sleeves ended halfway between elbow and wrist, and the balance of the suit clung tenaciously to my skinny frame.

Before the debacle I was broke and without a place to sleep, but my clothes were presentable, and all I needed to make a comeback was a decent job which I had hopes of finding. Now, through the gracious hospitality of the City of New York, I had become a disreputable bum overnight, no better and no worse than hundreds of others around me who must live by their wits to survive.

Through most of December I lived literally from hand to mouth, washing dishes in the kosher restaurants for my meals and a few cents a day. I swept and scraped the sawdust-covered floors of beer joints on Rivington, Delancey and Broome streets, cleaned cuspidors for five cents an hour and sometimes ate the leavings of free lunch.

During that time I was seldom able to spare more than ten to twenty cents each night for lodgings, which meant sleeping in the cheapest flophouses, but it was the middle of winter and space under cover was preferable to the cold and rain outside. Lodgings could be had at any price from five cents up. One place had a series of long, wide tables. Sleeping space on the floor beneath the table was five cents; on top it was seven cents. Others provided cot with blanket for fifteen cents; without blankets—ten cents. For twenty cents you could rent a cot in a small cubicle, with chair and one blanket, and even semiprivacy, in the shape of a thin partition six feet high.

While the price charged may have determined the degree of privacy or comfort, there was absolute democracy otherwise, as vermin infested the hide, hair and clothing of each sleeper in these flophouses without regard to the fee charged or the lodger's station in life. The stuffy air was always tainted with the lingering perfume of burned sulphur and other chemicals, indicating that efforts were made periodically to exterminate at least the weakest of the cooties, but their demise, if any, was never noticeable. Absolute extermination of vermin from the seams of one's clothing was possible only by a process such as was used at the City Dump. Then it was sudden death for the free rider, but your suit would never be its old self again.

Although most of my meals were part of the payoff for dishwashing, sweeping and other such chores, food was cheap enough. There were numerous hash houses around Chatham Square, upper Park Row and Bowery where bread sold for one cent a slice, a bowl of soup one cent, frankfurter and roll two cents, and three cents with coffee. Beef stew, coffee and a slice of bread, eight cents.

For the stumble-bums of limited means who must have their beer, there were stale beer dives on side streets like Hester, Canal and Broome, especially on Sunday mornings when it was not unusual to see a couple of bums busily upending tiers of beer barrels and draining the remaining drops through the bunghole into buckets. This harvest was sold to the stale beer groggeries generally located in basements, where in turn it was peddled out at two cents a mug.

Try as hard as I would, I never seemed to earn more than a few cents in one day. My clothes were faded, out of shape and beginning to wear threadbare.

After several weeks of the ten- and twenty-cent lodginghouses, I became so plagued with vermin that I made a voluntary trip back to the Municipal Lodging House to rid myself of the free riders. I was no longer worried about spoiling my clothes. That stage had passed. To add further to my physical discomfort, holes appeared in the bottoms of my shoes. I put a thick piece of cardboard in each shoe. As the holes increased in size, the false soles wore out faster, so I carried spares in my pocket for quick changes.

Christmas came, and again I joined the line in front of the Bowery Mission. This time the line was even longer, and a light snow was falling; but I hung grimly on, moving ahead step by step for long hours. Slapping my arms, like others in the endless procession of miserable creatures, all trying to keep warm in the biting wind and falling snow, I thought back to last Christmas and the folks at home.

For six weeks I had been "on the town," and now, here I was on Christmas Day, for the second time in one month, standing in line for hours waiting on the bounty of the Bowery Mission. If all this could happen in only a few months, and long before my eighteenth birthday, what was my outlook for the future? I shivered and moved forward another step on the heels of the bum in front of me.

Turkey and mashed potatoes, beans, pumpkin pie and coffee. And I was still hungry. The generous portions had gone into a bottomless cavern. Several hours later, still hungry, I moved into the circle of a Salvation Army group. I was a bit timid at first, but with a little encouragement I was soon singing hymns and Christmas carols with the rest of them. When they moved onto the next stand, I fell in line like an old trooper and followed. When they finally marched into Salvation Army headquarters, I was not at all surprised that they invited me to dinner. As no questions were asked, I enjoyed my second Christmas offering with a clear conscience. It was the first time I had ever sung for my supper, but not the last.

On the night of December 31, I mustered enough courage to wander off the reservation and stroll the several blocks down Park Row to City Hall Plaza, where thousands of our good citizens were gathered to celebrate the passing of the old year and the coming of the new. And there on the outer rim of the multitude, still hungry, still penniless, and trying to look as inconspicuous as possible in my ill-fitting outfit, the moisture from wet pavements seeping through cardboard soles of worn shoes, I cheered with the mob at the coming of the brave new year.

The City Hall was festooned with red, white and blue electric lights and draped with large American flags. John Philip Sousa's band played the "Stars and Stripes Forever," and a chorus of five hundred voices echoed into the night.

At midnight a gigantic fireworks set was ignited, and then while rockets screamed into the air, the face of New York's mayor, Robert A. Van Wyck, appeared, rimmed in fire. It was a glorious sight. Completely thrilled by the spectacle, I lifted my own voice with the others, singing "Auld Lang Syne," and almost felt myself one of the people until I realized that I did not even have the price of a ten-cent flop.

That night, however, because we were all Americans and, as

such, had even the right to get drunk and crawl into a doorway to sleep it off as Americans sometimes do on such occasions, the cops left me alone in common with other celebrants; so I cuddled up in my favorite alleyway undisturbed until time to look for breakfast.

On New Year's night I invited myself to work out again with the Salvation Army. Again I dined well. Things were picking up. In the days that followed, the captain helped me find several odd jobs and also allowed me to sing for my dinner when hungry. In one week I saved two dollars.

On Bayard Street near Elizabeth there were basement stores where one could pick up a better garment by turning in one not quite so good, plus a modest "fee for handling." For a dollar and a half I was able to make such a trade. What I received was not much better than my own, but it did fit me and was a decided improvement.

I was so enthusiastic at ridding myself of the shrunken suit that I bought a shirt for twenty cents and a cap for a nickel and discarded the worn hat. Feeling much more confident, I began to wander farther from the Bowery district searching for a job. Then something happened that completely altered my condition in life.

* 6 *

A WELL-DRESSED MAN beckoned to me and asked if I would like to earn a quarter. After trotting along with him for several blocks, I was handed a slip of paper and a check, and pointing to the entrance of a large store, Acker, Merrill and Condit Company, he said I was to have an order filled there, present the check and return with the package and change while he did another errand.

I took off, according to directions. In due time I was handed a package, some bills and small change and then I set out to meet the man, without stopping to wonder why he was such a trusting person. In a few minutes, however, he was beside me relieving me of the package and the change. Two other fellows were there also. They were detectives.

Once again I was in a patrol wagon, this time really en route to the police station. The check was a forgery and this was only one of several such transactions by the same man, only this time they had set a trap and caught up with him. I told my story truthfully and expected to be turned loose, but not so.

I had no home and therefore must be held under lock and key in the House of Detention at 203 Mulberry Street as a material witness until wanted. My patron was to be held in the city prison, charged with forgery and obtaining goods under false pretenses.

Having been pushed around by the East Side police during the past two months, I became quite panicky until the booking sergeant informed me that I would receive two dollars for each day I was held as a witness, plus mileage fees to and from court. He also informed me that it was my privilege to petition the State for suitable clothes in which to appear in court. It sounded too good to be true.

In the House of Detention I was assigned to a room in which there was already one occupant, whose name, I learned, was Charles T. Jones. The door of our room was kept locked and I noticed that the outside windows were protected with bars.

Meals were served in the room and, except for one hour of exercise each day under close supervision, Jones and I were kept pretty well isolated. He had a deck of cards and taught me to play pinochle; we played from early morning until lights out at ten o'clock.

Jones was frequently taken out of the room and many times

was not returned for hours. For several days he was morose and uncommunicative, seldom saying a word. Finally, he asked point-blank if I had been put in the room to spy on him.

Evidently I convinced him to the contrary because he loosened up and voluntarily told me some of the facts concerning his own case. He explained that for several years he had been employed in Houston, Texas, by a wealthy oil man named William Marsh Rice, as valet and secretary. Later Rice moved to New York, bringing Jones with him.

Suddenly Rice died and when it was found that the bulk of his estate had been left to an attorney, Albert T. Patrick, whom Rice had known only a few months, an autopsy was held and traces of mercury were found in his stomach.

The signature of Rice on the will and on several large checks cashed by Lawyer Patrick were more closely examined and pronounced forgeries. Patrick was arrested, charged with forgery and suspicion of murder. As the principal witness in the sensational case Jones, whose age was about twenty-six, was held in the House of Detention and had already been there several weeks when I was locked in with him.

I made a written request for suitable wearing apparel in which to appear in the trial court and was surprised and gratified when a deputy took me to a downtown shop and had me fitted with a good suit, shoes, linen and a hat, at the expense of the State.

I was taken to the Criminal Court Building twice. I was scared stiff in the witness box but got through without trouble.

At the trial I learned that the defendant, a member of a well-known New York family, had been free on bail while I, merely a witness, had been kept under lock and key. He was found guilty and then paroled.

I was discharged and given thirty-two dollars for witness and mileage fees. When I bade good-by to my roommate, Charles Jones, he inquired if the police had questioned me regarding anything he had said during our two weeks together. I truthfully said no.

I left the House of Detention with the best "front" I had ever owned. Now, if ever, I was determined to find a job, but was still timid about leaving the Bowery because in all of New York it was the only section in which I knew my way around.

From newspaper accounts published later, it developed that my former roommate Jones had made a confession in which he said that he had seen Albert T. Patrick holding a towel over the face of Rice as Rice lay on his bed. In a subsequent confession Jones admitted that he personally killed Rice by holding the towel, saturated with chloroform, over his eighty-four-year-old benefactor's face while he slept. He swore that Patrick had induced him to kill his employer by agreeing to pay him ten thousand dollars a year for life from the proceeds of the Rice will which purported to leave the bulk of his fortune to Patrick.

After signing the confession, Jones cut his throat with a knife which he said later was given him by Patrick. He recovered and repeated his confession at the trial. The trial opened on January 20, 1902, with Jones, the self-confessed murderer as the State's witness, and on March 26 Patrick was convicted of murder in the first degree.

Patrick married his housekeeper, Mrs. Addie M. Francis, in the Tombs prison before being sent to the death house at Sing Sing on August 7, 1903. Two weeks before he was to die he won a stay of execution and sentence was later set for January 20, 1906. Before that day arrived New York's Governor Frank Higgins commuted the sentence to life imprisonment. Finally, on November 26, 1912, Governor John Dix granted him a full pardon. Charlie Jones, who actually committed the murder, was sentenced to ten years in prison, but was turned loose in little more than a year.

American in the Rough

Houston, Tex., Nov. 17, 1954 (INS.):

The curtain fell last week on the final act of one of America's most celebrated murder cases when an old man, broken in health, fired a bullet into his brain. The suicide of Charles T. Jones in Baytown, Texas, thus eliminated the remaining actor in the William Marsh Rice murder saga— a drama of greed, betrayal and intrigue.

I found work in a penny arcade at 21 Bowery, directly opposite Chinatown's Pell, Mott and Doyers streets. The entrance was brilliant with clusters of electric lights, and the walls were lined with coin machines of every type, including some shocking peep shows. Facing the entrance was a gigantic electric banjo that played incessantly. A palmist, Madame Dora, enjoyed a fish-bowl existence in the glassed-in bay window facing the Bowery.

The place had always intrigued me, but on the only occasion I had mustered enough courage to enter, after being a guest of the City Dump, I had been given the bum's rush. Now, with a decent "front," I walked right in and faced the manager for a job. I could hardly believe my cleaned and polished ears when he said, "If you can use a mop and a broom I'll pay you eight dollars a week." In another week I was emptying coin machines and rolling pennies for the bank deposit.

Besides Madame Dora, there was her husband, Professor Cohn, who had the tintype concession; Charlie Englehart, who ran the shooting gallery; Barney, with the punching bags; and Smithy, who handed out a nickel cigar when you bounced a baseball against the hard skull of a grinning human target.

This group took me to their collective bosom with an invitation to midnight gatherings in Hung Far Low's restaurant on Pell Street.

The Chinatown of early 1901 was squeezed into two short blocks on Pell Street from Bowery to Mott and a curving, twisting little thoroughfare about two hundred yards long called Doyers Street, starting at Bowery and ending at Pell.

Sandwiched between the gambling joints, restaurants and shops, including basements connected by underground tunnels, opium dens did a flourishing business with both white and Oriental customers. The fumes of burning opium mingled with the odor of stale beer and other smells peculiar to the neighborhood.

Several well-known characters made a comfortable living exploiting Chinatown activities. One was old Tom Lee, a real Chinese, who controlled most of the gambling and vice in the district and who was also the active head of the On Leon Tong.

The other character, George Washington Connors, known as Chuck Connors, I came to know well. He was reputed to have been born on Mott Street and spoke reasonably good Chinese, which he turned to good account by establishing himself as Chinatown's chief "lobbygow," or tourists' guide, and made it stick.

When not earning an honest dollar in his chosen profession, he frequented the Chatham Club, at 6 Doyers Street, or he could be found just around the corner at the Pelham Club, operated by Mike Saulter, where several years later Irving Berlin was to begin his career as a singing waiter under his youthful name of Izzy Baline.

Charlie Englehart represented Chuck at No. 21, and it was from there, just opposite Pell Street, that most of the sightseeing groups were started to Chinatown.

Many a night, after No. 21 closed, Englehart indulgently accompanied me to one dive after another, until I knew my way around the East Side and entered most of the tougher joints without interference.

One of the favorites was Mike Lyons' bar near Houston Street. This bar never closed, and was patronized almost nightly by such men as Big Tim and Little Tim Sullivan, Gentleman

Jim Corbett, Bob Fitzsimmons, Terry McGovern, Mayor Robert Van Wyck, Teddy Roosevelt, and Sailor Tom Sharkey.

Steve Brodie's was a popular hangout for the sporting crowd. The walls were covered with trophies and pictures of celebrities. In a glass case near the bar was the diamond-studded belt presented to the great John L. Sullivan after his defeat of Jake Kilrain.

On the outside of the saloon, above the entrance, was painted the figure of a man perpetually suspended in mid-air between the Brooklyn Bridge and the East River below. Steve, hero of the doubtful jump, died later that same year, 1901.

Such places on the Bowery as McGurk's Suicide Hall, Mike Saulter's, The Dump, Cob Dock, the Fleabag were tough, but there were dozens of other dives in the neighborhood even more vicious, disreputable, and downright dangerous. These were known only by street numbers. One of the worst was handy enough, being next door to the arcade. The entrance to No. 19 looked like any other saloon. Once inside, a rear door opened into a room extending all the way back to New Bowery. There was a bar, scores of bare tables and a small space for dancing. This was seldom used, as most of the patrons were either full of "hop," or stupefied from drink. The piano player was a pasty-faced hophead who, when he reached the verge of exhaustion, would draw out a syringe and inject a shot of dope into his arm without any show of false modesty. After rejuvenation, he would bang out more tunes and fall into a routine of filthy songs.

Number 19 was a hangout for pickpockets, prostitutes, and users and peddlers of narcotics. The women hangers-on were the very dregs of the slums, disheveled and diseased. Nevertheless, large numbers of Navy men and deepwater sailors managed to find their way in, along with a few curious tourists, many of whom remained long enough to regret it.

It was a common sight to see figures slumped in chairs or reclining against walls, totally unconscious. A slight dose of

44

chloral hydrate dropped carelessly in the customer's glass just
before closing time made the going simple and easy. The back
alley was dimly lit and traffic was light in the early morning
hours, and when the rising sun or perhaps a cold rain caressed
the fevered brow of the sleeper, bringing him back to consciousness, his wallet was missing, and he felt as if he had met a
locomotive head on.

Such was New York's lower East Side at the turn of the
century.

* 7 *

A FEW DAYS BEFORE the unofficial opening of Coney Island on
Decoration Day, Charlie Englehart helped me to land a job at
George C. Tilyou's Steeplechase Park. The steeplechase was a
series of a half-dozen metal tracks, circling the entire lot, on
which an equal number of inanimate hobbyhorses, each bearing
a rider, chased up hill and down dale as the jockeys strove to
lead the pack to the finish line by lunging the body forward at
strategic times and places.

The acres of space within the circle of tracks were used for
freak shows, carousels, ferris wheels, chambers of horrors, shooting galleries, mystic maze, and a mammoth dance hall. I worked
in the shooting gallery from nine in the morning until six in
the evening seven days a week. With evenings free I looked
around for a night job on the side to pick up extra money.

Henderson's beer garden was the largest and most unique
place on the boardwalk. It featured grand opera with excellent
talent, and the price of admission was five cents for a large
stein of beer. It was there I found the extra work as a super-
numerary, working two tabloid performances each night.

In *Fra Diavolo* I carried a spear with a rubber tip, in *Carmen*
I carried a wooden musket; in those and other popular operas

45

I sang in the ensemble and made all the motions without learning either the words or the language in which they were written. My pay was one dollar in cash each night. This brought my weekly earnings to nearly twenty dollars.

When I had a bank roll of twenty-five dollars, I packed my bag and left for Buffalo and the Pan-American Exposition, clutching a letter from Charlie Englehart to the manager of Frederick Thompson's newest ride, "A Trip to the Moon."

In Buffalo the gentleman to whom my letter was addressed kissed me off to a subordinate who listened to my recital of past experience at the arcade, the steeplechase and Henderson's. Despite the fervency of my appeal, during which I took advantage of the carnival man's prerogative to exaggerate a trifle, I failed to land among the favored employees of Mr. Thompson's "Trip to the Moon," but I did wind up with a pair of scales, guessing weights on the midway. This happened on my eighteenth birthday. (Guessing one's weight is not difficult once the knack is acquired. When we failed to guess within three pounds, we looked properly mortified; whereupon, new customers stepped into the circle to be felt, prodded and pinched. If we lost, we were even. If we won, a dime was still the tenth part of a dollar. The gag was to ease your hands lightly over the knobs, bumps, angles, protuberances, and, if lucky, the curves of the prospect, while softly murmuring, "You weigh about . . . about . . . let me see . . . about umteen pounds," while gently propelling the giggling subject toward the scales.)

Four weeks of spieling my act while gently massaging fat ones and thin ones was quite enough and I was glad to shove off for Chicago.

Rather than ride the brake beams free and spoil my good clothes with the dirt and grime of the road, I chose to pay for a ride on the cushions even though the sacrifice would barely leave me in a solvent condition. I had learned the value of a good front when seeking a job.

In Chicago I looked up a theatrical booking office. After handing out a good line, I was given a card to the Sam T. Jacks Theater on lower Madison Street, where a singer of illustrated songs was wanted. I could sing fairly well and knew the melody and most of the words of every song turned out by Tin Pan Alley for years back. What could I lose by trying?

I was hired and did two numbers at the evening performance. One was a nifty little item, "The Mansion of Aching Hearts," followed by "The Fatal Rose of Red." Later my repertoire included "The Moth and the Flame," "Just Break the News to Mother," "The Star and Flower," "She Is More to Be Pitied Than Censured," and other tear jerkers.

The show was billed as the London Burlesquers, and featured a score of buxom beauties whom Mother Nature had done right well by. My pay was twenty-five dollars a week, but most of it went for meals and room, and keeping up with the Joneses, meaning the ladies of the ensemble. After several weeks in Chicago, the show moved on into Iowa and Nebraska playing one-night stands. At Omaha we played three nights. The show closed late in August after doubling back toward Chicago.

Until reaching Omaha, I had given little thought to the future, but when the show turned back, I cut loose with the hope of continuing west. In the hotel lobby I met Jim Parker, a tall, good-looking cattleman from Dawes County, Nebraska. He was shipping a carload of breeding cattle to Crawford in the northwest corner of the state. I was invited to travel with the car to water and feed the stock, and on arrival he would hire me as a ranch hand. This promised work for a few months and enough money to pay my way to California. I rode in the caboose with the train crew and was met by Mr. Parker on arrival at Crawford.

At the ranch, ten miles out of town, my boss undertook to make a cowhand out of me. Before a select group of cowhands, cooks, and hangers-on, who perched themselves on the rails of the corral fence like a flock of buzzards, I entered the corral to mount a Western cow pony for the first time.

I approached the pony from the nearest side, neglected to bring the reins up over the animal's head, placed my right toe in the wrong stirrup, and nonchalantly lifted my left leg up and over the pony's rumble seat. Fortunately no bones were broken. A kindly cowhand lifted me gently to my feet, then gave me a lesson in mounting a fractious cow pony.

Besides learning to mount and ride properly, my education included throwing the lariat and cracking a twenty-foot bull whip. All of this added up to "love's labor's lost" when Parker relieved me of my cow-punching chores after two weeks with the explanation that I was running all the meat off the cows' bones.

Unfortunately I had been left on the job long enough to invest my first half-month's salary in a lariat, spurs, bull whip and a horsehair rope. Being broke and in need of a job, I let Parker sell me on taking a job as a sheepherder at Chadron, twenty miles distant.

A Mr. Honeyman hired me at fifteen dollars a month and "found." Honeyman grazed twenty thousand sheep, divided into five herds. The headquarters ranch, located on the Niobrara River, was equipped with corrals, chutes, and shearing pens, but the great herds of sheep, each one the charge of a single herder, lived, grazed and frequently died on the great expanse of free Government lands on the open prairie without benefit of corral or permanent camp.

In the fall of the year the herds of ewes were corraled at the home ranch and allowed to run with the rams for a brief time. Then the herd moved out on the open prairie, followed by the herder in his lumbering wagon drawn by a couple of ancient horses. These two nags, a couple of collie dogs and four thousand dumb sheep would be his only companions as the scorching suns of the plains gave way to the rains and light snow flurries of late fall. Then would come the swirling blizzards of deep winter, while the sheep drove before the blast or huddled in canyons and the marrow almost froze in the sheepherder's bones.

Picture the prairie schooner of pioneer days; shorten it by a third, widen it to extend over the wheels to provide more living space, pull the canvas smoothly over the wooden ribs, put a small window in the front and a divided door in the rear, and you have the nice cozy home of a Nebraska sheepherder.

Inside is a small wood-burning stove, with stove pipe protruding through the canvas top. A bunk built crossways occupies the front. Hinged to the bunk and extending between two benches is a table. You furnish your own mattress and blankets. As for sheets, I never heard of them.

Tacked up in the wagon were the two "house rules": sheep are not to be killed for food under penalty of dismissal. Horses must not be used to herd the sheep. Rules, however, never prevented a fool sheep from stumbling into a prairie-dog hole and breaking a leg occasionally, in which case I assumed it was permissible to indulge in lamb chops for dinner.

With the dogs, horses and sheep I headed for the far horizon and a very indefinite future. Boss Honeyman spent the first few days with me so that I might have the benefit of experience acquired during a lifetime on the range. I was instructed how to feed, water, bed down and protect four thousand sheep who must manage to forage for themselves during fall, winter and spring on the open prairie.

I was told how to hold the herd together in fair weather or foul; how to detect missing groups of sheep by keeping track of the hundred black and brown ones, known as "markers"; how to locate and salvage strays; how to keep prowling and howling coyotes and timber wolves at a distance; and how to wangle the most help from the sheep dogs, which were efficient enough in the beginning but which, through mishandling, could quickly become useless as aides in guiding and guarding the flock.

There was so much to learn, and all for fifteen dollars a month. One thing I could vouch for: the job would be a steady one. Sixteen hours a day, seven days a week, thirty or thirty-one days a month. Fortunately for me, and probably for the flock, I was starting at the best time of the year—autumn.

At break of day the sheep were on the move, spreading out fanwise, nibbling the grass, as they moved slowly forward, until by midmorning they covered an area of a square mile or more. After a leisurely breakfast I lazed the hours away, generally on a slight elevation from which I could keep an eye on the herd. If "markers" were missing, it was a signal to look for trouble. Other sheep wore bells to give the alarm if the herd started moving at night.

The sheep dogs, Don and Shep, were invaluable. If the leaders of the herd, a mile distant, started spreading too fast, a word or a pointed finger was enough to send Don or Shep off like a rocket. Immediately the line of sheep would reverse and head back in the opposite direction.

The dog will wear himself out if he likes and understands the herder, but threats or blows will cause him to cringe until eventually he becomes useless. Then give him another master, and he will work as intelligently as before. He awaits your slightest command with pricked ears and expectant eye. When looking for stray sheep, he anticipates your every movement, rushes ahead and soon returns escorting a badly scared piece of mutton.

Early in November Mr. Honeyman arrived with my sixty-day allotment of potatoes, flour, corn meal, lard, molasses, brown sugar and bacon. There were also letters from the old home. Hungry for human companionship, I was glad to see him. He remained overnight, so I had someone to talk to for a few hours at least. Not that he brought much in the way of news, being almost as much out of touch with wordly happenings as I was. The Sears, Roebuck catalogue was his best friend and correspondent.

After he left, I became terribly lonesome and morbid, especially after the first cold spell and heavy fall of snow. Life seemed to be just one mess of sheep, coyotes, jack rabbits and prairie dogs. Don and Shep were my only companions and they stayed as close to me as two fleas. I repeatedly sang every song I knew for their sole entertainment and in order that I could at least hear my own voice.

My first real blizzard nearly proved to be the last for the herd and herder alike. I had chosen a large canyon as a temporary camp. The walls rose high enough for partial protection from the storms, some of which blew up quite suddenly. Here I could park my wagon and allow my hobbled nags freedom to graze during the day, while the flock spread out over the flat plain, sometimes pawing through inches of snow to reach the dry grass.

The advantage of partial shelter, however, was offset by additional danger from prowling wolves and coyotes. On the open prairie they kept at a distance, but in the canyons, hidden by deep shadows, they sometimes sneaked among the sheep, slitting throats before even the dogs were aware of their presence.

On a night in mid-December a light snow completely covered the bedded-down herd. It turned bitter cold and soon the wind began to howl through the canyon. Ready for trouble, I turned in fully clothed. I was awakened by a blast that nearly overturned the wagon. Bundled up to my eyes, I stepped out into the blinding gale to find the sheep already moving down the canyon before the driving storm.

Hurrying as best I could, at times stumbling and falling, I managed to head off the closely packed mass of sheep. Finding it impossible to stop the forward movement, I had only one course to follow: drift along with the oncoming avalanche while running the dogs up and down the line of sheep, hoping to keep them together in one solid pack.

Through the night we drove on, striving to retard the headlong rush, trying to prevent portions of the herd from breaking away. When daylight finally filtered through the darkness and storm, the wind partially died down and we were able to bring the mad rush to a gradual halt.

The exhausted sheep settled down while a light snow continued to fall. Soon the entire herd became just a white blob on the prairie. Too tired to move, I dropped down on the snow beside the two panting dogs. Then I noticed little holes forming in the snow and realized that hundreds of sheep would soon smother unless rousted out. I began hauling them out and soon, with the excited dogs nipping at legs right and left, the mass of flesh began to erupt and stagger free of the jam. A rising temperature helped, but when we finally began moving back toward camp several hundred dead and dying sheep were left behind to furnish a feast for lurking coyotes.

Hours later when we reached our camp, I found one of the hobbled nags standing patiently in the lee of the wagon. Days later when the snow melted, I found the bones of the other far up the canyon.

In the months to come there would be other storms, light and heavy, but none that would offer such a challenge as the one through which I was lucky to emerge alive, even though I lost part of my herd.

Daylight melted into darkness; wolves howled; dogs barked; sheep bawled. The wind blew icy blasts, and the drops of moisture that fell from the panting jaws of Don and Shep froze before touching the ground. Time meant nothing except that with the coming of darkness another day had passed and spring was that much nearer.

Christmas came and went, and I was not even sure what day it was. The same was true when the new year of 1902 made its bow. My last Christmas, on the Bowery, had been nothing to remember with pride. Now my lot seemed to have improved, if only slightly. I was earning my board and lodging and even had a little something on the credit side of Mr. Honeyman's ledger. Not overlooking the fact that I exercised no little influence in my own particular sphere as boss over two dogs, one horse and four thousand sheep.

The boss arrived early in March. I told him the story of the blizzard, the lost sheep and the horse. He was upset but agreed that I had done everything possible under the circumstances. I was prepared to quit the job even if not fired, but he painted such a picture of happiness and contentment waiting just around the corner when spring would come, when the green grass would sprout overnight, when the prairie would be covered with strange wild flowers, when the little lambs would arrive, and the big sheep would be sheared of their wool, I fell for the blarney. Besides, I needed to add to my slim bank roll.

Early in April a man arrived leading a horse just about a year removed from the glue factory. Following instructions, I began working the herd back toward Chadron. Then overnight, just as the boss man had predicted, the prairie was covered with a sheen of bright green grass.

The sheep had lived on dry grass throughout the winter. Now, with the tender green blades barely visible above the ground, they literally went wild. A nibble here, a nibble there, then run six feet for another. The grass was always greener somewhere else. Don and Shep wore the pads off their feet trying to hold the herd together.

As the grass grew longer, the herd settled down to steady grazing. But not for long, for this was spring and with the spring came the lambs. Such cute little things, like all new arrivals, provided you don't have to do for them. In this case, however, the pleasure was all mine.

Mr. Honeyman suspected there might be lambs, so he came out one day and gave me a lecture on the subject. Told me how to receive and take care of the first stragglers. Later, when the deluge came there would be help, but for the first few there would be nothing to it. So said my boss, who should know, for it had been his responsibility to play Cupid last fall when the little matter of time and place had been arranged according to plan.

I'll never forget my first lamb. It was something only a mother sheep could love. It was the color of an orange, then faded to a brownish tinge, gradually losing color until it became a dull gray.

Following instructions, I separated the mother sheep and her gangling youngster from the herd, and this being the first arrival, I took considerable interest in its welfare. The old sheep babied him, answered his every little bleat with a queer kind of throaty rumble and within an hour had him standing on long, wobbly legs doing his best to hang on long enough to finish his first meal.

Next morning the lambing crew arrived and before noon little bundles from heaven were dropping all over the landscape. The crew workers seemed to know by intuition which ewes were about ready to lamb. These were rapidly cut out from the herd and soon the prairie was littered with little white dots indicating that blessed events were happening thick and fast.

There were dozens of cases where mother and lamb became separated. It was the job of the lambing crew to match up mother and lamb wherever possible, and they resorted to many ingenious subterfuges whereby an anxious mother was sometimes persuaded to adopt an alien lamb.

I heard of one practice that verged on downright deceit. It is a fact that once a ewe has smelled her offspring, she never forgets. Even when a lamb is stillborn the mother knows its odor and tries to encourage it to suckle, so the alert sheephand quickly skins the dead animal and with a few strokes of a sack needle stitches the skin to a foundling who has lost its own mother; whereupon the mother of the dead lamb smells the skin and clasps the prodigal to her breast and there you are. It may be deception, but two souls are made happy, not to mention the sheep owner.

With the coming of spring we kept a lookout for rattlesnakes that appeared in considerable numbers after being holed up during the winter. My most uncomfortable moments were the few seconds between the time when I heard the snake's warning rattle and when I located its whereabouts in prairie grass a foot high.

My first impulse was to jump but the direction in which to jump was the all-important thing, so I learned to shiver and stand motionless until I was sure. If let alone, the rattler would crawl off and disappear, but if you wanted a fight you could have it. He would gather half his length into a coil, loop the balance into a figure S and then, with beady eyes flashing, tongue darting in and out, head slowly swaying, he would lash out using at least two-thirds of his length for the strike. All the while, the rattles on its tail in the center of the coil would be buzzing ominously.

By the middle of May the lambing job was over and I had worked the herd toward the home ranch for shearing. Each morning I turned five hundred heavily coated sheep into a corral and, in turn, received back a similar number of skinny, frightened-looking creatures from which the fleece had been removed. The shearer merely grabbed the sheep, snapped it over on its back and presto! soon the trembling animal was struggling to its feet practically naked.

It was at shearing time that the weathers, the older ewes, and certain lambs were selected for market and segregated for shipment. It was also at this time, the first week in June of 1902, that I decided to draw my pay and bid good-by to Mr. Honeyman and four thousand sheep to whose welfare I had devoted nearly a year of my time. On June 10, I headed for Denver and civilization.

* 8 *

EN ROUTE to Denver, two days and one night in a passenger coach attached to a string of freight cars, I thought of all that had transpired since leaving Omaha nearly a year before, under the mistaken impression that Crawford, Nebraska, would be only a whistlestop on the way to California. Winter on the prairie, an endless succession of lonesome days and troubled nights, enlivened only by bleating sheep, barking dogs and howling coyotes, had been long and tough. The sunny days of spring with plenty of green grass and hordes of frolicking lambs had already mellowed some of the memories of those months, but for a long time I would remember a panicky night in December when the blizzard shrieked and the herd drove blindly on while the dogs fought a losing battle and I wondered more than once what would happen if I should falter and be overwhelmed by that avalanche of flesh moving slowly forward. Anyhow, it was over and I was on my way again with accumulated savings of nearly one hundred dollars.

No one would think of visiting Denver in those days without journeying to the top of Pikes Peak. With a group of other simple-minded tourists, I went to the little town of Manitou nestling at the foot of the peak. Entering a car, we were pushed by a funny little engine up a cog road to the top of the peak some fourteen thousand feet in the clouds.

Arriving at the summit, our party was huddled together for the usual souvenir group photograph. During the excitement incidental to the picture-taking, a major operation was performed whereby a lump in the form of a wallet was removed from my left hip. In the official photograph a gentleman of the city-slicker type cuddles close to a slim young man wearing a white Stetson hat. And there we have the story of the missing purse and nearly a year's wages.

In Denver I packed my lariat, bull whip, spurs and hair rope into a box and shipped them home to Aunt Lina. Then I climbed into an empty freight car heading west.

Arriving in Salt Lake City, on my nineteenth birthday, I learned that I might sign up for work at a railroad grading camp in Nevada with fare advanced. With a dozen other nondescripts, I was let off at a desert signpost inscribed ROKEBY. Besides the signpost there were about twenty tents equipped with bunks, including one for cooking and another where meals were served to some four hundred other laborers.

Salt Lake was five hundred miles behind me and Reno was sixty miles west. I was progressing. The contracting firm was Cory Brothers and my wage was two dollars a day and "found."

Steam shovels bit their way through the hills, and as fast as the ground was leveled, redwood ties were dropped, rails were laid over them and spikes were driven.

After two days of laying ties I fell into a prize job driving the camp water wagon, a huge iron tank on wheels drawn by four horses. Twice a day I drove to the nearest pipeline five miles distant, filled the tank wagon and drove back to camp.

Half a mile from camp were several tents, privately owned, including a bar and gambling tables. Here, after a hard day's work, the boys from the grading camp could relax and be painlessly relieved of their silver dollars as fast as they were earned.

Cory Brothers paid off every Saturday night and, like other

contractors of the time, used the quaint custom of paying by time check, which was a good thirty days hence. Rather than wait a month for their pay, the men cashed the time checks at the saloon and accepted a discount of five per cent, which meant they worked one day out of every twenty for nothing.

The payoff at the bar was in silver dollars. Between the pay-off bar and the exit were half a dozen green-covered tables featuring roulette, dice and faro layouts. It took a man with steady nerves and resolute will to run the gantlet without taking a whirl at the wheel or the galloping dominoes. That oasis was my downfall. Not that I was a gambler or even had funds for the purpose. But it was July in Nevada and hot!

On the fourteenth day I allowed my overheated team to relax in the shadow of the gambling tent while I placed a small bet on number seventeen just as a straw boss walked in the door. I was discharged forthwith.

I had worked fourteen days including two Sundays. After train fare from Ogden to Rokeby was deducted, and my time check cashed at the tent bar, I rolled into Reno the next morning with sixteen silver dollars.

Gambling was wide open in Nevada, then as now, and every public place, from the smallest saloon to the well-equipped Palace Club, had two or more gambling layouts.

I did not lose my entire sixteen dollars at one sitting. After losing only half of my nest egg, I arose on the pretense of needing a bit of food, walked into the Old Horseshoe restaurant, which was a part of the Palace, and ate a hearty meal before I returned to the table to watch with fascination while the little ivory marble persistently skipped my number. The dealer patiently added my remaining coins to the small-sized silver mine stacked in front of him.

With silver no longer burning holes in my pockets, I was anxious to reach my final objective—San Francisco.

I had been told by fellow travelers in side-door Pullmans

that the best way to get to any place quick, aside from "riding the cushions" at prevailing rates, was to ride the top of passenger trains.

That night, while the westbound passenger train stood at the station, I climbed to a car roof, flattened myself out, and took a firm grip on a ventilator. After a wild ride around the mountainous curves of the High Sierras, I ducked my head just as we flashed into a dark, cavernous opening which I thought was the usual short tunnel. It was not a tunnel but the forerunner of miles of sheds built over the tracks for protection against snow slides. A heavy pall of smoke from the coal-burning engine lay over me like a shroud. It drove into my throat, eyes and nostrils and threatened to strangle me.

When the train pulled into a little Sierra town, my feet hit the ground before we stopped rolling, and I spent the next several hours in agony while my stomach revolted from the effects of the smoke I had involuntarily inhaled.

Hooking onto a passing freight train, I was thrown off at Roseville. I went inland to forage for food.

And there was California hospitality at its best—a great big tree literally groaning under its weight of big black figs. I had eaten nothing since leaving Reno and even that had deserted me after my hectic ride the night before. I ate the luscious figs without stint, but with almost disastrous consequences. I never left the shade of that tree for twenty-four hours. I did not dare. Finally, I felt up to moving on again and made my way into Sacramento and then to San Francisco, where I arrived in July of 1902.

II

* 9 *

IT HAD TAKEN nearly thirteen months to cross the continent and in between there had been plenty of excitement, but at last here was the end of the trail, or so I thought. There came a fleeting memory of another day, nearly two years before, when New York seemed to be the answer to all things desirable; but once there, the mirage had faded. New York had looked good, but only from a distance. Well, here I was at journey's end again; but this was California, the end of the rainbow. Now for the pot of gold!

In the washroom of the Ferry Building I discarded my grimy overalls, smoothed out the wrinkles in my clothes and started out eagerly to look for a job. Not expecting too much the first day, I was satisfied to wash dishes for food, which I needed badly.

In the days that followed I discovered that when you are broke and without influence one place is much like another. My clothes looked shoddy and slept-in. My shoes were worn and run-down at the heels, and my only linen was the faded blue shirt on my back.

I gravitated to Skid Row, which was Howard Street between Third and Fifth. There I could get a room for a quarter and eat in the cheap hash houses for a nickel or dime. I applied at every place where I thought there was a chance for a job.

At night I walked the length of Kearny Street to the Barbary Coast district and, having nothing better to do, just hung around the dives on Pacific, Jackson and Commercial streets watching the activity and hoping something might turn up. Occasionally I washed dishes for meals and sleeping money. I reasoned that if I could raise enough cash to buy a decent "front" I might apply for a job as a singing waiter, but at the end of two weeks I had not accumulated as much as a dollar at one time.

One afternoon, almost in desperation, I approached a man in the lobby of an office building on Market Street and asked him for help in getting a job. He was sympathetic, asked a lot of questions, and then, to my surprise, took me to a suite of law offices in the same building. I poured out the story of my wanderings. When I explained that I had been hanging out on Pacific Street, he said that I would probably get into trouble there and that I should get a job in the country.

Calling in a husky clerk, he repeated part of my story and asked him to take me to the employment agency of Murray and Ready and get me a job on a ranch.

As he shook hands and wished me luck, he left a ten-dollar gold piece in my palm. At the employment office the clerk paid a fee of two dollars, and I was handed an order to report to the J. H. Glyde ranch near Dixon, California, at thirty dollars a month and "found." The clerk then took me into a store, paid for a pair of blankets and handed me my fare to Dixon. *

At Dixon I was picked up by a man who looked over my slip and drove me to a ranch house miles from town. My first assignment was the task of delivering twelve mules to a ranch ten

---

* The man who did this for me was George D. Collins, at that time one of California's most prominent attorneys. Three years later, at the peak of his legal career, he was indicted for bigamy. The jury disagreed, he fled to Canada, was extradited, tried and convicted of perjury in connection with the bigamy trial and sentenced to fourteen years in San Quentin prison. He always claimed to be falsely convicted and refused parole several times, demanding a full pardon.

After serving ten years, he was pardoned and passed away a free man in June of 1944. Whatever failings George D. Collins may have had in his personal or professional dealings, he was kind to a friendless boy and I shall always remember him with gratitude.

miles distant; I rode one of the two leaders while the other ten strung out behind me in pairs. Each mule was equipped with its own complete wagon harness, which jangled up and down on its back as we proceeded down the dirt road at a slow trot.

Leading six pairs of mules, even in harness, is not too much of a problem for the average farm hand, but on this trip I came to a creek, the waters of which were usually only knee-high. Water had broken through an irrigation project and lifted the creek water to a depth of several feet. The mules lost footing and began to swim. The harness floated and became entangled in the legs of other animals pushing along behind.

Within a few seconds I was the center of a dozen scared and squealing mules completely tangled in harness, floundering around in a sort of mystic maze. As we scrambled ashore, the confusion increased, with the mules trying to kick the harness free, hoofs flying in all directions, and me in the center of the mess like the ringmaster of a circus. I was scared speechless. The excitement brought farm hands to the scene, who rushed in and cut harness right and left until the animals were under control.

In the Big House on the home ranch that night my future was debated, but instead of being discharged, I was transferred to another ranch in the hills back of Winters. I was assigned a saddle horse and instructed to keep the fences repaired and see that scattered groups of cows were periodically driven toward the few places where water was available.

For weeks I performed routine duties, chasing lazy cows from under shade trees to the water troughs and repairing a fence here and there. Then on a hot afternoon, after running my horse up hill and down dale, I dismounted on the summit of a steep hill, tossed the reins over the horse's head and sat down to rest.

Suddenly my poor horse settled to the ground, folded up like

an accordion, then slowly rolled over the side of the hill, turning over and over as he disappeared from view.

I found him on his back wedged in a gully. There he lay on
his back, feebly waving his legs in the air as if the whole thing
were completely futile. He was wedged so tight that I was
unable to free him, but I shoveled away enough dirt to allow
him to roll gently over on his side. The net result of my excavation work was that he expired lying there comfortably on
his side instead of in the more ridiculous position of being
propped up on his back fanning the air with his feet.

It was tough on the horse, but he had nothing on me because
I was discharged forthwith, and twenty dollars were deducted
from my pay to cover his loss. James Parker of Nebraska was
right when he said I was not cut out to be a cowhand.

I returned to San Francisco to try my luck once more.

The net result of my sojourn in California's back country
could be summed up literally as "working off a dead horse." I
had left San Francisco with only the ten-dollar gold piece placed
in my palm by George D. Collins. I returned with the same
gold piece, plus eight silver dollars. After having my suit
cleaned and buying new shoes, linen and a hat to replace the
old Stetson, I still had a few dollars left to tide me over while
seeking work.

In a hotel room I washed and polished myself up and started
out, determined to land a good job. I called at the Orpheum on
O'Farrell Street, at that time a beer garden with tables on the
main floor.

Backstage, the manager listened patiently while I stated my
qualifications, particularly my tour with the London Burlesquers. He gave me a friendly pat and invited me to come
around some other time.

Next, I tried the Oberon Music Hall at Eddy and Powell
streets and then the Belvedere with the same result. Without

wasting any more time in the downtown tenderloin, I went back to the Barbary Coast.

Skipping the larger show places like the Thalia, Hippodrome, and Midway, I canvassed the small ones and was hired to work in a place called the Cave. The pianist, singer, comedian, juggler and all-round master of ceremonies was a character known only as Nickey. Nickey was so versatile I was never quite sure why he took me in, except that once in a while he had to rest, and while resting he played the piano and I obliged with popular songs.

Nickey's act was half man, half cigar. As he cracked jokes or sang sophisticated songs out of one corner of his mouth, he took sly puffs on the ever-present cigar drooping from the opposite corner, which was never allowed to go out entirely; and if the applause justified an encore, he would go into a juggling act which featured the cigar and was supported by a derby hat and a cane.

My partner's talent for juggling reached its zenith when the time came to divide the evening's harvest of tips. Nickey, the senior partner, assumed the burden of counting the offering which he divided neatly into four equal parts.

He gave me one part and took the other three parts himself, cutting in his cigar and the piano for equal shares. Realization that Nickey furnished most of the entertainment was little comfort to me on slow nights, when I was lucky to receive two dollars for my cut.

In the Cave it was customary to accept invitations to drink with patrons, and it was not unusual for one round of drinks to cost more than my earnings for an entire evening. My financial condition was such that more than once I wished the invitation might extend to a dish of ham and eggs. But human nature being what it is, you could drink yourself under the table at the customer's expense and still be mighty hungry.

One night, just before closing, I had drinks with two men

who looked like foreign seamen ashore for a good time. They claimed to have seen everything in Pacific Street and wondered if that was all the town had to offer. I suggested several choice spots, including the House of All Nations, where the company of carefree ladies could be solicited in any language, from pidgin English at the bottom of the social scale in the basement to the finest Gallic at the top balcony; from these Elysian heights one could gaze down upon his fellow adventurers circling around the several balconies below and in the open court on the ground floor.

I accepted an invitation to guide the party and we made the rounds, including the Nymphia on Stockton Street, the Bella Union at Washington and Kearny, and Purcell's Negro dive, the So Different. After that, I remember walking the length of Jackson Street toward East just as day was breaking.

My last recollection was of standing before the bar in a waterfront saloon. My knees were sagging and wobbly despite every effort of will to straighten them out. I remember crumpling to the floor in a heap, a feeling of utter irresponsibility sweeping over me as I lapsed into a state of blissful unconsciousness.

I never did discover what happened after I passed out or the time that elapsed before I became conscious again. My awakening was accompanied by all of the elements of a tormented soul atoning for past misdeeds—a horrible nightmare coming true.

I was lying on a cot, face down, with my head hanging over the edge while I retched violently, striving to empty my stomach of every single thing not fastened down. My head ached, creaked and cracked, and seemed swollen to such proportions that I put up a shaky hand to make sure it would not pull loose and float upward toward an overhead skylight where a ghostly light just barely broke the darkness of the dingy room.

I must have lapsed into unconsciousness again because when I came to, it was so dark that not even the skylight was visible.

Painfully struggling to my feet, I located a door and beat on it, making a terrible racket.

Suddenly the door opened and two pairs of hands grabbed me and threw me violently on the cot, which collapsed to the floor. Then a voice shouted, "Keep quiet, you bum, or I'll blast you again." I subsided, and the door was slammed shut.

For a long time I lay in a sort of coma, my head feverish and throbbing, my throat parched and my stomach in severe cramps. Sometime after daylight a man came into the room and, without even asking how I felt, told me to open my mouth, then poured steaming hot coffee and rum down my throat until my insides almost sizzled.

As soon as I was able to speak, I asked for a doctor and demanded to know where I was and what had happened. He replied that a doctor had seen me the day before and had said I would be all right, that I was in Mr. Brewer's boardinghouse on Steuart Street, that I had been there for two days and owed more than twelve dollars for medicine, food, lodging and the doctor and that I had better pay up.

Without even searching my pockets, I groaned that I had no money and no prospects of getting any soon. "We'll see about that," said he. "Mr. Brewer says you'll pay or work it out."

Coming back later with more hot coffee and rum, he pointed to a bucket of water and a washbowl and told me to clean up; we were going visiting.

He led me down a flight of stairs and through a saloon past several bleary-eyed men lounging at the bar. Out on the street I was hoisted into a horse-drawn delivery wagon. Dizzy and miserable, I lay on the bottom of the wagon while the driver flapped the reins and we started off. The jolting ride over several blocks of cobblestones almost finished me.

At our destination I managed to get on my feet long enough to be pushed into a room and to a counter where my keeper volunteered my name and nationality, as he handed me a pen with which I scratched my name feebly. Afterward I was handed back into the wagon and given a shot of rum which almost put me out again.

On the return trip I was so far gone that I only remember being carried bodily upstairs and dumped into the room. In the late afternoon food was brought in and I tried to eat, but my stomach was still upset and rebelled so badly that my jailers finally gave me a mug of hot coffee and rum which put me to sleep again. I awoke several times but it was always pitch-dark in the room, and, remembering the manhandling I had received before, I decided to wait until morning before making a move.

Daylight came and with it the same two men.

"Get going," one of them said.

"Get going where?" I groaned.

"Put your shoes on and start moving. You'll find out soon enough," was the reply.

The same wagon was waiting outside, but this time there were six of us besides the driver and the two men in charge, each of whom carried heavy sticks as "persuaders." We were driven to the foot of Howard Street and hustled out of the wagon to a rowboat tied up at the dock. Four of us were shoved down the ladder and the other two, both drunk, were swung over the wharf and dropped like sacks of wheat into the arms of the boat crew. The boardinghouse runners dropped into the boat and shoved off.

* 10 *

I HAD LONG since realized what was happening to me, but under the influence of drugs, liquor and manhandling, I had cared little whether I lived or died. Now, feeling much better for the first time, I began to think things out.

No amount of liquor could have produced such terrible effects as I had suffered during the past three days and nights; consequently, I must have been drugged before being taken to the boardinghouse on Steuart Street. I decided to tell my story to the captain and ask to be set ashore at once.

We were heading for a cluster of three large sailing ships, swinging at anchor. As we came close, I saw that two flew the British flag. Rowing close to the nearest ship, one of the men at the oars shouted, "Ahoy, the *Belfast!*"

A dozen heads showed over the rail; a line was thrown and made fast and then a rope ladder came hurtling down.

My heart was beating like a trip hammer as I climbed the rope ladder, stepped on a broad rail, missed my footing and fell four feet to the deck. The fall almost knocked the breath from my body. I struggled to my feet, confused and bewildered, just as an officer, whom I later learned was the second mate, grabbed my arm and demanded to know if I were a sailor.

"I've sailed on a schooner," I answered.

"Then if you've sailed before," he shouted at me, "why don't you say Sir?" And with that, he plunged his fist into my midriff with such force that my breath left me completely and I caved in, rolling over and over in the scuppers, gasping like a dying fish.

As I wallowed in the gutter trying to regain my feet, three

other men came over the rail and jumped to the deck without assistance. Next came a drunk, pushed from below and hauled from above until his body rested on the wide rail, from which he was allowed to roll over and drop to the deck. After a struggle the second drunk was hauled aboard in the same manner. The officer gave both a good booting, then turned on his heel and walked away.

As he disappeared down a stairway into the cabin, a crew member hauled me out of the scuppers and led me forward into the starboard fo'c'sle. A half-dozen men, some looking more dead than alive, sat on a bench drinking coffee which they dipped from a large can, as I entered and took a seat.

One said, "Get your pannikin out and dip some hot coffee. You look as if you need it. Where's your dunnage?"

"If you mean baggage," I replied, "I have none."

"No dunnage?" he said. "Didn't you even bring a farewell bottle?"

As I shook my head, a deep groan went through the fo'c'sle. I felt terribly depressed.

The sailor who had helped me dipped his tin cup deep in the coffee can, brought it over and sat down beside me. He explained that his name was Arthur Gribble and that he was a native of Greenock, Scotland. He had been an A.B. (able seaman) for years and had joined the *Belfast* nearly nine months before when she had sailed with a general cargo from Cardiff, Wales, to Hong Kong.

From Hong Kong the *Belfast* had sailed for San Francisco in ballast, arriving a month before, and in the meantime had loaded twenty-five hundred tons of wheat at Port Costa. She was now waiting for the last few members of the crew to be delivered before heaving anchor and sailing by way of Cape Horn for Queenstown, Ireland, for orders.

I asked Gribble how long the voyage would last and almost fell off the bench when he replied that we would sail nearly seventeen thousand miles and be at sea from five to seven months, depending upon wind and weather. During all of this time we should be lucky even to sight land more than once before reaching the Irish coast.

I then told him how I had been beaten up and brought aboard the *Belfast* against my will and that I wanted to get ashore. I asked if it would do any good to complain to the captain. He asked if I had signed anything, and I remembered with a shock that I had.

He said that there were several aboard in the same fix and that any attempt to get aft to see the captain would be prevented by the mates, who could make it mighty tough for me in the months at sea.

Gribble explained more about the *Belfast* and its officers, and how to avoid abuse as much as possible by being quick to respond and at least pretend to know something about working ship.

During the remainder of the day I made myself useful coiling ropes but kept clear of the mates. The second mate, having already put me in my place by knocking the wind out of my sails, made life miserable for the other newcomers by hazing them unmercifully. The drunks, having been alternately kicked into insensibility and revived by buckets of cold sea water, were tossed into bunks in the fo'c'sle and left to stew in their own juice.

After the decks were cleared and things made shipshape, the men were told to be ready to turn to at short notice and then were dismissed. I asked Gribble what would happen if anyone should hail a passing boat and ask to be put ashore.

He pointed to a dim figure lounging on the poop deck and remarked that the officers would keep anchor watch throughout the night, allowing no vessel to approach except the expected boarding master's boat with crew members yet to come. He further explained that of sixteen able seamen and two ordinaries

73

shipped in Cardiff, eight had deserted in Hong Kong, had been replaced there by others at regular "blood money" rates and that the same eight had jumped ship after docking at Port Costa. With them went four additional able seamen and one ordinary, leaving on board only five of the *Belfast's* original crew.

Gribble was one of the original five, all of whom had remained aboard only because their wives and families lived in Britain and they could not afford to desert and forfeit their right to sail on British ships in the future.

At present on the *Belfast* were nine A.B.'s and one ordinary seaman (myself) for whom Captain Davies had already paid "blood money" of seventy-five dollars each to boardinghouse runners.

I thought of the long voyage ahead and suddenly wondered what my aunt would think if she failed to hear from me for half a year. Seeking out Gribble, I asked if there would be a chance of getting a letter ashore before we sailed. He said the pilot would take the last mail ashore when leaving the ship after taking her through the Golden Gate channel. I wrote my aunt a brief letter merely explaining that I was leaving on a long voyage and telling her not to expect to hear from me for several months. This done, I made my way on deck, where I stood for a long time beside the rail staring at the flickering lights of the city less than a mile distant. I fervently wished I were ashore and wondered when, if ever, I should see San Francisco again.

At midnight I went back into the fo'c'sle to find only a dim light showing from a smoky coal-oil lamp, and everyone asleep. Dead tired, I climbed into a vacant bunk and soon fell into a troubled sleep.

I was awakened by hands pawing at me and a voice shouting, "Come on, son, rise and shine. Bring the coffee and step lively."

I looked at Gribble. He nodded toward the galley, so I rolled out of my bunk, went out on deck and soon came back with the hot coffee.

74

It was daybreak. All hands had been roused out, even the drunks. They were a sorry-looking bunch, unshaven, probably unwashed, for days. One brought out a farewell bottle. After making the rounds, the bottle was empty, but it set everybody up and the hot coffee topped it off.

The second mate thrust his head in the fo'c'sle and shouted, "Turn to, you loafers! Someone throw a line to the pilot boat."

There was a rush for the deck as a boat came alongside. The pilot climbed aboard, shook hands and chatted with the mates before he walked aft to have breakfast with the captain. While we were busy on deck making preparations for getting under way, there was a shout of *"Belfast,* ahoy!" and soon another boat was alongside.

Over the rail came two men looking very wobbly but able to navigate under their own power. With a heave-ho a third was hauled aboard and temporarily rolled into the scuppers after being baptized with sea water.

Dunnage bags hurtled over the rail, followed by a vicious-looking boardinghouse runner who went aft to settle with the captain for deliveries just completed. Signal flags were run up, and a towboat was soon alongside. A heaving line was thrown and the heavy hawser drawn aboard and made fast. The capstan on the fo'c'sle head had been clicking merrily while the anchor cable was being shortened; and as the mudhook broke water, the tug steamed slowly ahead.

The *Belfast* swung into line. Her bow was pointed toward the Golden Gate and the open sea.

As we passed Meiggs Wharf, the crimp came hustling out of the cabin and clambered over the side. He grinned and shouted, "Good-by and good luck!"

A sailor muttered, "It's too bad we couldn't knock him on the head and take him for a trip around the Horn."

Most of the men seemed to be sailors who knew their way about a ship, but it was evident that several were making their first sea trip. I was badly frightened, but the knowledge of seven days on the *Millie R. Bohannan* from Savannah to Philadelphia gave me some confidence.

When the mate shouted, "Lay aloft and loose courses and tops'ls!" Gribble leaped into the main rigging. I followed right after him.

After loosing mains'l and tops'ls, the other men dropped below to help sheet home the sails, leaving only Gribble and me aloft. When the topgallantsail (pronounced t'gans'l) hung free, Gribble asked if I could loose the royal without help. I could only gulp and answer yes as he hustled down to the deck while I continued some fifteen or twenty feet higher. Loosing the royal was not difficult, but I was not used to working on a job at that elevation while holding on for dear life.

We were still being towed, but the breeze was light, so the loose-hanging sails merely gave us additional headway to lighten the strain on the towboat and move us along a little faster.

By then we were passing through the Golden Gate and into open water, and from my position, high on the royal yard, I could see San Francisco fading in the distance. As we rounded Land's End, I could plainly see the Seal Rocks, the Cliff House and the glassed roof of the famous Sutro Baths.

From my swinging perch, far above the *Belfast's* deck, I looked down just in time to see the towboat's hawser cast off and also to see the mate staring aloft while shouting through his cupped hands, "Aloft there, look alive, and skin down here, unless you want to ride up with that royal yard." I "skinned" down in a jiffy. The tug ran alongside the *Belfast* just long enough for the pilot to change ships, after shaking hands with the officers and wishing us fair winds and a safe passage home.

Maybe it was homeward bound for Gribble, the officers and a few others, but for most of us it was just a long voyage with a dead end on arrival in Great Britain. I had already learned that it would be almost impossible to get a ship out of Britain without agreeing to a clause in the ship's articles calling for a period of three years and return to the United Kingdom.

With the departure of the tug and our pilot, there went our last link with the rest of the world for nearly half a year.

The breeze was light and the sailing smooth, but all was not running smoothly with the crew on deck. For many hours every member of the crew had been on the job, including the last drunk tossed aboard early in the morning. Evidently it was a part of the religion of our ship's officers to let no one make a mistake as to who was boss aboard ship. Blows and kicks were frequent, and in most cases with no reason except to display authority.

I jumped at all commands, pretending to know my way around, and tailed on to the braces and halyards along with the old-timers; but my inexperience was too evident to be overlooked entirely. Once when I was told to go aloft and loosen buntlines, I looked bewildered and hesitated. The second mate let go with a kick that "shivered my timbers" and almost lifted me into the rigging.

On the ship's articles as A.B.'s were two Canadians, who had never even seen the ocean before. Instead of looking sharp and following the experienced men, they appeared bewildered. As a result they were hazed and unmercifully beaten until they seemed undecided whether to fight back or jump overboard.

On a windjammer, especially a "lime juicer," one might choose to jump overboard if so inclined. But as to fighting back, the skipper and the mates, by virtue of British maritime law, had power almost of life and death over a ship's crew at sea. Even back talk usually brought a crack on the jaw by a fist or perhaps an iron belaying pin.

Among the seagoing fraternity any man making a first voyage was referred to as a "farmer" regardless of previous occupation. By a coincidence, the two Canadians, Felix and Celle, actually were farmers from Quebec who had happened to stray into the wrong saloon on San Francisco's water front at the time the *Belfast* needed men.

* 11 *

Just before dark, with all sail set and running gear coiled on the deck ready for instant action, all hands were called aft and lined up in a row; then watches were chosen in the same manner in which sandlot baseball teams are picked by the American boy.

The sixteen A.B.'s and two ordinaries standing stolidly before the mates, like slaves at the auction block, were a scurvy-looking aggregation. But beneath the dirt and the scraggly whiskers and the hangovers, they were still a husky, brawny bunch—with one exception.

None of the eighteen stood less than 5 feet, 8 inches in height or 170 pounds in weight, with a single exception. I was the guilty wretch, standing 5 feet, 6 inches and weighing 135 pounds. And this in a windjammer where beef on the hoof was rated higher than in Chicago's stockyards.

Looking the crew over, the mate beckoned to a husky Finn, named Elka, as lead-off man in the port watch. The second mate selected Gribble for the starboard watch. Then the mate took Fitz, a big Irishman, and the second took Bill Potter, the only other American aboard except me. Mr. Jarvis picked Lutes, a Dane; Mr. Atkins selected Duck, an Englishman. And so it went until fourteen A.B.'s had been chosen. Finally, Jarvis took the farmer Felix and Mr. Atkins took the other Canadian, Celle.

With the able seamen disposed of, there remained only the two ordinary seamen. Mr. Jarvis took the strapping young Eng-

lishman, Ollie, who had made the trip from Cardiff, leaving me
as the last choice from the bottom of the barrel, so I was
awarded to Mr. Atkins by default.

As he sized up my entire hundred and thirty-five pounds and
waved me over to his side, I felt like the bat boy on the team.
Mr. Atkins was the gentleman who had tried to bore a tunnel
through my midriff on the morning of arrival and who, only a
few hours ago, had done a little uplifting by kicking me into
the main rigging. As the "Patsy" of the starboard watch I was to
curse him for one hundred and fifty-three days before giving
him a receipt in kind.

All crew members worked watch and watch except the cook,
steward, sailmaker and carpenter. The last two, known as Sails
and Chips, were subject to call when all hands were needed on
deck to reef sail or tack ship in stormy weather.

The *Belfast* was a three-masted bark of eighteen hundred
tons net register, with a cargo capacity of twenty-five hundred
tons. Her figurehead was a lady with classic features and a trim,
well-carved body, clothed in flowing white robes, and, as the
ship's slick-looking hull, measuring 250 feet in length, was also
white and marked with square, black-painted ports, she was a
beautiful vessel.

From the fo'c'slehead looking aft, the mast farthest forward
was the foremast with its topmast and t'gallantmast, next was
the mainmast, also with topmast and t'gallantmast, and third
was the mizzenmast, equipped with a long boom to carry fore
and aft sails only.

Both fore- and mainmast carried five square sails each. Looking upward from the deck, these were fores'l, lower tops'l, upper
tops'l, t'gans'l, and royal.

Sails were set by hauling on the ropes, called sheets, attached
to the clew in the lower corner of the sail, so that each sail
was spread between its yard and the yard below. All yards

were controlled by braces, with which to swing the yards from port to starboard tack, etc. The yards above the lower tops'ls were controlled by halyards for hoisting.

Being bark-rigged, the *Belfast* carried no square sails on the mizzenmast, but instead carried a large three-cornered sail called the spanker and above that the gaff-tops'l.

Far forward was the bowsprit extending outboard beyond the ship's bow, with a further extension called the jib boom. From the end of the jib boom looking aft were the triangular fore and aft sails, the flying jib, outer jib, inner jib, and fore-topmast stays'l.

Between foremast and mainmast was the main topmast stays'l, main t'gallant stays'l, and main royal stays'l, with a similar set of stays'ls between main and mizzenmast.

All fore and aft sails were controlled by halyards for hoisting and downhauls for snuggling down, before furling. Every halyard, brace, downhaul, clew line, sheet, buntline, or rope of any description which was a part of the ship's running gear must be memorized not only by name but by position on the ship so they could be located by sense of touch on the darkest night or in the worst weather. Releasing the wrong halyard, brace or sheet in a storm could endanger the ship.

Watches were four hours on deck and four below, night and day, except from 4 to 8 P.M. This was divided into two periods, four to six and six to eight, called dog watches. Thus the starboard watch would be on deck the first night from midnight to four in the morning, and on the second night from 4 to 8 A.M. and so on.

As we left the deck for our first watch below, a problem presented itself—I had no eating utensils, no blankets, no oilskins, nothing except the clothes I stood in. In most cases, when delivering the "body," the crimp tossed aboard a small dunnage bag containing these necessities. For that the victim signed a note for two months' wages in advance, collectible thirty days after the ship left port.

Gribble had lent me his own utensils for the few meals thus far, but now I was to be initiated into the mystery of the slop chest. The slop chest was a store of selected articles carried on the ship, and was the skipper's own little racket. Here the men could purchase needed articles at a price limited only by the captain's greed.

Timidly, I went aft, met Captain J. E. Davies for the first time and signed for oilskins, sou'wester, hip-length sea boots, underclothing, cotton blankets, a tin plate, pannikin, knife, fork and spoon, two flannel shirts and two pairs of dungarees. For these articles I was charged a month's wages; so here I was, one day at sea and already three months in debt.

My next move was to select a bunk, which was made easy by the simple fact that only one was left. The two best bunks were occupied by holdovers from the last voyage. The next best were taken by the biggest bullies in the fo'c'sle, according to size and pugnacity. Mine was the leftover in the very nose of the ship, just above and to one side of the hawse pipe-opening through which led the anchor cable. When the ship was on the high seas the heavy cable links were unshackled from the anchor and allowed to slide into the chain locker below. Then a wooken plug twelve inches in diameter was driven into the opening from the outside.

In stormy weather when the ship's bow plunged in the waves, sea water would squirt through the hawse pipe, sprinkling the surroundings, mostly my bunk. In heavy seas the ship's bow would rise up, up, until I seemed to be standing on my feet in the bunk, then down and down she would plunge until I almost stood upon my head.

It was the first day of October 1902, and while the way might be long and the going might be rough, at least I knew where I was heading, which was something new for me.

Ten minutes before midnight there was a loud shout, "Turn to, the watch!"

One man stumbled aft to stand a two-hour trick at the wheel and another climbed the ladder to the fo'c'sle head, on lookout, where he paced back and forth timing his turns to walk slightly uphill as the *Belfast* rolled lightly from side to side.

The rest of the watch lounged on deck, alert for changes of weather and commands from the afterguard. That is, all except the ordinary seaman, meaning me. I was supposed to stand just below the break of the poop, constantly at the beck and call of the deck officer, who, like the lookout on the fo'c'sle head, also paced up and down on the poop deck or lounged behind a square of protecting canvas called a weather strip.

Every half hour I climbed to the poop deck, taking care to use the lee side, watched the ship's chronometer until it registered the time to the second, then hit the ship's bell one stroke at twelve-thirty, two strokes at one, and so on until eight bells.

The lookout on the fo'c'sle head would repeat the signal on a larger bell and in a loud singsong voice call out, "All's well!" And the Lord help either of us if I missed the time by a few seconds or if he failed to give the answering signal.

At four in the morning, after our first watch on deck, we went below. At seven-twenty we were called for breakfast before reporting on deck at eight o'clock to relieve the port watch. As the only ordinary seaman in the starboard watch, it was my duty to fetch the meals and clean up the fo'c'sle afterward.

When I reported to the galley expecting to be handed an assortment of breakfast dishes, the cook, a coal-black Barbados Negro called Jonah, gave me a bucket of coffee and a wooden tub full of hardtack. These were four-inch disks, dark brown in color, made from a mixture of flour, oatmeal, ground straw and water. It was almost impossible to bite through them, so they were generally cracked with a belaying pin and soaked in coffee long enough to become edible. The standard breakfast was ersatz coffee and hardtack. The evening meal was the same except that tea was drunk instead of coffee.

The only real meal of the day was served at noon and the menu seldom varied: a pannikin of soup made from dried peas, and sixteen ounces of salt beef or salf pork. Placing the "kid" containing the chunk of pork or beef on the deck where all could view the operation, Bill Porter, who had already bullied himself into the leadership of the starboard watch, drew out his sheath knife and carved it into portions.

Potter then speared the first piece, the next important man in the watch took piece number two, and so on. Being the "Patsy" of the watch, I received the ninth piece, by no means the largest or the leanest. That's how it would be for the rest of the voyage.

On Sunday the menu was varied by serving "fresh" meat. This was tinned Australian mutton, from which the blood had been squeezed to make the popular drink Bovril. It was dry and stringy and had a leatherish taste, but at least it was a change. Served every seventh day, it was also a reminder of the passing weeks.

At five o'clock in my first dogwatch below, I was sent aft to the steward for our whack of extra supplies. This, it seems, was the "Queen's Birthday" when each man would receive sixteen ounces of brown sugar and a like quantity of marmalade which must be made to last a full week. The marmalade was a special mixture of orange peel and crushed carrots; but bad as it was, it was welcome to use as a spread over the rocklike chunks of hardtack, besides covering up traces of the weevils. Later there would be one addition—a cup of lime juice served each day as an antidote against scurvy.

And now, lest it be feared that our ship's crew was discriminated against in the matter of food, let the record show that the items and portions described were the official issue for all deepwater ships under British Board of Trade rules as posted in the ship's fo'c'sle.

Naturally the afterguard fared much better. They even took along a coop of chickens which disappeared two by two each Sabbath day as the voyage progressed. There was also a pig, which grew fatter with the passing months, until he met the fate of the chickens, but that was on Christmas Day, after we had rounded the Horn.

Sacks of fresh potatoes were spread out in the cold lazaret below the cabin, and these lasted the afterguard from eight to ten weeks. White bread instead of hardtack was also served in the aftercabin.

* 12 *

WITH MODERATE WINDS the *Belfast* drove south and slightly east day after day. Sometimes the wind freshened enough to cause the lighter sails to be furled. But before long would come the cry, "Loose the royals!"

And away I would scoot up the rigging to the royal yard to unwind the gaskets and drop the mass of canvas, to be sheeted home by the men below. Loosing the lighter sails was the ordinary seaman's job.

During the daylight watches in the first few weeks at sea I was kept too busy doing the dirtier jobs usually assigned to beginners to learn splicing, rigging or patching sails. My specialty was more along the lines of swinging in a bosun's chair greasing masts or tarring down the standing rigging.

One morning as I was working in the main lower rigging, smearing tar on ratlines, shrouds and backstays, the inevitable happened. The bucket slipped and down went the mess, splashing tar in every direction over deck and white-painted bulwarks.

Shaking from the panic inside me, I scrambled to the deck and reached for the bucket. As I did so, I received a boot from the second mate, delivered with such hatred and venom that I was lifted from the deck and landed on all fours several feet away. The act was so deliberate and cruel I almost went berserk.

I hesitated for an instant, coldly deliberating whether I should grab an iron belaying pin and smash his brains out. Then reason returned, and when he again lifted his foot, this time to crash it into the small of my back, I rolled into the scuppers and lay there.

Captain Davies stood at the break of the poop and watched the scene without batting an eye. Someday I would get even.

Down below, the watch would curse, rave and threaten among themselves, but on deck they knew better than to fight back, so they grinned and took it. The abuse was not general but mainly directed toward several of us who never seemed to please.

Captain Davies, personally, never raised his hand or even his voice against any man on his ship, but never at any time did he forbid his officers to do so. Incidentally, the first and third mates were pretty decent chaps, though firm enough when occasion required. At a time when single passages lasted from four to seven months from port to port, men would get restless and unruly and must necessarily be kept under control. But the second officer abused the privilege.

Gribble gave me a partial answer. My wages as ordinary seaman, American scale, were twenty-five dollars a month, while Mr. Atkins' wages as second officer, British scale, were five pounds, or slightly less than mine. This fact griped him, and I suffered because of it.

In the meantime I had my first experience with the trade winds, so important in the maneuvering of sailing ships and in the lives of the men who sailed them.

The northeast trades took us bowling south at a fine clip, blowing steadily in the same general direction day after day. The weather was balmy and there were so many things to see that I began staying on deck when off duty. I would work my way out to the very end of the jib boom, straddle it and then watch the ship sail toward me, her bows cleaving the blue water and leaving two boiling streams of white foam gushing along her sides. Aloft, the great white squares of canvas bellied out before the wind until it seemed the tremendous strain must soon burst the seams. Below me, schools of frolicking bonitos or albacores would race along, always keeping just ahead of the cutwater of the oncoming ship.

Sometimes Gribble and I would make a heavy hook fast to a strong line, hide the hook with a bit of bleached linen and drop it just ahead of the churning mass of foam. As the *Belfast's* bow rose on the next wave, lifting the tempting bit of white above the water, there would be a sudden rush and a bonito would rise to take the bait; then I would slide down into the chains and smother the big fish in a gunny sack.

For a share of the prize, Jonah would condescend to cook it, and the watch would enjoy a change of diet—a bit dry but still acceptable.

By November first we had lost the trade winds and were deep in the tropics a few degrees north of the equator. For days it was deadly calm, as we floated lazily on a glassy sea. The sun was so hot that the pitch in the deck seams would boil up into little bubbles and pop. We were in the well-known doldrums, a sort of vacuum between the northeast and southeast trade winds.

We went barefoot day and night, even climbing the sharp tarry ratlines on callused bare soles. At times it rained so hard that the deck became a shallow swimming pool before the water escaped through the open ports.

The helmsman would stand listlessly; the deck officer would moisten a finger and hold it up hoping to trace the direction of the next breeze. Suddenly there would be a puff of wind, generally from the wrong direction, catching the sails aback, a shout, "Man the braces, and about ship!" And the heavy yards would swing slowly around. The ship would straighten out and begin to make headway; the helmsman would set his course; the watch would start clearing up the mess of ropes; and then —once again, a dead ship on a sea of glass.

This happened a dozen times in as many hours, but no matter how often a catspaw breeze started and as suddenly stopped, it was proper seamanship to take advantage of every single puff of wind.

At intervals schools of flying fish skimmed to the surface, sailed through the air, then dropped into the sea. At times one would miscalculate and hit a sail, dropping to the deck with a loud "plop." A near-by sailor would make a dash for it, just as Tommy, the ship's cat, took the same notion.

Slowly we edged across the Line, sometimes sailing a few knots, sometimes drifting. Then the fluctuating breezes gave way to the southeast trade winds and soon we were booming along on our course at twelve to fifteen knots.

When off watch, I climbed to the royal yard far above the deck, there to sit by the hour searching the horizon, hoping to sight some other ship sailing those lonesome seas. Barefoot, wearing only dungarees and singlet, the balmy wind riffling through my hair, I could look down at the long narrow shape below—a white strip of foam streaking along on either side, merging into a wider path of foam in her wake.

Far forward, I could see the long heavy rollers gathering force for a strike, and just when it seemed that the next rushing sea must break over her, up would go the bow and she would fall off slightly as the long green rollers slid harmlessly under her forefoot. We were still a long way from the turbulent seas where two oceans meet, but I was beginning to imagine what it must be like down there.

On the morning of November 28 there was a shout, "Land on the port bow!"

Both watches piled out to have a look at the island of Juan Fernández rising from the sea like a small cloud. By late afternoon we drew abreast of it about ten miles off our beam. The island was high and mountainous, and looked to be about fifteen miles long.

At nineteen I was still impressionable enough to hope the skipper would find some reason for going ashore on Robinson Crusoe's legendary island, but we continued on our course and by morning it was far astern.

Almost overnight the weather cooled and the wind blew harder. One by one, the good-weather sails were replaced by newer and stronger canvas in preparation for heavy weather ahead. Additional tarpaulins were stretched over the hatches and battened down. We must have a tight ship with a cargo of wheat. Not only would sea water spoil the grain; it would swell and strain the seams of the vessel dangerously.

Well into the "roaring forties" we ran into hurricane weather and for forty-eight hours lay close-hauled under a reefed main tops'l. Walls of greenish water broke over the weather bow, smothering the deck from rail to rail, smashing every loose thing in its path, before spilling itself over the afterdeck.

As the gale shrieked and howled through the rigging, and the seas piled aboard, orders went forward that the watch would not be relieved and all hands were to stand by. With yards pointed up into the wind and only the reefed main tops'l showing, the old *Belfast* rode out the storm.

When day broke there was no line of demarcation between gray seas and gray skies. The wind blew with the same unabated fury, driving before it sheets of hail and sleet. As it grew lighter, all eyes swept the ship's rigging aloft and the overflowing decks below, seeking out the damage. The main royal had been blown right out of its gaskets and the fore-t'gans'l was beginning to blow free, threatening to go any minute.

Above the roar of the wind we could hear Jarvis shouting, "Lay aloft and secure that fore-t'gans'l!"

Gribble, Potter and Kosky sprang into the forerigging, and I followed. The force of the wind flattened our bodies against the ratlines, almost driving the breath from our half-frozen lungs as we climbed slowly upward, timing ourselves to move only as the ship swung to leeward, hanging on as she swung back into the wind.

Reaching the foretop, we eased our way through the lubber's hole and began the climb to the t'gallant yard. Gribble and Potter took the weather side and I followed Kosky out on the lee yardarm. The yard was snapping and jerking with the violent motion of the ship.

As we slid along the ice-coated footrope, the ship's head veered off a bit. As we reached for the flying canvas, the sail bellied out in the wind, its frozen surface as hard and round as sheet metal. Trying frantically for a hold on the canvas, I used both hands, while literally gripping the jerking yardarm with the muscles of my stomach. A sea hit the ship's bow, causing her to broach to, as the sail shook free of wind. The heavy storm canvas thrashed upward and backward over my head, as my two hands clawed at the empty air.

Instead of falling backward into space, my foot slipped and I straddled the icy footrope, dangling upside down and holding on with both hands and a leg. As the sail filled again and bellied out before the wind, Kosky reached over and helped me slide along the slippery footrope toward the futtock shrouds, where I regained my equilibrium, and once again moved out on the yard to battle with wildly flapping sail.

We finally stowed the sail and dropped to the deck, but in all the years I would sail the seas there would never be a closer call. One of the first expressions I heard aboard ship went something like "One hand for the ship, one for yourself."

But don't ever tell that to a sailor on wind ships. It takes two hands to reef, or even loose, a sail, so hang on by your stomach muscles and pray.

The storm ran its course and when we came on deck for the regular watch the wind had hauled westerly and dropped from hurricane force to a moderate thirty miles. As the seas leveled off, all hands were put to work clearing up the mess of tangled ropes. Reefs had been shaken out of the lower tops'ls, and a new royal was sent aloft.

Overhead, the flying scud revealed a cold-looking disk that was the sun, but even though the hail and sleet had ceased for the time being, the air was bitter cold. In the fo'c'sle below, every straw mattress and blanket was in a condition ranging from just damp to sopping wet. My bunk, far forward, had taken so much water the blankets were saturated.

From now on, every man would turn in "all standing," which meant he slept in sea boots and oilskins. We were all done up and badly in need of rest. The wet blankets, the lack of sleep, the cold and misery would be with us for some time to come.

Squaring around to leave the wind several points free, the *Belfast* plunged ahead on a course south and east. We passed close enough to the Diego Ramírez Islands to see the white foam breaking against the rocky face of the cliffs. In midafternoon the breeze freshened, and Captain Davies began to look anxiously up at the royals, but the sky was now clear, and we continued to plow along at twelve knots on a course east-south-east, with all sail standing.

During the graveyard watch, from four to eight in the morning, it was customary to serve coffee at two bells—five o'clock. After coffee would come the order to turn to and wash decks. This was a ritual on all British sailing ships, in fair weather or foul.

One morning, with all sail set except royals, and bowling along before a wind so strong that every yard of canvas was under a terrific strain, we had coffee as usual and then began the scrubbing job under the watchful eye of the second mate, who always bossed the job from a sheltered position behind a weather strip on the poop deck.

Suddenly there was a blast of wind followed by a loud report. I looked aloft to see the main t'gans'l writhing in the wind, as it disappeared to leeward making a noise like a thousand firecrackers.

As the skipper and mate rushed headlong up the after companionway, Mr. Atkins shouted, "Call the watch! All hands on deck!"

For hours we clewed up and hauled down, furled and reefed, while a gale screamed and howled through the rigging; hail, snow and sleet beat upon us unmercifully. Almost completely spent, we huddled under such shelter as we could find after stripping the ship down to tops'ls, stays'ls and storm spanker.

Lifelines were strung the length of the deck, but getting aft or forward, between seas smashing aboard, was a hazardous business. It was my turn to relieve Ollie of the port watch; I waited for the next sea to crash over and then, as the ship's bow reared high, I stepped from under the fo'c'slehead, looped my arm over the lifeline and started aft on the run.

As her bow plumped down again, a great wave poured over and raced along the deck, picking me up like a chip. I felt myself being propelled along the line at lightning speed, until, badly shaken up and half strangled by salt water, I brought up against the after companionway with a mighty crash.

I spent the balance of the watch at my station below the break of the poop, wet and shivering in the icy blast. I wondered what would happen next as I listened to the whine of the wind, the booming of seas breaking aboard, and the creaking of timbers, ropes and blocks. The group of officers on the poop above me were merely dim outlines, but above the sound of wind and waves I knew they were discussing the ship's position. Apparently we were far off our course somewhere south of Cape Horn and were making leeway at an alarming rate, despite being "hove to."

Each half hour I struck the bells as usual, but there was no answering signal from the lookout, now stationed on top of the galley amidships where he could neither see nor hear what went on aft.

Daylight revealed a forlorn and desolate scene. On all sides were tracts of field ice. On the lee quarter, becoming visible as darkness gave way to a sort of dim twilight, was a bluish-white mass of ice that looked at least a quarter-mile long, its top out of sight in a snowy mist.

On deck, above the bulwarks, all running gear and standing rigging were coated with bluish-white ice, giving the old *Belfast* a ghostly look. Icicles hung from the lower shrouds. Aloft, the lee side of the main royal had loosened.

Kosky and I started up the weather rigging to secure the flapping sail. We were a dozen feet below the main top when, with a sound like a clap of thunder, the weather sheet of the main lower tops'l parted, and a length of iron chain whipped and snapped in the wind and threatened to demolish everything within range.

The sail gave way and a section of canvas with chain attached flew straight into space and disappeared in the distance. After securing what was left of the blown-out sails, the *Belfast* was snugged down to ride out the storm.

The drift was toward the huge chunk of ice on the lee quarter. Toward night, when the gap had closed too much for comfort, it was suddenly decided to "go about" on the opposite tack to get more sea room. With a gale at its worst and a tremendous sea running, the skipper decided to "wear" ship.

All hands were called to braces and sheets, including not only Chips and Sails but Jonah and the steward as well. The steward, though seldom called upon to work ship, was not afraid to pull ropes on deck with the other men, but Jonah was a badly frightened colored boy, so he was assigned to the lee side of the wheel to help Gribble.

A few words here will explain the difference between "tacking" and "wearing" ship. When "tacking," the vessel's head is quickly brought up into the wind by suddenly jamming the helm *hard down,* causing all sails to shake and flutter; in neutral, one might call it. Then, at the right instant, the lee braces are released and the yards are hauled around by concerted pulling on the weather braces, just as the wind fills her sails and she heels over on the opposite tack.

When "wearing" ship, the helm is put *hard up,* allowing the ship's head to pay off, and as she turns *from* the wind, the yards are hauled around and she slowly turns to leeward. The bow describes the greater part of a circle as she turns her stern to windward and then comes up with her head to the wind and sea on the opposite tack.

"Hove to" as we were, under reefed tops'l, fore-topmast stays'l and storm spanker, we had no headway; therefore, we could not "tack" ship if we wanted to, so "wear" ship it would be, an extremely dangerous operation in a hurricane, with a tremendous sea running.

As the *Belfast's* head wore slowly around, the seas stopped piling over the bow for the time being, allowing us to make our way to the braces where we would at least have something to hang on to. Atkins and Wilkinson, with Potter and Lutes, slacked away braces and sheets while Mr. Jarvis stood on the poop deck directing the job, with the Old Man close by. Watching his chance between heavy rolling seas, Mr. Jarvis slowly worked her around, shouting to Gribble at the wheel, "Port the helm. Steady there. Starboard a bit. Hold that!" Finally she was running directly before the wind, but all hands expected any minute she would be pooped by a great roller and smothered from end to end.

If this happened, there would be little chance of the officer and the two helmsmen surviving the deluge. Then with no one at the wheel she would broach to and come broadside to the sea, the sails would go flat aback and in an instant the masts would be ripped out and the ship become unmanageable.

She escaped being pooped, but as wind and sea hit her starboard quarter, solid green water swept her from stern to stem; we on the main deck made a leap for the lower shrouds, barely reaching the sheer poles as the avalanche of water swept forward and over the bows.

Then we dropped to the decks again and continued to haul braces until the ship was finally snugged down. The hurricane blasted away, driving the ship farther south with each passing hour.

Then, on the poop deck, a near miracle happened. Captain Davies popped out of the companionway with a bottle of brandy, handed Gribble a rousing drink and told Mr. Jarvis to call all hands aft to "splice the main brace."

In all my life no single glass of liquor ever before or since had the same effect on me as did that glass of brandy. I was wet, half frozen, and tired enough to drop in my tracks. As I drained the glass, fire, starting deep down in my stomach, seemed to flash through every vein until even the ends of my fingers and toes tingled.

We were kept busy sweating braces and halyards, already as taut as fiddle strings, untangling ropes and even climbing aloft in the freezing gale to wind extra gaskets around sails already securely furled.

My knuckles were raw and the few fingernails still left were torn half loose and bleeding. Sea cuts had opened up, splitting the skin between the fingers. My ankles and knees were beginning to pain me badly, and on investigation I found my skin beneath the damp underwear was breaking out in salt water boils. Nothing could be done about it because no change of clothing was available even from the slop chest, and there was no heat on the ship with which to dry anything except the small cabin stove and the galley, jealously guarded by Jonah.

Once I wondered aloud why we were not left alone in our misery, while the ship was under control, "riding it out." And then Potter said, "That's how it is on all ships, son. They haze you around to keep you from brooding and feeling sorry for yourself, and then when you do get below, tired and worn out, you're damned glad to pull a blanket over your head and sleep it off instead of complaining."

Many a time we looked aft longingly, hoping for another call to "splice the main brace," but it never came. For twenty-four hours there was no watch below while we drifted among ice floes; then four men in each watch were sent below to sleep in two-hour spells during the night watches.

There was no watch below during daylight as all hands worked to replace the damaged sails. The lower tops'l was sent down, after which the second-best tops'l was hauled aloft, bent and sheeted home. A new main t'gans'l was sent up but was furled until better weather. Sails immediately went to work repairing the tops'l which might be needed at any time. Then the crew went back to regular watch and watch.

* 13 *

AT NOON, just before going to the galley for our pea soup and salt horse, the overcast broke away, showing a frosty-looking sun in a light-blue sky. The skipper and mate were eagerly engaged in getting a "sight" so badly needed to work out the ship's position after days and nights of being blown all over the South Atlantic.

There was speculation about how far south we had blown. We never actually knew, but the "fo'c'sle navigators" estimated we were approximately five hundred miles below Cape Horn, and also far eastward of our course.

Through the dogwatches and the first night watch, the skipper kept the mates company on the poop deck, frequently casting anxious looks aloft, where every shred of canvas was drawing and looking as though something might crack under the strain at any moment.

When the starboard watch reported back on deck at four o'clock, there stood the Old Man behind the weather strip, facing the sleet and flying spume, still staring aloft through the mist and still "cracking on" with lower and upper tops'ls, fores'l and mains'l, spanker and a couple of stays'ls. The old *Belfast* was taking it, but we wondered for how long. We soon found out.

Apparently the glass took a sudden drop because all hands were hurriedly called on deck, and orders were shouted to shorten down to reefed lower tops'ls, and storm-stays'l. We had stowed the lighter sail and were preparing to reef tops'ls when the storm struck like a blast from a frozen Hell.

It hit with terrific force. The *Belfast* keeled over and plunged her bow so deep into the rolling seas that her stern lifted out of the water high in the air. For a long moment the forward half of the ship seemed to linger beneath solid water, then up came her head as she leveled off, with sea water filling the deck from stem to stern.

The second and third mates were in the waist of the ship. Both men leaped into the shrouds as the ship took the dive. The crew was aloft, some stowing the upper tops'ls, others on the way to the deck to clew up the main lower tops'ls preparatory to reefing. With the gale came driving sleet and spume that enveloped the entire ship in a thick mist.

Four men led by Kosky worked their way to windward, feet sliding cautiously along dripping, ice-coated footropes, numb fingers trying to grip the iron jackstay, so enlarged with ice that the small space between jackstay and yardarm had become a solid part of the yard itself. Kosky slowly inched himself out to the extreme end of the weather yardarm, precariously straddling its very tip, and balanced himself there in order to pass the weather earring (rope) through a ring in the leach of the sail, haul it tight and lash it to the end of the yard.

In the meantime, Lindy was straddling the opposite yardarm to pass the lee earring. In between were the rest of the watch, with Wilkinson, the third mate, in the center ready to haul up the bunt. Hunched over the crazily jerking yard and holding on by the creases in our bellies, we dragged at the ballooning sail, easing it over to leeward while Lindy hauled fast the lee earring.

Nine half-frozen men beat at the hard wet square of canvas with bruised knuckles and torn nails until the upper half was drawn to the jackstay, where the reef points were knotted over the yard and the signal given the mate below to sheet home the closely reefed tops'l.

Then we dropped to the sea-battered decks, manned the clew lines and set to work reefing the fore lower tops'l. When eight bells had struck, we went below for pea soup and salt junk and were ready to call it a day.

Evidently the Old Man had taken a shot of his own grog, or the glass was rising rapidly, for instead of heaving to, as we expected, he continued driving due north, steering a course "Full and Bye" in a wind that strained every bit of canvas. Soon the wind dropped to only a mild gale, the clouds broke and the sun came shining through.

Reefs were shaken out, and soon every sail was showing, including the royals. By midnight we were streaking along at twelve knots an hour. Land was reported. The skipper hopped around with Mr. Atkins, "taking bearings" on Falkland Islands. It was then little more than a dot on the horizon and we never did get any nearer to it. The Old Man had his bearings and knew exactly where he was, and that was all that mattered just then.

It began to blow harder and many an anxious eye was cast aloft, but aside from sweating up the braces and halyards not a sail was disturbed and we continued to race along. As the wind hauled further south we squared the yards, and drove north at nearly thirteen knots an hour. We were really "cracking on."

Two men were needed to handle the wheel as the seas began to roll up on our quarter, and spray burst high over the bows. Cape Horn and the Falklands were getting farther behind us every hour. As I hauled in the log just before going forward for the morning coffee and hardtack, one lone albatross, symbol of stormy weather, wheeled overhead and, with its great wings spread and long legs dangling, sailed majestically toward the south and disappeared.

A few days later we picked up a strong wind from the southeast and, with every sail swelling before the steady breeze, began a fine run through lazy, rolling seas as the air grew warmer each day. We had already doffed our oilskins, and now off came the sea boots and the underwear that had not been really dry for weeks. Every day was washday on the *Belfast*. We scrubbed ourselves and we scrubbed our clothes. The sun shone warm, and soon the damp blankets and even the stinking "donkey's breakfasts" (straw mattresses) were steaming on deck.

As for me, I felt like shouting Hallelujah.

And then, one morning Ed Duckworth said it was Christmas. He was sure of it because he had seen the steward stick the ship's pig, and stewards just don't go around sticking ships' pigs unless it is a festive occasion for the afterguard. Fortunately no one forward expected any part of the pig, so no one was disappointed. When we filed aft at exactly noon, Tom Jackson suggested we might get a noggin of rum instead of the usual lime juice and vinegar, but it tasted like lime juice and vinegar to me.

When I went to the galley for the midday meal, I was not expecting the fresh pork, but I did think we might get a bit of tinned plum duff to mark the occasion. I was wrong.

So it came about that my third Christmas dinner since leaving the old homestead was a cup of pea soup and a bit of salt beef, served at sea some three hundred miles off the coast of Argentina and opposite the Río de la Plata, where the temperamental Pamperos frequently act up and sometimes leave a ship dismasted or on her beam ends.

Gribble had frequently mentioned the Pamperos that had a habit of slipping up suddenly off the river Plate. Until mid-afternoon the sun shone bright and warm without even a wisp of cloud to mar the deep-blue sky.

The only concession made by the ship's officers to the possibility of trouble was to order the royals, flying jib and gaff-tops'l furled during the afternoon watch. Maybe they broke out a noggin or two of rum with which to wash down the roast pig and plum duff, and then decided to ignore or defy Pamperos, if any. Anyhow, the wind was fair, a nice brisk breeze was blowing and all hands forward gathered around the forehatch to enjoy the second dogwatch while Ollie played his accordion.

From aft came a sharp order, "All hands shorten sail; port watch clew up t'gans'ls."

We jumped fast and worked with a will. The sky was entirely clear except for a few light fleecy clouds directly overhead. A stiff breeze was blowing from the southeast. Lindy said, "Maybe the bottom dropped out of the glass." Duck, the Englishman, replied, "Most likely they want to give us a bloody good time on Christmas night."

The wind dropped to a mere breeze and within minutes we

lay absolutely becalmed, rocking gently on the ocean swells while the few sails still hung straight up and down. Then came orders to square the yards though not a breath of air was stirring.

The sun was beginning to drop below the horizon. In the southwest we noticed for the first time that whitish clouds had formed and were getting darker. Then came a flash of lightning as the clouds grew blacker. Almost as if it were a signal Mr. Jarvis shouted, "Get those upper tops'ls in."

It was still clear in the north and east, but in the southwest trouble was brewing, with flashes of lightning more frequent.

A shout from below, "Aloft there, get on deck; all hands at braces." I slid down the backstays to the rail and dropped on deck. Still not a breath of air stirred as we stood about expectantly waiting for something, anything, to happen.

The *Belfast* lay on a calm sea idly rocking on the ocean swell like a duck on a pond. An instant later, like a bat out of hell, a blast of wind laden with hail and sleet struck over the port quarter with such force that the ship heeled to a forty-degree angle, drove her starboard bow fathoms deep under solid water, then righted herself and leaped forward like something alive.

We picked ourselves up from the scuppers, where we had tumbled like so many tenpins, and hauled hard on the braces. Gribble and Nelson at the wheel struggled to bring the plunging ship under control.

The wind shrieked and moaned through the network of wire rigging, and masts and yards creaked and groaned under the strain. Fortunately the ship's head had been coaxed around and the yards squared enough so that the squall struck us fair on the quarter. Had we been caught aback in that blast the masts would have snapped off like so many match sticks.

For hours we drove before a wind of unbelievable force, helped along by seas rolling up under our stern, reminiscent of

Cape Horn weather, but instead of attempting to haul the yards close to the wind and heave to until the storm blew itself out, the Old Man kept the yards square and her nose pointed to the north while we ran before the gale and toward better weather. A few hours later the storm petered out. We picked up the steady southeast trades and boomed along under a full spread of canvas.

During weeks of stress and strain and just plain misery, we had talked of our troubles and the sleep we had missed. We had daydreamed of the things we would do when we got back into fine weather.

But when the flying fish began to skim through the air and the dolphin, the bonitos and the albacores began playing leap-frog with the *Belfast's* cutwater, I was back at my favorite spot on the end of the jib boom, dungarees rolled to my knees, singlet open to the breeze, bare feet dangling and almost dipping into the surging foam as the ship's bows dropped low into a receding sea and then pointed high into skies as blue as the deep tropical waters beneath.

As I looked aft from my spot on the tip end of her nose she seemed always to be moving eagerly forward, sometimes easing her way along before the warm moderate breeze, at other times rushing faster, with a "bone in her teeth," spilling streams of white on either side.

* 14 *

ON JANUARY 1, a day dedicated to new resolutions, it would have been fitting to make a short entry in my own little log-book proclaiming my complete freedom from debt.

Having worked three full months, I had now met my obliga-tion for two months' pay advanced to Mr. Brewer, the crimp, and an additional month's pay for slop-chest purchases, and the "dead horse" could be respectfully interred. Henceforth, until voyage end my daily wage of nearly one Yankee dollar a day would be my very own. I began to feel important again.

For nearly two weeks we drove steadily on our course northward and slightly east, seldom touching a rope except to tighten up braces and halyards. We finally lost the southeast trades a few degrees before reaching the Line. Whether driving along with steady trade winds or lying becalmed in the Equatorial Stream, as helpless as a sea turtle on its back, there was no loafing on the *Belfast*, particularly now on her homeward-bound passage.

I was put to work on the teakwood trimmings of the poop and the deckhouses. With a pad of canvas I would scoop up some wet sand, then scrub until the old surface was removed from the teakwood and also from my hands. Then the wood was given a coat of bright linseed oil.

As the *Belfast* lay motionless on an ocean resembling an immense mirror, we hung staging overside from which we worked, scraping rust from the ship's iron sides. From time to time, sharks six to fifteen feet in length would nonchalantly swim by just beneath, causing us to lift our dangling legs hurriedly to safety.

Masts and yards were scraped and oiled. Slack rigging was taken up. On bended knees we holystoned decks until the weather-stained planks were virgin white, ready for a dose of linseed oil.

During these hours of tarring, painting, scraping, scrubbing and greasing we would drop our tasks and rush to braces and halyards when a catspaw of wind encouraged the ship's officer to shout, "Man the braces."

Mile by mile we edged northward, wallowed across the Equator and then, as the breeze hung on a little longer each time, finally picked up the northeast trades and began driving along at a good clip.

Early in February the steward ran out of flour and for a few hours the afterguard faced the appalling possibility of having to eat hardtack with the rest of us. Then Mr. Atkins, bright fellow, came up with an idea. During the night watches I usually passed the time sitting in a coil of rope near the companion ladder within call of the poop, stirring myself only to heave the log and strike the half-hourly bells. Now, the second mate broached the ship's cargo and provided me with a tub of wheat and a small coffee grinder, with orders to grind wheat into flour during my leisure times. This became a nightly chore for me until we reached port.

After passing the Azores we ran into heavy gales and were blown far westward before sighting Cape Clear on the southern tip of Ireland on February 21.

A day later, when almost in sight of Queenstown, a hurricane, estimated later by Captain Davies at eighty miles an hour, blew both reefed tops'ls to pieces, leaving us under bare poles except the small storm-stays'l that somehow or other clung to the stays.

The series of gales left us "hove to" on March 2, just below the Scilly Islands off England's Land's End. We had learned that storms are "where you find them," whether south of the fifties, off the river Plate, in the Indian Ocean or in the North Atlantic.

With the *Belfast* badly battered, sails blown to pieces and the crew run ragged, Captain Davies decided to skip Queenstown and put into Falmouth, England, only a short distance away. Falmouth was also a port of call where ships waited for orders as to final destination. The irony of Captain Davies' decision to skip Queenstown lay in the fact that when our orders came a week later, they read to proceed to Cork, Ireland, which is up the river Lee and can be reached only by passing through Queenstown Harbour, our original destination.

With a fair wind and only a short distance to sail from our position off the Scilly Islands, we soon passed Lizard Light, picked up a tug and were towed into the inner anchorage of Falmouth Harbour, where we dropped anchor on March 3, 1903, 153 days after passing through the Golden Gate. The last landmark I saw when leaving San Francisco was Land's End. The first landmark we picked up when sighting England was also Land's End.

As the anchor chains rattled through the hawse-pipes, I was aloft with other crew members giving the sails a neat harbor stow. Looking toward the docks, I could see a dozen small boats racing toward the *Belfast*. They were bumboats fighting to make first contact with the newly arrived ship. They soon hooked on, and men swarmed over the rail, gathering around Captain Davies on the afterdeck. After much shouting and arm waving, all were dismissed except four, who followed the skipper down the companionway.

These runners represented small shopkeepers who would now make their separate deals with the Old Man whereby crew members might purchase anything their hearts desired at a price high enough to take care of the captain's percentage. You merely signed for your purchase and later the bookkeeping would be taken care of at the shipping office where the crew would be paid off. Soon the runners scooted off toward the docks in their little bumboats to return at knock-off time, loaded down with all of the things the crew had missed and longed for during the long voyage.

In the meantime, we were kept hustling to make everything shipshape while waiting for orders that might read London, Glasgow, Belfast, or even a port in Continental Europe. If the latter, fare would be paid to transport crew members to the nearest port in Britain. Whatever the port, in the British Isles or on the Continent, the contract between the Crown and the individual would be concluded and the crew discharged.

Several of the crew would receive only half pay, or one pound, ten ($7.50 American money) a month, for the thirteen-month voyage. The other half pay had been drawn monthly by their wives. These men would go home and spend a few quiet weeks with their families until again standing before the commissioner they heard the ship's articles read, including the words: ". . . and back to a port in the United Kingdom, the voyage not to exceed three years."

When shipping out again they must content themselves to remain on the same ship, wherever her path might lead, for the period of their contract with the Crown, and on their return, another ship and another three years of bondage would be waiting. The alternative? Desertion in a foreign port and forfeiture of accumulated wages. That apparently would also be my lot if I should seek another ship after leaving the *Belfast*. And if not another ship, how else would I get out of Britain and back to California?

The prospect of getting out of Britain was far from encouraging. That could wait, however. The immediate future was much more inviting. It was six o'clock, things were shipshape, and work was over for the day. We would sleep "all night in" for the first time in five months. And the bumboatmen were spreading their attractive wares on deck for inspection: pies, cakes, pickles, cheese, cold meats, butter, jellies and white bread. White bread, after five months of hardtack garnished with wriggling weevils. Cold roast pork, beef and mutton instead of rancid salt horse and fat salt pork.

Seeking out an isolated spot far forward on the fo'c'slehead, like a half-starved dog afraid someone might take away his hoarded bone, I laid a cloth of clean wrapping paper and then spread out my delicacies.

A bit of sausage and a nip of headcheese. The cold pork was excellent, but then so was the beef and mutton. If concessions *must* be made, I could eat a little less of the white bread, although it *was* good, especially with butter, real butter. As for the cakes, pies and jellies, they were much lighter and less filling than the more solid meats, so one could afford to eat more of them. Pickles didn't count, of course.

I finished dinner feeling like an overstuffed balloon. An hour later my head hung over the rail, eyes watery, stomach convulsed and as empty of food as it was before I started dinner. My poor stomach couldn't take it after five months of abstinence from all decent food.

It was a blessing to be able to turn in and sleep ten full hours. The following night the bumboatmen were back again, this time with clothes as well as food. I selected shirts, underwear and shoes, then allowed myself to be measured for a suit of clothes. Bumboat merchants take no chance on having a ship move out on them. The following night they were back with the new suit.

The material was heavy broadcloth, navy blue and square cut in the English style. I also ordered a heavy pea jacket of the same material and topped it off by selecting a blue cap with a short visor. I learned later that the cap was the style referred to as a "second mate's discharge," meaning that I had favored myself with an undeserved promotion. English money had great purchasing power. Total bumboat purchases, including clothes, shoes and food, was only five pounds, four, or about $26 American money.

Mail forwarded from Queenstown was brought aboard, including three letters from my aunt. Evidently, in my farewell note, I had failed to make clear how long the voyage might last, because her first letter was written immediately after receiving mine. Her second letter, written in December, berated me for not answering the first, and the third and last indicated that she had given up hope of hearing from me again. In reply, I wrote a twelve-page letter describing all that had happened since leaving San Francisco. That letter came into my hands twenty-five years later, and from it I was able to reconstruct the details of my first voyage around Cape Horn.

Early in March orders were received to proceed to Cork, Ireland. Having already had a taste of March weather in the North Atlantic and off the Irish coast, we were glad enough to tag along behind a powerful tug for the last lap of our long voyage.

The trip up the river Lee from Queenstown Harbour to Cork was interesting, especially a number of ancient-looking Irish castles on the bluffs overlooking the river. The following morning we were paid off at the British shipping office and walked out of the door to be greeted by a noisy mob of water-front hangers-on, all anxious to help the crew get rid of their pay. In the van of the shouting crowd were a dozen elderly women vendors, carrying trays loaded with red apples, roasted chestnuts, sea food, "chips and taties" and steamed snails.

My earnings for the voyage totaled twenty-six pounds, twelve shillings, but after deductions of ten pounds for the advance note to Brewer, four pounds, four shillings for slop-chest charges and five pounds, four shillings for bumboat purchases at Falmouth, I received only seven pounds, four ($36 American money) to show for nearly six months of hard work. However, I did own a good outfit of clothes.

Most of the discharged crew planned to take the regular night boat across the Irish Channel to Fishguard in Wales and then proceed to either Cardiff or London, from which they would sign up for an outward-bound voyage after spending their pay.

With money burning holes in our pockets and all day on our hands, Jackson, Duck, Gribble and I hired an Irish jaunting car and set out to see the sights in and around Cork.

Up one street and down the other we bounced, sitting back to back in the rickety old contraption. Our driver was a typical old Paddy, clucking, coaxing and threatening his lazy old nag, as he took long drags on a clay pipe held so firmly between his clenched teeth that it stuck straight out like the prow of a ship.

Leaving behind the cobbled streets of Cork, we struck out for Blarney Castle, several miles out in the country. Past rows of fine-looking homes and through long lanes of drooping beech trees, we jolted along, with a fine view of the river Lee, until we reached the village of Innescara. We stopped before a quaint roadside pub to give the nag a well-earned rest, and Paddy joined us in "splicing the main brace" with Flaherty's Irish whisky, pure white and with the kick of a donkey.

Then the last lap along the little river Martin and a jog up the hill to Blarney Castle, a towering mass of gray stone and boulders, surmounted by huge turrets that had withstood time and the elements for over four hundred years.

Up we climbed, in and out of steep winding passages and over stairs of hewn rock to the very topmost turret, before we got our first glimpse of the old Blarney stone itself and found that to do an authentic job of kissing, one must be either acrobat or sailor. The stone was a projection of rock, a foot below the rim of a rocky shaft, but it was on the opposite side from where we stood, and therein lay the trick.

At that point Paddy of the jaunting car took over and bossed the job. Following instructions, Tom Jackson lay flat on his back, extended his arms over his head, grasped two iron bars imbedded in the rock and then drew his head down until his lips touched the projecting stone while Duck and I held onto his feet.

When Tom's equilibrium was duly restored, each of us went through the rite in the hope of acquiring that eloquence promised in song and story to him who should be so fortunate as to kiss the magic stone. For a sailor, well used to having his ups and downs, it was not much of a feat; but most visitors contented themselves by merely leaning over the shaft, reaching down and touching the rock and then gently kissing the finger-tips that had touched the famous stone.

* 15 *

THE NIGHT of March 10 was a rough one on the short stretch of turbulent water between Ireland and Wales, so rough in fact that nearly all the passengers kept to their staterooms. The small assembly hall was left mostly to us former members of the *Belfast's* crew, to whom a badly rocking boat was certainly no novelty. Then who should stroll into the cabin of the channel steamer *Killarney* but the second officer of the *Belfast*, now just another bucko-mate without a berth.

As he seated himself on a bench opposite, I was busy with my own thoughts and paid no attention until he pointed at me and smirked, "Well, well, and I thought we were bloody well rid of the Yank at Cork."

Then something went off inside of me and, like a jack-in-the-box suddenly released from its spring, I hurled myself across the narrow deck space and smashed my doubled fist directly into his grinning teeth. His head crashed against the wall and, as he slid to the tilting deck of the badly rocking little steamer, I landed on top of him; and there we rolled over and over, clawing, tearing and gouging at each other.

The ex-officer of the *Belfast* fought tooth and nail, not because he wanted to, but because he had to; and as for me, I actually enjoyed every bit of the wild scrap, give or take, because at last I was getting even for the pushing around aboard ship. I had spent many a long watch, in good weather and bad, crouched on the bottom rung of the companion ladder, serving as lackey to this fellow and whiling the hours away in dreaming of just such an opportunity as this. Now it had come in the

stuffy cabin of a little steamer, rolling and tossing in the middle
of St. George's Channel. I made the most of it.

Just as the men kept hands off when a row started aboard
the *Belfast,* so did they stand aside while Mr. Atkins and I
pummeled each other, until a ship's officer appeared in the
doorway demanding to know, "What goes on here?"

Then the ring of delighted spectators closed in and separated
us, but not until I had achieved at least a measure of revenge
for some of the kicks and blows I had taken from him aboard
ship.

That night, while nursing my bruises, the thought occurred
to me that with most of us hoping to ship out of Cardiff, I
might find myself outward bound aboard some "lime juicer"
with Atkins again my superior officer. I broke out in a cold
sweat at the very thought of it. (On the train en route to
Cardiff we both looked a sight with our swollen and lacerated
faces and blackened eyes.) With only six months of seafaring
experience in my discharge book from the *Belfast,* I would be
lucky to get a berth even while living at the Sailors' Home.

Registered with me at the home were Elka the Finn, Lloyd,
the two Irishmen, Fitz and Jerry, and the two French-Canadi-
ans, Felix and Celle. Some would try to eke out their pay and
take it easy for a few weeks, paying board of one pound a
week at the home. Others would spend every shilling in a few
days and perhaps be outward bound in a week.

All other members of the *Belfast's* crew continued to London by train, including my best friend, Arthur Gribble. From
London he would go home to Greenock, Scotland, where his
wife and two children would greet him after the voyage of
more than a year. During his absence Mrs. Gribble drew one
pound, ten, half his monthly pay. How they could exist on that
pittance, even in Scotland, is beyond me. Arthur would reach
home with additional pay of some fifteen pounds. After a few
weeks with his family there would be another voyage and an-

other long absence, possibly two or three years. I bade him good-by at Cardiff and never heard of him again.

At the Sailors' Home I met with a bit of rare good luck. My battered and bruised appearance attracted the attention of a young Dublin Irishman, Johnny McGee. Through Johnny, I signed as one of a four-man crew in the British three-masted coasting schooner, the *J. H. Barrow*. As she was a coastwise ship carrying only A.B.'s, I thus became an able seaman after serving only a six months' apprenticeship instead of the customary three years. The *J. H. Barrow* was only one hundred tons register, and at that time was lying at anchor in Milford Haven, a port on the eastern tip of Wales, loaded with barrels of salt herring consigned to London.

On my first night in Cardiff I held on to my pounds, shillings and pence, not knowing how long I might be on the beach before landing a ship. On the second night, however, with my future assured at least as far as London, I celebrated by treating Johnny to a lively evening. We were joined by my two former shipmates, Fitz and Jerry. With this quartet of three-fourths Irish and one-fourth Yankee, all in funds, we proceeded to paint the water front a bright Irish green, with perhaps a dash of Yankee red.

Perhaps it was because that night was my first real letdown after a long voyage or because first memories linger the longest; in any event, the morning light found the Irish-American quartet sprawled athwartships a narrow bed in a haven called the Angel Hotel. After consuming gallons of "arf and arf" and Shandygafs, the only angels we could recall were barmaids who refused to desert their posts at our invitation and several promenading ladies of the "midnight patrol" who required no invitation and who had no posts to desert.

A roll call of the quartet brought out an inharmonious note: not a single one-pound note, not a gold sovereign, not even a half crown of silver remained in our collective exchequer. The fruits of our long voyage had gone down the rat hole in numerous pubs and brothels, with perhaps a pound or two clinging to itchy fingers of newly found friends.

We were broke, one and all. And then I learned about the luck of the Irish. Johnny McGee took Fitz and Jerry to see Captain Muldoon of the good ship *Barrow*, which was still in Cardiff, and then, "praise be the saints!" Captain Muldoon hired the two of them. We learned later that he had fired a Swede and a Finn to "make way for the Irish."

To add to my own woes, I discovered that I had lost my heavy pea jacket, which I had bought in Falmouth and had counted on for the tough cold trip around Land's End and through the English Channel to London. But there seemed no limit to the ingenuity of the Irish, as represented by Johnny McGee.

He had an acquaintance with one Jones the Goat, a marine outfitter who furnished slop-chest goods to most of the deep-water skippers. After a fifteen-minute parley with Mr. Jones, he not only bought a pea jacket for me on the cuff but also borrowed train fare to deliver the four of us to Milford Haven.

The *Barrow* was a fine-looking schooner, registered from Dublin and so Irish that her figurehead should have been a harp intertwined with shamrocks. Besides Captain Timothy Muldoon, there was Mr. Tooney, the mate; Aleck, a redheaded Liverpool Irishman, who was the cook; and the four foremast hands, Fitz, Johnny, Jerry, and me (the only non-Irishman aboard).

We hove anchor at daylight, hoisted sail and under a light breeze moved along toward the harbor entrance just in time to meet a big steam trawler coming in from the open sea. As she came abreast, less than twenty feet away, with a small-sized mountain of fresh herring rising ten feet high on her deck, Captain Muldoon shouted, "Throw us a fish." Whereupon her crew bombarded the *Barrow* with herring until we passed beyond range. We scooped the mess into hampers and then for the next several days Aleck served herring in more ways than we ever thought possible.

By morning of the fifth day out of Milford Haven, we had clawed our way around Land's End with the lights of the Scilly Islands visible on our starboard beam. A fair wind carried us into the Channel, past the Lizard Lights almost to Start Point beyond Plymouth, then deserted us as the fog closed in.

For two days and nights we were blasted by March winds laden with hail and sleet. Then the heavy mist lifted, the sun broke through and Captain Muldoon, taking full advantage of the clearing weather and strong-fair wind, made a fine run around Beachy Head, past Dungeness and through Dover Straits to the Downs, without losing sight of the English coast all the way.

We dropped anchor among a score of other sailing craft with the lights of Deal and Walmer flickering only a few miles away. A few ships like ourselves were only waiting overnight before towing upriver to London, but mostly they were big square-riggers, outward bound and merely standing by for a fair wind down-Channel to the open sea and the long haul around Good Hope or the Horn to ports of the Orient, the Indies, Australia or the Americas.

At daybreak we were at the windlass heaving anchor. Rounding North Foreland, we passed close enough to Margate to see objects ashore, and then, with the wind almost directly astern, headed for the Thames estuary.

After passing Nore lightship off Sheerness, we lost our fair wind, so Captain Muldoon accepted a tow from a fussy little tugboat, after a sharp argument with its skipper over the fee to be charged.

Down came our sails, and before they were snugly furled,

we had moved into the two-way traffic stream of the world's busiest maritime highway, the river Thames. Then followed an ever-changing panorama of moving ships along forty miles of turning, twisting river that took us into the very heart of the world's largest city.

Plowing along ahead of us, in a continuous procession, were ships of sail and ships of steam; majestic ocean liners, the last word in speed and luxury; sleek-looking private yachts, all white, polished and shining; and excursion steamers, rails crowded with sight-seers.

Sturdy old colliers loaded with "black diamonds" from the coal mines of Wales; dingy-looking tramp steamers blotched with dabs of red lead ("sea dogs with the mange"). And then, like a midget leading a sleek greyhound on leash, a puffing little tugboat towing a large ship with graceful lines, tall spars, a magnificent spread of yards and beautiful tracery of rigging; a great four-masted bark flying the "red duster" of England from its monkey gaff.

More ships. Flags of nations passing in review. A man-of-war —the Royal Navy on parade—its scores of blue-jacketed youngsters swarming over every vantage point. Then came Gravesend and, directly abreast of it in a bulge of the river, a great fleet of sailing ships idly swinging at anchor.

A half circle around the Isle of Dogs and there was Greenwich, longitude zero! And over on the north bank, West India Docks, Limehouse, and Billingsgate, London's great fish market where eels are a choice morsel and where thrives the costermonger, or fish peddler, whose quaint costume and quainter Cockney speech add to London's attraction for the Yankee tourist.

Next came Tower Wharf, beyond which was a great, deep moat completely encircling the irregular pentagon-shaped mass of buildings that is the city's most cherished historical relic, the Tower of London.

Only a short distance farther was the pool where scores of ships anchored overnight, waiting to be hauled into their docks. It was after dark by the time we dropped anchor and snugged down.

I drew the ten o'clock to midnight watch and found it no hardship to kill time staring at the interesting sights on every side, including the traffic crossing the Tower Bridge only a short distance away.

Early next morning we were warped into St. Katherine Dock, and soon the barrels of herring were being transferred from ship to shore.

Johnny was familiar with the city and knew most of the "right places." This time there was no wild binge like our night out in Cardiff, owing mostly to an acute shortage of pounds, shillings and pence. With our fast eight-day passage from Milford Haven to London, and only five or six days needed to discharge cargo, we were lucky to get an advance of ten bob, meaning ten shillings.

Deciding that we should see as much as possible within our limited means, Johnny led me a few blocks to a high monument of Fish Street Hill near the bridge, and there we paid three-pence for the privilege of hiking up several hundred steps to the top where, from a platform enclosed in an iron cage, we gazed down on the busy traffic crossing old London Bridge and at the scores of ships at anchor in the pool.

Having indulged our economy streak, we descended from the sublime to the ridiculous, paying a shilling and sixpence to spend the balance of the evening at Madame Tussaud's chamber of horrors on Marylebone Road. There, among other fearsome objects, we saw the wax likenesses of Queen Anne, Lady Jane Grey and Marie Antoinette, who had lost their heads for one reason or another, and also gazed upon the chopping block presumed to have been used for the decapitating job.

The average deepwater sailor seldom strayed far from his

native habitat, the water front; he preferred to spend his loose time in the kind of place and among the sort of people he could be comfortable with, while ridding himself of his pay without undue strain.

Taking a cab to Limehouse, near West India Docks, we had no difficulty finding our type of divertisement in Charlie Brown's Railway Tavern. We paid cash for the first few drinks and then became a trifle befuddled and let the chit pile up a bit, forgetting that we had less than four shillings between us.

When the hour of reckoning arrived, we could only fish through our pockets and shout that we had been robbed. Robbed right there in Charlie's place. Apparently even Limehouse tavern keepers have their sensitive moments. Our Cockney waiter shouted the equivalent of "Hey, Rube" in the purest of Billingsgate and things began coming our way, hard knuckles and ale bottles predominating. A flying wedge of bobbies rushed in and quelled the riot, then booked Johnny and me at the Bow Street police station for defrauding a tavern keeper.

Next morning we succeeded in getting a telegram to Captain Muldoon, who at first threatened to discharge us, then relented, settled with the tavern and paid a ten-shilling fine for us on condition that we remain aboard ship until sailing day.

In the state we were in, physically bruised and financially broke, it was no additional hardship to keep our parole, but I hoped that some day I should be lucky enough to see a bit of London, other than Billingsgate, Limehouse, and Madame Tussaud's, even if it be only Big Ben or Cleopatra's Needle.*

* Excerpt from a diary written on June 4, 1953, "Coronation Time," exactly half a century later: "I took a cab to Charlie Brown's Railway Tavern, but was sorely disappointed. In my earlier visit the tavern walls were adorned with pictures of famous ships of the line and the Clippers that rounded the Horn and ran "the Easting" down. The shelves bulged with models of square-riggers, and the atmosphere was one of appeal to men who go down to the sea in ships. But alas, fifty years have taken their toll, and the beautiful models have been sunk without trace, leaving Charlie Brown's tavern just another pub.

∗ 16 ∗

Two MORNINGS LATER the *Barrow* was again a part of the river scene, this time being towed down the Thames bound for Antwerp in ballast to load general cargo for Dublin, her home port. We dropped our towline at the estuary and headed across the North Sea, pushed along by a brisk wind. Without special incident, except frequent blowing of the foghorn and dodging ocean liners hurrying down-Channel, we picked up the light off Flushing on our third morning out. Then we plowed through the tumbling waters that overlie the Flemish shoals and sailed well up into the Scheldt River before picking up a tow.

Antwerp was competing with Hamburg at that time as the world's second busiest seaport, and the Scheldt, like the Thames, was literally clogged with ships arriving and departing. Captain Muldoon quickly accepted the first towboat offer and soon we were threading our way up the river to the Quai Van Dyck, where we made fast to a great overhanging wharf. By mid-afternoon we were loading case goods into the ship's hold.

As we finished work for the day, two boardinghouse runners swung aboard ship. They hoped to persuade the four of us to leave the schooner for a few days of rest ashore, after which, according to them, berths would be waiting on a fine ship at much higher wages. We were promised a nice, comfortable boardinghouse and plenty of wine, women and song.

In the midst of their plea, the mate came hurrying forward and ordered them to leave the ship. An argument followed and suddenly, without warning, Fitz stepped up to one of the runners and slugged him. As he dropped limply to the deck, the second man reached into his pocket for brass knuckles as Fitz closed in on him. Johnny put an end to the whole thing by gently tapping the second runner over the head with a wooden belaying pin, knocking him out cold alongside his friend. We hoisted the two of them to the wharf above and left them to recover and wander away at their leisure.

Then Fitz recounted his own story which I had heard once before on the *Belfast*. In Antwerp, two years before, Fitz had been slugged and robbed of nearly thirty pounds. Being broke, he took refuge in a boardinghouse with the understanding that he would be shipped on a coastwise vessel. He awoke one morning to find himself aboard the British ship *Peter Iredale*, headed down the English Channel bound around Cape Horn to Portland, Oregon.

He deserted the *Iredale* in Portland, leaving eight months' wages behind, and worked his way to San Francisco. After being on the beach two months, he awoke with a headache one morning and found himself on the *Belfast* bound around the Horn again and headed right back to Europe where he started from. He had never seen these two runners before, but to quote Fitz, "All boardinghouse runners looked alike after that."

In those days Antwerp was the home port, or port of call, for nearly two hundred shipping lines, and more than a thousand vessels cleared the harbor each month. In addition, it was the favorite payoff port for scores of sailing vessels after voyages of from one to three years' duration. Even at prevailing low wages a ship's payoff after a long voyage averaged several thousand dollars, and with such a harvest to work on, the place was infested with crimps and boardinghouse masters. They met every incoming vessel.

If the crew had recently signed on and had little pay coming, boardinghouse runners enticed them ashore with a promise of better jobs. If the ship was a homeward-bounder, with payday yet to come, they advanced money to the crew, gave them bottles of liquor and then hung on to them like leeches after they left the shipping office, devising every possible scheme from the "badger-game" to knockout drops to pry loose the last franc or shilling.

Having separated the victim from past earnings, they set out to mortgage his future by furnishing him room and board until such time as they might dump the drink-sodden wretch aboard a ship and, with the connivance of the ship's master, collect "blood money" and an advance note, thus reaping a profit both coming and going. The art of shanghaiing was practiced as frequently and as brazenly in Antwerp as in San Francisco or Hong Kong. As a result, it enjoyed the unenviable reputation of being the worst and toughest of all Continental ports.

However, despite its deserved reputation for iniquity, the cesspool flavor of its water-front dives, its gilded if slightly tarnished Lilies of the Scheldt Valley and its Continental disregard for inhibitions, we managed to see and enjoy what went on without getting into any serious trouble. Our financial rating, after paying for the debacle in London, was something less than nil, but Captain Muldoon advanced us two francs each day, which was enough to pay for beer and wine at a *café chantant* in the Place Verte. And what was lacking in Antwerp we found in near-by Brussels.

Our pugnacious shipmate Fitz claimed to be an authority on Brussels, especially on what was known as the Lower Town where anything that Antwerp had to offer might be duplicated but in a manner less crude and with more appeal; in other words, the same merchandise served in more attractive packages. We accepted Fitz not only as guide but also as a banker *pro tem,* he being the only one of the crew still in funds.

On a Sunday morning, followed by the skipper's warning that if we should get into trouble we could jolly well get ourselves out of it, we boarded the Brussels Express, rolled out over a great viaduct above the streets of Antwerp, and little more than an hour later emerged from the Gare du Nord and strolled over to the Boulevard de Waterloo in Belgium's capital city.

Smoothing out the wrinkles in our shore clothes, we hied ourselves over to the Grande Place, or public market, and killed time until nightfall, sipping wine and liqueurs at little pavement cafés.

Thus far, our Brussels adventure was decidedly a flop, but after dark our shipmate's talent as a night prowler asserted itself and we set off for a more picturesque section of town. First, the Moulin Rouge, largest cabaret in Brussels. Droves of girls at the tables. Tough-looking, lonesome, thirsty and ambitious. Stockings rolled below their knees. Curves and angles much in evidence through peekaboo waist or skintight sweater. Faces calcimined like shopwindow manikins; eyes darting here and there looking for companionship and a place to light. We move toward a table, and here they come; one wants a light, another a cigarette; all want an invitation.

A couple waltz by. Of all things—two men dancing together cheek to cheek. Many girls dancing together. Evidently people *must* dance. Now a mixed couple. Mixed is right: the woman is white; the man is coal black. All male dancers wear hats. Now the cabaret numbers. A young man impersonates a woman and does it too well. Other acts. Then a middle-aged woman dressed as a man sings sophisticated songs, with gestures. We pretend to understand and applaud. Now the performers pass the hat, their only compensation.

Three sailors on the loose in gay Brussels are spending too much time in one place, so we excuse ourselves to our partners for "just a minute" and forget to return. Around the corner another garish-looking place with the doorman dressed in droopy Turkish trousers.

The Oriental Palace. Something new. Scores of girls dancing together; sitting at table—but something *is missing*. Not one wears a stitch of clothing. All are absolutely nude and there are scores of them. Not a bit self-conscious. Nude girls were no novelty in Brussels. But here in the Oriental were scores of them. Then we notice that every wall is a mirror and a scant dozen nude ladies are made to look like a hundred. Yes, it was all done with mirrors, but it was tremendously exciting and might also prove equally expensive, so we ignored the friendly invitations to sit it out and ordered at a small bar instead. Our order was wine, but in this elegant House of Mirrors, wine was construed to mean champagne, and that's what we got. We decided not to argue the point, so paid and made our exit. After all, we did get our money's worth.

Now, Fitz leads the way and we come to a dark, narrow street, just wide enough for the three of us to walk abreast and still clear the walls on either side. Fitz explains in purest Liverpool Irish that our narrow thoroughfare is named the Rue d'Une Personne, which means Street of One Person. This could certainly be true if the one person were "Mr. Five by Five." Fitz rings a bell. A blue-eyed girl looks through a peephole and evidently three men of the sea pass muster, as the door swings wide.

Inside is a miniature bar. Fitz says nothing less than champagne will do, so Johnny and I, remembering Charlie Brown's Tavern and Captain Muldoon's warning, fervently pray that our banker's money will hold out. In this miniature Temple of Elysian lure, dedicated to the fleshpots of Belgium's capital city, it is fitting that the events of the evening be passed over lightly with the comment that Brussels' claims as the widest open city in all Europe were fully substantiated.

Safely away from the Rue d'Une Personne we took stock and found that every pocket had been picked and the last sou removed. Our actual loss was small because we had little to lose, which no doubt was a disappointment to our beautiful hostesses, but we were still in Brussels, our ship was in Antwerp, and the hour was late. And then Fitz, our guide, proved that the Irish are smarter than the Belgians any day. He removed a shoe and triumphantly hauled out a ten-franc note.

Our jubilation was tempered considerably, however, when we reached the Gare du Nord and found that the last train had left for Antwerp. Next morning, when we reported late aboard ship, the skipper was so mad he would have discharged the lot of us except for the bother of hiring replacements.

We battened down the hatches and followed a towboat through a maze of incoming river traffic as far as Flushing, where we cut loose and hoisted sail for the run through the Straits of Dover and down-Channel. Bucking a deadly west-sou' west wind, we made short tacks back and forth for forty-eight hours before getting a slant of wind that carried us through the Straits and well down the Channel.

* III *

☀ 17 ☀

BETWEEN SQUALLS and April showers, fog alternately closed around us like a trap, then cleared completely. Captain Muldoon knew his English Channel almost as well as the skippers of the fishing smacks that were a constant menace in the narrow waters between the Channel Islands and the English coast. We turned Lizard Point and headed up through St. George's Channel on the ninth day out.

Three days later we picked up Mizen Head light, forty miles south of Dublin Bay, and early next morning docked in Dublin. Then followed a week I still like to remember, because for me it was an experience I had not known for three years. At no time since I had left my own home and people had I entered a friendly home or known a really nice girl. In Dublin I found both. Johnny lived with his widowed mother and his sister Maggie. Invited to their home at their insistence, I moved in, sharing Johnny's room at night while the two of us worked cargo on the *Barrow* during the day.

After dinner Maggie proudly showed me the sights. We paraded up and down Sackville and Grafton Streets, sat on O'Connell's Bridge and watched members of the gaudily uniformed Irish Fusiliers courting their sweethearts. We visited Dublin Castle, Chapel Royal, Malahide Castle, and Guinness's brewery where the stout comes from. We drank Irish whisky, but only in our tea, which was a new idea to me but evidently an old Irish custom in the McGee family.

On Sunday we strolled in Phoenix Park. We hired an Irish jaunting car and were driven out Blackrock Road along the

Irish Sea to Kingstown, where our ship had dropped anchor a few nights before. We saw ancient Irish castles on the cliffs overlooking the sea. Then back to the McGees' where Maggie's mother had cooked a fine dinner of kidney and mutton pudding, calves' hearts and chutney, washed down with tea spiced with a dram of Paddy O'Flaherty's best.

After dinner who should join us but Skipper Muldoon, who, it turned out, was a long-time friend of the family. No wonder Johnny had taken liberties and wangled favors. But pleasant as the party was, the captain brought bad news for me. As soon as the schooner's cargo was unloaded, she would be sailed across to Lancaster, England, and placed in a drydock for overhauling, which meant the end of my job.

With my pay and a fine discharge from Captain Muldoon I shook hands with shipmate Johnny, kissed Maggie good-by with a promise to write frequently and took the night boat across the Irish Sea to Liverpool. On the advice of Captain Muldoon, I skipped the boardinghouses and registered at the Sailors' Home, paying several days in advance.

Britain's second largest seaport was loaded with deepwater sailors, most of them broke and waiting for a ship, any ship, to any port and at any wage. Most of them, entirely without funds, were living in sailors' boardinghouses that lined both sides of Paradise Street, Park Lane, and Duke Street, and would remain in hock to their boardinghouse masters until lucky enough to sign on for a voyage. Then they would leave behind an advance note covering the first month's wages to cancel out their board bill.

As the supply of seamen more than equaled the demand, there was no shanghaiing of men against their will in British ports; therefore, ships' crews were signed up in an orderly manner. But most of the sailors, being what they were, shunned the Sailors' Home because of strict rules and placed themselves in the hands of boardinghouse runners, who in turn had to hustle up berths for their boarders to prevent being eaten out of house and home.

On my second day in the Sailors' Home, the bulletin board in the lobby read:

FOUR-MASTED BARQUE CELTICBURN, DESTINATION HAMBURG AND SANTA ROSALIA. SIGN UP AT FOUR O'CLOCK. SAILMAKER, CARPENTER. TWO ORDINARY SEAMEN. TWENTY ABLE SEAMEN.

I became so excited that my stomach began doing tricks. Santa Rosalia is a Mexican port in Lower California. It would mean another voyage around the Horn, but that must come eventually, anyway, and I was determined to get back to the West Coast; so the sooner the better.

At four o'clock the lobby fairly swarmed with men, hoping and praying for a berth. The captain, a stout, red-faced man, stood on top of a table where he could look the men over and appraise each one for evidence of sobriety, seamanship, reliability and, most important on a sailing vessel, beef, to throw on the end of a brace or halyard in heavy weather.

To most of the men selection meant a job, an opportunity to eat again. To me it meant more than just a job. It meant *going home*. It might be months before another ship would sign up for the West Coast. Nervous and feeling sickish at my stomach, I stood right beside the table, holding my Board of Trade discharge book.

My experience on the *Belfast* and *Barrow* totaled only seven months. And me, hoping to land one of the two ordinary-seamen berths! The captain chose his carpenter and sailmaker, then called for two ordinaries. Two-dozen hands went up. As he motioned one man after another to come forward, I impulsively tugged at his trouser leg. He looked startled and asked, "What's the matter?"

"Please take me," I said.

"Are you an A.B.?" he inquired.

"Yes," I answered. "Here is my discharge book."

Without reaching for my book, he handed me a slip and continued making his selections. Backing out of the excited crowd, I went outside to gloat over the slip in my hand and only then realized that it called for an *able seaman* instead of an *ordinary*.

Later I noticed a happy-looking fellow examining his slip and ventured to ask him where the shipping office was. After becoming better acquainted as prospective shipmates, we spent our last evening in Liverpool together. His name was Scotty McLeish and he had six years in his discharge book. He had never been around the Horn or to America and was as excited as I, so we decided to be mutually helpful.

Hours later, while we were enjoying a steak and lark pie and mugs of ale in a place called Old Mother Smerden's Pub, I became confidential and showed him my discharge book, asking if he thought I would get along all right aboard the *Celticburn* as an A.B. He suggested that I sit tight because, at worst, I could only be disrated to ordinary seaman if unable to perform the duties of an A.B.

From Old Mother Smerden's we drifted over to Copperas Hill, where sailors' talk was the universal language and where a round of shandygaffs, "arf and arf," Bass ale or Guinness's stout for a party of four could be had for sixpence, with a snack at the bar thrown in. Still excited over our new berth and unwilling to risk missing the sign-up at the shipping office next morning, we excused ourselves early and backed out of the Bluejay Inn as Lizzie, the Irish barmaid, shouted in derision, "Sure, it's bloody easy for you sailors, sitting on your stern posts, letting the wind blow you along, at three quid a month."

At ten next morning the commissioner gathered the new crew around him and read aloud the ship's articles, finishing with, ". . . and back to a port in the United Kingdom, the voyage not to exceed three years."

As each man signed, he was asked if a month's advance note was desired. I hesitated, then, recalling the last paragraph of the ship's articles, requested the advance. God willing, I had no intention of being a member of the *Celticburn's* crew when she returned to Britain.

On the *Belfast* my wages as ordinary had been five pounds a month, the American scale. Now, on the *Celticburn* wages for an ordinary seaman would be only one pound, ten, and my wage as an A.B. would be only three pounds, under the British scale. I cashed my advance note at the Sailors' Home and used one pound to purchase a "donkey's breakfast," a double blanket, and other needed items and stowed the balance away for future use.

After lunch Scotty and I, dunnage bags over our shoulder, joined other seamen in a rickety horse-drawn wagon and were driven from the Home to the Princess Docks, where the ship lay ready to be towed to sea. A representative of the Home accompanied us to check all men aboard whose advance notes had been cashed.

At the dock the *Celticburn's* towering masts and spreading yards stood out over all neighboring ships. She was one of Britain's largest four-masters, twenty-five hundred tons register, which was a fourth larger than the *Belfast*. Her royal yard was 160 feet above the deck. She was to proceed to Hamburg in ballast and there load coke and bricks of patent fuel for Santa Rosalia, a Mexican copper-mining town in the Gulf of California, opposite Guaymas. Besides those who had signed on in the morning, there were already aboard a steward, a cook, two apprentices, Mr. Douglass, the chief mate; Mr. Lane, the second mate; Mr. Thomas, the third mate; and Captain Alfred Davis.

The layout on the *Celticburn* was not very different from that of the *Belfast*. She was larger by seven hundred tons, carried one more mast with its complement of yards and rigging, two more A.B.'s and also two apprentices, but like the *Belfast*, her fo'c'sle was far up under the bows, and she looked just as dark, wet and uncomfortable. In many British ships the fo'c'sle was a separate house on deck. And on many ships, the wheelhouse on the quarter-deck was enclosed for protection against wind and sea and a large net was strung under the jib boom to prevent men from being washed overboard. The *Belfast* had none of those safeguards. Neither had the *Celticburn*.

However, those things seemed very unimportant when I compared my lot with what it was on that morning only seven months before when I was unceremoniously dumped aboard the *Belfast*, bewildered, beaten and without even an extra shirt.

Now, as A.B. on one of Britain's largest ships, I took stock of myself to determine what was lacking and what should be done to fill the gaps. It is the privilege of the ship's master to disrate any seaman unable to perform his duties and I did not want that to happen to me. I was a lightweight, which is almost a crime aboard a windjammer, and I looked much younger than my twenty years. As for seamanship, my first three months on the *Belfast* were almost a total loss, but I had partially made up for it during the last half of the voyage when I took my trick at the wheel and learned to handle myself aloft.

Six weeks as A.B. on the *Barrow* had helped a lot. I lacked finesse in splicing ropes and wires and sewing sail, but there would be little call for those duties until we were loaded at Hamburg and outward bound. By that time I could learn more, and I did. I had no illusions about what lay ahead, particularly the return passage around the Horn, but warm clothing, good oilskins and the knowledge of how to handle myself should make a difference. Now I had good sea boots and heavy underwear and also nearly three pounds to purchase additional comforts before leaving Hamburg. I felt happy and optimistic.

One of the first to report on board, I selected a bunk in a good location and staked it out with my dunnage bag. I wondered what I should do if my choice was challenged, but fortunately I was not put to the test.

On May 3, two months after the *Belfast* had dropped anchor in Falmouth, a great oceangoing tug, the *Sarah Joliffe,* drew alongside, passed a towline and soon we were on our way down the Mersey River. We crossed the bar and dropped our pilot opposite the North-West lightship, but the breeze was light, so Captain Davis megaphoned the tug's skipper to continue towing us until abreast of Great Ormes Head, where we cast loose and, with a strong easterly wind, began to scoot along at a good rate.

As soon as the mess of running gear was cleared and ready for action, all hands were assembled aft to be appraised and selected for watches, according to their respective gifts of height, weight and seamanship. Without casting any aspersions on the judgment of Mr. Douglass, the first mate, who turned out to be a nice enough fellow, I mention that his first choice was Henry, a husky, coal-black Negro, while I was his last choice.

By midnight we were around Holyhead and driving south toward Saint George's Channel. The fine run continued all the way to the tip of the Cornish coast, and three days after leaving Liverpool we were well up in the English Channel, where stiff head winds were encountered, necessitating short tacks every hour or two. When the wind finally hauled fair, we slid through Dover Straits into the wider reaches of the North Sea.

There was no moon and several times we narrowly escaped colliding with other ships. One night, in inky darkness and a drizzling rain, a scream was heard and the lookout, straining his eyes in the gloom, just barely made out a fishing smack sliding along toward our stern, so close the very paint was rubbed from the little vessel's side. The smack was still afloat and apparently all right as it drifted astern in the ship's wake, the crew of three men shouting and shaking their fists in rage as we slid out of sight.

Thirteen days out of Liverpool we made Cuxhaven, accepted a tow from a prowling tugboat and moved up the Elbe River toward Hamburg. It was Sunday and, along with the usual traffic, a dozen gaily decorated excursion steamers cruised slowly up and down the river. Crowds lined the rails waving and shouting, bands played waltz music and people were dancing on deck. As the tug slowly hauled the *Celticburn* up the river, a dozen of us were spread out on the yards aloft, giving the sails a neat harbor stow. I straddled the yardarm, almost able to reach out and touch hands with excursionists leaning over the rails on the top decks of the flag-bedecked steamers. It was dark when we dropped anchor and looked longingly at the bright lights of Hamburg, flickering a short distance away.

We need not have been impatient because we were to remain in Hamburg for a full month. Next day we docked in the Saint Pauli District, which seemed so separate and apart from the rest of Hamburg that there were times when it was difficult to believe it was part of a German city. English was spoken in all of the water-front bars and beer stubes, and half of the vaudeville acts in the theaters and music halls were also in English.

This, however, did not keep Scotty and me from spending evenings in other sections of Hamburg; we soon learned where to go and what to do even though expressing ourselves in sign language. After all, money did talk and with the remainder of our advance notes, each had nearly a hundred marks to spend. First, I bought woolen socks and a heavy woolen sweater. From experience I knew that memories of beautiful Fräuleins, Strauss waltzes, and marvelous nights on the Kleinermarinastrasse would not keep me warm while standing a trick at the wheel or reefing a tops'l off the Horn.

In Cardiff, London or Antwerp, with only a night or two to

kill, I could afford to go broke all in one piece, but here in Hamburg, with weeks to tarry, I became cautious and budgeted my fund. Or perhaps it was the influence of my Scotch shipmate.

There were mammoth beer gardens with fine orchestras, sometimes numbering one hundred and twenty musicians, many of them teen-age youths. One pfennig would buy a stein of beer and an hour of wonderful music. With another pfennig we could buy pretzels from a lovely Fräulein who strolled among the tables with her stock of pretzels strung on a long cane.

On Sundays we stretched our budget for excursion trips on the Elbe. Aboard the steamer, we would stand alone at the rail and enjoy the scenery. There were swarms of lonesome girls aboard, out for a good time. Soon we would have company and then there would be dancing on deck followed by beer and pretzels.

After a while there was dinner in a large café at Cuxhaven on the edge of the North Sea. A dinner worth remembering. Anchovies and pickled herring. Partridge pies with rich flaky crust. Wursts served with spiced red cabbage. Wine. Cheeses and tasty pastries. Tariff for two couples was four marks. Cognac served in a giant snifter glass was extra but well worth the price. Moonlight. The river Elbe. Band music and dancing. Beer and pretzels. Wine and sausage. Jolly, happy people who knew how to enjoy life. That was Hamburg. That was Altona. That was Saint Pauli and the Kleinermarinastrasse in June of the year 1903.

Day by day work progressed, loading several thousand tons of cargo into the *Celticburn*. Heaping trucks were lifted twenty feet above the yawning hatches, a bolt was knocked out, the bottom opened and tons of coke dropped into the hold until the last crevice was filled, the hatches battened down and the ship made ready for her fifteen-thousand-mile voyage.

A month after arriving in Hamburg we were again following

a tugboat, this time in the opposite direction. A few miles before reaching the open sea we caught a mild easterly wind, so in order to lighten the strain on the tugboat, which was making slow time hauling our heavily laden ship, we set all but the lighter sails.

No sooner had we done so than the wind suddenly increased, the *Celticburn* shot forward and the excited tugboat skipper shouted to hold her back as we were about to trample all over his little tug. We hurried to the braces and backed the main and mizzen yards just in time to slow the ship's progress and prevent her from swamping the panicky Dutchman ahead.

We soon hit open water, and Captain Davis signaled the German skipper that we were cutting loose. The yards were hauled around, the royals, flying jib and gaff-tops'l set, and we headed down the North Sea on the first lap of the long passage that lay ahead.

On the third night out, during the middle watch, with the darkness thickened by a heavy overcast, I was frightened almost out of my wits by the sudden appearance of a great ocean liner that popped out of the darkness ahead. She passed close by with hundreds of lights streaming from windows and portholes and disappeared into the black night. No doubt the officers of both ships knew exactly what they were doing, but for a moment my eyes popped wide.

Battling head winds in the North Sea, we had squeezed nearly through the Straits and, on the eighth night out of Hamburg, were just off Gris-Nez light on the French side when the wind fizzled out completely. A thick, soupy fog closed in and there we lay rocking gently in the choppy channel, helpless without steerageway and directly in the path of inbound channel traffic.

It was a spine-tingling business as the foghorn wailed and all hands stood by, nerves taut and eyes strained, as answering signals indicated the nearness of approaching vessels. Ghostlike hulls loomed dimly through the mist, then silently slipped by and disappeared in the enveloping fog.

Toward morning a breath of air fanned itself into a breeze, catching the ship's sails aback. With both watches standing by for quick action, yards were trimmed and once again we began the zigzag battle against head winds.

On the starboard tack, heading toward the French side several watches later, still feeling our way through almost impenetrable fog, the curtain lifted to reveal the dim outline of Alderney Island just to leeward, while straight ahead, blinking through the clearing mist, was the Casquets Light. Orders were shouted, the helm was jammed hard down, the ship's head came up into the wind and we swung over on the port tack just in time to avoid plunging into the swirling, churning waters that twist and turn all ways at once around the Channel Islands off the French coast. A few hundred yards more would have meant the destruction of the *Celticburn*.

The wind veered to the north with heavy, stinging rain squalls, but it was a fair wind. We squared away and just before dark watched England's Land's End and the twin lights of Lizard Point fade out behind us for the last time. Four times in less than three months I had circled that tip of the Cornish coast and I was not sorry to see it drop astern. At last the big *Celticburn* was in the open Atlantic with elbowroom to spread her great white wings as she pointed south with six thousand miles of open water ahead.

Beyond was Cape Horn and plenty of trouble, but that was too far away to worry about—yet.

* 18 *

ALTHOUGH the afterguard was strictly British, the rest of the crew, including the steward, cook, sailmaker, carpenter, two apprentices, twenty A.B.'s and two ordinaries, could rightly be described as a motley lot. They included a Dane, a Dutchman, a Scotchman, a Frenchman, an Italian, an Irishman, six Englishmen, four Norwegians, two Swedes, two Finns and two Americans—the Negro Henry and me. Despite the mixture of nationalities, it was already evident they were a good crew with no greenhorns or troublemakers among them. The reason was obvious. The men had been signed on in an orderly manner without force or coercion. Each had received his own advance note and if some of them turned it in on an overdue board bill, at least they received a farewell bottle of whisky as a receipt.

It would be a far different story on the return passage, however, because most of these same men would desert and be replaced by "bums and misfits" slugged, drugged, and forceably recruited by the crimps in Sydney Harbor and the nitrate ports of Chile and Peru. But now, on the outward passage, it was a harmonious crew, working ship with a will and making things easy for the afterguard.

At the same time, the officers, although enforcing strict discipline, seldom had occasion to use the brutal methods practiced on the *Belfast*. There were occasional fist fights and quarrels among thirty-odd human beings who sometimes grew irritable from close association with their fellows during half a year at sea, but they were allowed to fight it out among themselves without interference.

There was little difference in the food. Tacked up in the fo'c'sle was a faded notice from the Board of Trade listing the minimum food allowance, and that minimum was good enough for the shipowners, one and all. The wriggling things in the *Celticburn's* hardtack may have been a trifle more palatable, but the small whack of salt horse, the thin pea soup and the dry, stringy Australian bully beef looked and tasted about the same in all of the deepwater ships.

One sign indicating that the *Celticburn* was a happier ship than the tough *Belfast* was the singing of sea chanteys, which was encouraged by the ship's officers, who knew that a lusty chantey sung while engaged in any task of manpower was as good as a shot of grog. And less expensive!

Broadly speaking, there were three kinds of chanteys: those used around the capstan when weighing anchor; those used for the long haul on braces or halyards; and the short, snappy ones for hand-over-hand work when hoisting the lighter sails.

Although the titles and the tunes were familiar to the old-timers, the lyrics were almost as varied as the men who sang them. The lead-off, or chanteyman, improvised verses about such things as home, ports of call, whisky and, most of all, his sweethearts, who naturally were many and varied because, after all, the erratic nature of his occupation often prevented his return to the same port twice in succession, thus necessitating frequent replacements to fill the gaps in his social life.

On the *Belfast*, because her crew was a miserable, surly lot, few chanteys had been sung, most of the heavy rope pulling having been synchronized with a long-drawn-out "Yo-ho" or equally expressive grunt. From shipmate Gribble, I had memorized the words and tunes of the most popular ones, but in my capacity as a lowly O.S. I had wisely refrained from bursting forth in song lest our worthy second mate think I was getting too much fun out of life and break into my enjoyment with a swift kick in the tempo.

On the *Celticburn* I was now an A.B., entitled to all rights and privileges, and so it happened that one night a few hours out of Cuxhaven, when the port watch was strung out on a halyard ready to haul away, I suddenly broke out with "Whisky is the life of man."

Immediately the watch responded with a chorus, "Whisky-Johnny," and a heavy pull on the rope. Then the next line: "I drink whisky when I can," followed by the chorus, "Whisky—for my Johnny" (and another lusty haul).

Right then and there I became chanteyman on the bark *Celticburn*, and many a time thereafter, often in swirling water, hip deep, I led the port watch in "Blow, boys, blow," "Away—Rio" and "The Banks of the Sacramento" in competition with wind shrieking through the rigging like a thousand complaining demons. Lined up ten deep, grasping a half-frozen rope, bodies swaying in rhythm with the violent jerky movements of the ship, beset by raging wind and crashing seas, men forgot the petty grumbling, the weariness, the misery of wet body and hungry gut as they hauled away with every ounce of energy and sang lustily.

CHANTEYMAN: "Oh, blow the man down, bullies.
Blow the man down."
CHORUS: "Way—ay—blow the man down."
CHANTEYMAN: "Oh, blow the man down in Liverpool town."
CHORUS: "Give me some time to blow the man down."

And reminiscent of the days when the sailormen were willing to face the gales of Cape Horn, beckoned on by the twin sirens, California's gold and Frisco's Barbary Coast, they sang this old chantey at the capstan while heaving anchor.

CHANTEYMAN: "Sing and heave, and heave and sing."
CHORUS: "To me hoodah, to me hoodah!"
CHANTEYMAN: "Heave and make the hand spikes spring."

CHORUS: "To me hoodah, hoodah—heigh!
And it's blow, boys, blow,
For Californi—o.
For there's plenty of gold, so I've been told,
On the banks of the Sacramento."

Another favorite was the nostalgic "Away—Rio."

CHANTEYMAN: "Oh, the anchor is weighed and the sails are set."
CHORUS: "Away—Rio!"
CHANTEYMAN: "The maids that we're leaving we'll never forget."
CHORUS: "We're bound for Rio Grande.
And away—Rio! Away—Rio!
Sing fare-you-well, my bonny young gel,
We're bound for Rio Grande.

Other well-known songs of the sea included "Reuben-Ranzo," "Storm-along," "Good-by," "Fare-ye-well," and "The Yellow Rose of Texas." The colorful verses were limited only by the imagination of the chanteyman himself.

As if to compensate for the dense fogs and head winds that had plagued us night and day during the Channel run, a strong northerly gale swept us on alongslant from the Bay of Biscay, down past the Madeiras and soon we were in the belt of northeast trade winds.

The ocean around us was alive with shoals of bonitos, albacores and skipjacks, all keeping pace with the racing ship. Sometimes a solitary frigate bird would come sweeping along, then suddenly dive at the sea and come up with a fish wriggling in his beak. With a whirring sound like a covey of partridges flushed from a country roadside, flying fish would rise from the blue expanse of ocean, their glistening wings flashing like silver in the bright sunlight. They would glide a full quarter-mile through the air before dropping into the water to wet their wings, only to reappear a moment later in another mass flight. In the distance porpoises (hog fish) played nautical leapfrog; one followed the other with almost mathematical precision, looking much like the undulating coils of a prehistoric sea serpent slithering through tropical seas.

The steady trade winds carried the *Celticburn* gently but speedily along, and we logged nearly two hundred miles every twenty-four hours. The almost motionless helmsman kept the ship on course by lazily giving or taking a spoke of the wheel now and then.

We passed Cape Verde Islands, a dim blur in the distance. A few days later our fine breeze fizzled out completely, leaving the ship rocking gently on the ocean swells a few degrees north of the Line. Far off to the westward, little more than a smudge against the dim line separating sea and sky, could be seen Saint Paul's Rocks, a volcanic formation that juts well out of the Atlantic almost midway between the bulge of Brazil and the west coast of Africa.

Without the benefit of even a vagrant puff of air, we rocked back and forth as gently as a babe in a cradle for three blistering days. The sun, like a bronze ball of fire, beat down upon the ship until heat waves actually seemed to be visible, rising from the deck toward a sky that looked like a purple-colored metal basin turned upside down.

From the royal yard 160 feet above the deck, the placid ocean was an unbroken expanse of rich, deep blue, flat and clear, extending as far as the eye could see, and the ship itself, including its top hamper of yards, masts and rigging, and drooping sails, was reflected upward as if the *Celticburn* were a ship's model set in the center of a gigantic mirror.

While aloft, we spotted dozens of large green turtles asleep on the surface of the smooth water, the reflection of the bright sun on their backs making them shine like green jade. Since sea turtles are both fish and flesh, they furnish not only soup and stews but steaks and cutlets as well; so Mr. Douglass, the mate, ordered the ship's gig lowered overside and had it rowed toward a sleeping turtle as large as a wash tub. We took care to drift silently alongside. Then cautiously reaching over, Mr. Douglass suddenly grabbed a hind flipper and, with an ingenious twist, flopped the turtle completely over. Then while it was floating helplessly on its back, unable to swim away, a line was fastened to a flipper and it was towed to the ship and heaved up on deck. The crew forward received a liberal share, which provided a welcome change from the monotonous diet of salt junk and pea soup. Incidentally, whales were frequently seen spouting in the distance, and several times on the voyage razor backs rose from the depths almost alongside the ship.

Occasionally, after hours of extreme heat, as the ship floated idly on the smooth surface like a duck on a pond, a black cloud would suddenly appear over the horizon, followed by flashes of forked lightning and sharp peals of thunder. Commands would be shouted, followed by a rush to halyards, downhauls and braces. The wind would strike like a flash, the ship would heel over and begin to gather headway. Yards would be squared or backed sharp up, and we would seem to be on our way at last, when, as suddenly as it had begun, the wind would cease, and once again the *Celticburn* would lay like the celebrated "painted ship on a painted ocean."

Early one morning toward the end of July word came from aft that we were straddling the Equatorial Line at about longitude 24 degrees west. It had long been the custom of the sea to initiate those novices who were crossing the Line for the first time, but on my first voyage the *Belfast*'s crew had either overlooked the event or felt it too far beneath their notice to bother, so I had escaped going through the embarrassing ceremony. On the *Celticburn,* however, the crew and even the afterguard were eager for any excuse to break the monotony of heat, rain and dead calms, so elaborate plans had been made in advance to celebrate the invasion of King Neptune's domain.

By a coincidence, all six victims were British. There were the three A.B.'s, including my friend Scotty, all of whom had made the Atlantic crossing many times but had never sailed below the Line. Then there was Slush, the cook, who had served mostly in steamers on the Mediterranean run, and the apprentices, Hughes and Johnny, who were making their first sea voyage.

Word was passed to go easy with the cook, but this was superfluous because we seamen could hardly afford to antagonize the autocrat of the ship's galley. He could accidentally drop a cake of soap in the pea soup, shortchange the already small rations, refuse to allow clothes to be dried in the galley and do endless things to inconvenience all hands.

By acclamation, the chief role was assigned to Henry, the giant Negro, which of itself was unique because none present had ever heard of a coal-black King Neptune. His consort, Queen Amphitrite, had a lily-white complexion beneath her brown whiskers, so for the sake of uniformity that part of her map not covered with hair was plastered with a light coating of lampblack, and all was well.

Royal robes were made of sackcloth, and each wore a wig of long curly hair made from raveled rope yarns tucked under a cardboard crown. As no gilt or gold paint was to be had, the crown was painted a sickly ochre yellow. Neptune wore whiskers of plucked oakum whitened with flour and both he and his queen carried pronged tridents of wood.

After being suitably announced, King Neptune and Queen Amphitrite clambered over the ship's bows, dripping with water and seaweed as though emerging from the deep, and took their places on thrones facing the candidates, each of whom was blindfolded and seated upon an upturned bucket. Directly behind the victims was a large canvas trough filled with sea water, ready to receive its prey. Near by was a slush bucket filled with a smelly mixture of tar, rancid grease and soapsuds, an old paint brush to be used for lathering and a length of steel barrel hoop which would serve as a razor.

When all was in readiness, the blindfold was removed from Scotty, the first candidate. Neptune propounded a few silly questions, then ordered the victim to be initiated in due form. An assistant lathered Scotty's face with the gruesome mixture from the slush bucket, then proceeded to scrape it off with the improvised razor. A hocus-pocus ritual was mumbled, after which he was asked his name and, as he opened his mouth to speak, the greasy tar brush was thrust into the cavity while at the same time he was tipped over backward into the water trough. Each candidate received the same treatment except Slush, the cook, who was dismissed after receiving a once-over shave. As nautical legend has it, "God sends food, but the Devil sends cooks," and the crew were taking no chances with the "Devil's Disciple."

After wallowing across the Equator, we took advantage of every vagrant breeze, inching far enough south to pick up a light wind that swept us into the path of the southeast trades off Brazil's Cape San Roque, and soon we were booming along with every rag of canvas drawing. After more than two weeks of excessive heat, blustery rain squalls and almost constant pulling and hauling of braces, it was a welcome relief to drive ahead on our course, logging a steady ten knots an hour, and never a call to man the braces for days on end.

It is night and the middle watch. You lazily climb aloft, bare toes clinging to the stiff tarred ratlines as you ascend step by step, pausing occasionally to glance at the scene around, above, below you. You rest on the slender royal yard, one hand lightly clutching a swaying rope. The moon is full and directly overhead. The trade wind is strong and as steady as a clock, yet it is warm and soft, and clings to your bare hide like a caress. Every sail is taut and straining gently, each a separate picture framed in magic moonlight.

As the ship's bow dips into the rolling seas ahead, the swirling foam separates into two narrow bands of white that stream along her slim sides, merging into a broad wake of churning silver, silver that sparkles and glistens under the beaming rays of the full moon suspended from the very center of the great dome above.

There is no noise except the rhythmic sound of wind flowing softly through the spidery web of stays, shrouds and gently swaying ropes. Far below on the quarter-deck the officer on duty leans against the weather shrouds. Behind the great wheel the helmsman stands motionless, the light from the binnacle casting a halo around his head.

Far forward, the man on lookout has momentarily ceased his incessant pacing back and forth and now stands gazing into space, his body swaying slightly with the slow motion of the ship. You wonder what are his thoughts. And what of the silent helmsman. And of that officer who has just now resumed his slow pacing up and down, up and down, timing his steps to the rise and fall of the ship as she lifts herself slowly out of the depths, then rides high as the next sea slides under her stern.

Suddenly there is a change in the wind, the watchful officer sings out an order; the helmsman snaps to attention; the spell is broken, and you reluctantly climb down from the heights of Olympus and find yourself a soft coil of rope on which to doze away the remaining hours of your watch on deck.

Under the spell of the tropics, the days and nights passed quickly. Soon the temperate trades were far behind us and heavy weather loomed ahead. Storm sails had replaced the old patched canvas.

We had crossed 54 south, well inside the Falklands, when

144

word passed that we were headed for Lemaire Strait, a twenty-five-mile stretch of water separating Staten Island from Tierra del Fuego. Captain Davis planned to take a chance and drive directly south through the narrow passage in the hope that he might turn and make the necessary westing around the Horn and into the Pacific while wind and weather were favorable.

At daylight we picked up a point of land jutting out from the eastern end of del Fuego, like a giant finger pointing across the strait. As the tip of Staten Island on the opposite shore came clearly into view, the wind veered too far to the west to allow the ship to navigate the narrow passage in safety. Yards were hurriedly squared and the ship headed east. Our course lay parallel to the irregular coast line of the island, which was clearly in sight most of the day, showing a rugged terrain broken by snow-filled crevasses and occasionally dark splotches indicating stunted vegetation. By nightfall we had rounded the east end with plenty of sea room to spare and were headed on a direct slant toward the Horn.

* 19 *

ON SEPTEMBER 3, 1903, we were treated to a sight shared by few seafarers, even among those who have made the rounding many times: the sight of rugged, desolate Cape Horn itself, from a vantage point so close that a moving object ashore could have been seen with the naked eye.

For hours we had been under close sail in thick, misty weather when suddenly the clouds broke, showing patches of blue sky. Just then a voice from aloft shouted, "Land on the starboard bow."

All hands lined the rail or climbed aloft for a better look as the great snow-capped mass of land loomed into full view, a dark, silent sentinel standing guard at the very bottom of a continent.

As interested in the unusual sight as the lowliest member of the crew, the skipper and mate stood by the break of the poop, sextants in hand from sheer habit, but there was no need for an observation at noon on this day with grim old Cape Horn directly abeam, staring them straight in the eye. How well they knew the latitude and the longitude of that squat mass of barren, desolate land standing guard over swirling waters where two oceans meet, and before which countless iron men in wooden ships had passed in review, fighting and winning the battle against odds of wind, wave, sleet and snow, and sometimes losing, too.

It was not often given the crews of ships making the Cape Horn passage to take a bow before Old Cape Stiff in person, while favored by moderate winds and clear skies. Most shipmasters preferred plenty of sea room in those latitudes and generally aimed to make the rounding by passing south of Diego Ramirez, some fifty miles below Cape Horn, instead of risking the passage between the two dangerous land hazards.

Captain Davis, disappointed by failure to complete the short run through Lemaire Strait, now found himself just below the Horn with clear weather and a favorable northwest wind, so he swung the *Celticburn* over on the port tack and headed on a southwest course that in twenty-four hours of good sailing weather would have enabled us to clear Diego Ramirez and head up into the South Pacific with only open water ahead. We were not to be that lucky.

A moderate northwest wind suddenly changed to a withering blast from the west, dead ahead; a heavy mist closed in, blotting out the islands, and the ship heeled over almost on her beam ends. Pitching and tossing on windswept seas, at times balanced precariously on the crest of a foam-topped wave, then

146

sinking into the trough between masses of gray-green water, the ship battled for survival.

Struggling for footing on slimy decks sometimes completely under water, the badly spent crew hauled home the clew lines that slowly drew the giant fore and main courses close to the pitching, jerking yards above. The canvas bellied out before the gale in huge wind-filled pockets as the men climbed the thin ratlines, swung out over the futtock shrouds and inched their way out on ice-coated footropes to grapple with the flapping sails, each an expanse of stiff frozen canvas fifty feet in depth and ninety feet in spread.

Soaked to the skin, hands torn and bleeding, clinging desperately to the rigging, one wonders how sails can be loosed or furled, how men can avoid being blown from yards high above the decks; but someway, somehow, the job is done, done because it *must* be done. For if we fail, the ship will perish and with it the crew.

As the last two men dropped from the forerigging to the heaving deck, watching their chance between boarding seas, a terrific blast tore the furled foreroyal free of its gaskets; the sail opened out like a balloon. The *Celticburn* heeled so far to leeward the tip of her main yard seemed to dip into the seas that raced alongside.

With a grinding crash the fore-t'gallant mast broke just above the yard and down came the wreckage, including the royal yard, the heavy spars bringing up in a tangled mass of lifts, shrouds and stays as they swung in the wind, smashing against the upper tops'l yard with every plunge of the ship. We scrambled up the forerigging again, this time to battle not only the elements but the banging spars and the deadly wire stays and lifts that writhed in the wind, at times wrapping themselves completely around the rigging to which we clung for our lives.

At the risk of being smashed into pulp we cut away most of

the wreckage and even lashed the broken t'gallant mast, but the royal yard swung wildly back and forth like a giant pendulum. As the ship rolled far to leeward, the lifts parted and the heavy spar plunged overside. Day after day the westerly gale blew with such murderous violence that we were unable to carry any sail other than reefed tops'ls and stays'ls, and because the heavy overcast never broke, we were unable to determine the ship's position except by dead reckoning.

Our drift south and east became more noticeable each day because of the increasing bitter cold weather. With our best t'gans'ls, royals and jibs blown to pieces, Sails requisitioned every man who could use a palm and needle and these old-timers worked under cover in the after cabin, while others of us, less fortunate, took the tricks at the wheel and did other jobs on deck.

All large windjammers carried an extra spar lashed on deck for emergencies. Several of us were delegated to assist Chips in trimming it to size. While "hove to," we wrestled with that spar, watching our chance between icy seas that roared over the weather bow until we felt tempted to give up and just allow ourselves to be swept over the rails and out of our misery.

The seas became so heavy and dangerous that we filled canvas bags with storm oil and oakum, pricked small holes in them with sail needles and tossed them overboard. The drift of the ship strung them well out to windward where the seeping oil left a thin scum over the water. This helped greatly in flattening down the tremendous seas while we "fished" the shattered t'gallant mast aloft and jury-rigged it into place along with the new royal yard.

After battling head winds or lying hove to and riding out the storms south of the Horn, it was the end of September that all hands felt like shouting "Glory Hallelujah" when a cloudless day broke and word came forward that we had crossed 50 south on the Pacific side.

The "roaring forties" were still ahead, however, and soon we were running before a screaming southeaster. Suddenly a "long graybeard" broke astern, completely smothered the poop deck, tore Frenchy loose from the wheel and whirled him over the break of the poop and along the length of the main deck until he crashed against the forecastle ladder more dead than alive. As Frenchy lost his hold, the wheel spun around with such force that Sarky, a six-foot Finn, holding tightly to the lee side, was whirled overhead, his feet making a complete arc in the air before he was smashed to the deck on the opposite side.

Third Mate Thomas and Mr. Douglass, huddling against the rigging with a turn of rope about their bodies, cleared themselves in time to grab the wildly spinning wheel and steady the ship, while the Finn's unconscious body brought up against the foot of the mizzenmast in a tangle of ropes.

We hung on with tops'ls, the two courses and storm-stays'ls while the storm raged and blew us farther north toward better weather.

Dozens of great white albatross circled and screeched above us. Only once in a great while did one come to rest on the stormy water; then it would have difficulty in taking off and use tremendous energy paddling the water into foam.

We fastened a hook to the end of a long line and, after baiting it with a chunk of fat pork, attached it to a section of board and lowered it overside. Soon a big white fellow with a five-foot wingspread swooped down and gobbled bait, hook and all. It was hauled aboard and put up a terrific battle. Frenchy wanted to dry the skin of its feet and make them into fancy tobacco pouches, but the skipper ordered it let loose, thereby sparing not only its feet but its neck as well.

Since becoming a chanteyman shortly after leaving Hamburg, I had gradually promoted myself into leadership of the port watch; in fact, I had become what is known among the seagoing fraternity as a sea lawyer, of which there was at least one in the forecastle of every "lime juicer." The sea lawyer was prone to emphasize the misery and all-round sad lot of the lowly foremast hand, as compared to the better food and living quarters of the afterguard. As most deepwater men were foreigners not too sure of their English or even their rights aboard ship, they were content to sit and listen while the self-constituted leader of the watch loudly proclaimed the rights of one and all and swore that justice should be done.

Now that we were back in nice weather with nothing to do but make trouble, I noted that our daily whack of salt pork or beef seemed to be little more than a few handfuls of messy grease held together by a few streaks of lean and that the wriggling things in it only gave up the ghost when dropped into the cook's boiling pot. Also, in warm weather the hardtack began to show signs of animation. If it were left on deck in the sun, it began walking sidewise like a turtle.

One day when our whack seemed to have been scraped from the sides of the barrel, I pointed out the injustice of it all to my watch mates and, taking their grunts for approval, suggested they follow me aft to complain. It took a bit of prodding, but they trailed along behind as I walked aft with dignity, carrying the mess "kid" in the center of which reposed a small chunk of highly scented pork.

I was met at the break of the poop by Captain Davis, who asked what the trouble was. For reply, I handed up the offering with a request that he please smell it. He sniffed carefully, remarked that he had smelled better and worse, then turned on his heel and walked away. As I gulped and fumbled for an adequate reply, my faithful followers turned and marched back to the forecastle. I followed, feeling much like Napoleon on the retreat from Moscow.

Apparently I had lost my first case as a sea lawyer, but I decided to try again. At eight bells next morning I remained in my bunk. The mate came forward to investigate. Between grunts and groans I complained of severe stomach pains, probably brought on by tainted pork. He expressed sympathy and prescribed the usual shipboard remedy for any malady from scurvy to a broken collarbone—castor oil. I must take it or go to work. I took it.

Twenty-four hours later, when I still failed to turn to, Captain Davis came forward, felt my pulse, looked at my tongue, said my symptoms were bad and ordered me aft for special treatment. I was given a bunk in a small room and, after another dose of castor oil, was served a large dish of marmalade, nothing else. At six o'clock more marmalade was served, followed by another helping for breakfast. I waved it away and asked for a cup of coffee. The steward kindly explained that coffee, or in fact any food other than marmalade, was bad for stomach ulcers. I could eat marmalade or else. On the fourth day, still on a diet of marmalade, I received permission to convalesce on the lee side of the quarter-deck. The sun would be good for me.

As eight bells were struck at noon, I sat in the bright sun, my back against the cabin skylight, browsing dreamily through a borrowed book, a gob of partly eaten marmalade exposed temptingly in the tin pannikin beside me. Scotty McLeish paused on his way to relieve the wheel and handed me a note; it suggested that I cease soldiering at once and come forward.

I stepped gingerly over the forecastle threshold to be greeted with a series of swift kicks and right hooks that left me with two beautiful black eyes, a series of red welts gracing my posterior upholstery, and an urge to stand erect while indulging in my next meal of Liverpool pantiles smothered in delightful pork scrapings. I have never cared for marmalade since.

Thinking of food aboard ship reminds me of the toothsome cracker hash, sometimes known as "dandy funk," that some of the crew used to whip up occasionally for a change of diet. Recipe: Sew a piece of canvas into a small sack, put into it several disks of hardtack, then beat the biscuit into flour with a belaying pin. To this add leftover bits of salt beef or pork, season with brown sugar, then add water and stir into a smelly, mushy mess. Pour into an empty bully beef tin and coax Slush, the cook, to bake it in the galley oven. Continue to use this recipe until face, neck and hands break out into boils and the skipper starts treating you for what he fears may be scurvy; then change your diet.

* 20 *

TOWARD MID-OCTOBER we were still booming along but nearing the northern limits of the warm steady trade winds when my watchmate, Tony, had a mishap that caused the skipper to cuss a blue streak and almost cost Tony his life.

I was back at my favorite pastime spending my watch below straddling the jib boom and jiggling a fishing line up and down in front of the onrushing ship's bow, hoping that a bonito or albacore might grab the hook hiding behind the fragment of white linen. My friend Tony, however, preferred more direct action.

Having acquired a harpoon from somewhere on the ship, he lashed a small platform across the martingale chains several feet above the water, and there he balanced himself, hanging on precariously with his left hand while with the right he made cast after cast at the big fish playing about in front of the plunging cutwater.

Whether Tony really expected to spear a fish in this fashion is a question, but spear one he did, a four-foot bonito. Greatly excited by his catch, he hauled the big fish up and at the same time tried to open a gunny sack and bring it up under the struggling fish still fastened to the harpoon. I yelled, "Hold everything," and raced along the footrope to lend a hand, but Tony was too excited to notice my offer. The big bonito was putting up a terrific struggle and it was a case of the fish or Tony.

The fish won. Tony, bonito, gunny sack and harpoon, all dropped into the churning water and slid out of sight toward the ship's stern. I stood up on the end of the jib boom screaming "man overboard" to the helmsman, who left his wheel, grabbed a life buoy and, when Tony's head emerged from the ship's wake, tossed it in Tony's direction.

Within a few minutes the main yards were backed and the ship lay hove to. A strong sea was running and by the time the after lifeboat was clear with six men at the oars, Tony was out of sight.

For an hour all hands were congregated on the poop deck, with eyes glued on the ship's boat in charge of Mr. Thomas which rose and fell far astern, making slow progress in the choppy seas.

If the Old Man noticed the invasion of his sacred quarters, he kept it to himself. We waited, hoping that Tony was still afloat, and no sharks around. The small boat was a mere dot rising on the crest of occasional swells. In due time there was the ship's boat under the stern and in it Tony, looking very sheepish indeed.

After a stiff drink of hot rum and a few hours under warm blankets, Tony recovered sufficiently to listen to a cussing from the skipper that fairly shriveled him. He wondered if the Old Man really wanted him back after having him fished out of the sea.

153

Following his mishap and the caustic tongue lashing, Tony lost interest in harpooning and settled down to the safer pastime of stuffing tiny ships through the necks of small bottles to while away his spare hours.

From his ancient dunnage bag he resurrected several flasks, a slab of soft wood and a small carving knife, together with spools of thread, bottles of glue, beads and sail needles, and then set to work on the models, each of which required days of tedious and exacting work and, incidentally, each of which would eventually change ownership ashore for the price of a few drinks.

First, the small hull was carved, then miniature masts, yards and jib booms. The point of a sail needle was then filed flat and the needle twirled around to drill the small holes in hull and spars. Through these holes were drawn strands of silk for running gear; beads were used for blocks. After the hull, spars and running gear were put together just as the model would look later when upright in the bottle, the silk strands were released, allowing the spars to collapse and lie flat on top of the hull. It was then pushed, stern first, through the neck of the bottle and imbedded in wet putty. The silk forestays were pulled tight through the holes in the jib boom, raising masts and yards until all backstays and braces were taut. Then the silk strands, or forestays, were touched with glue and, when dry, cut off close to the jib-boom end.

The miniature deckhouses, lifeboats and other fixtures were each in turn touched with glue and shoved into place with a long knitting needle. And there he had the model in the bottle.

While Tony worked on his models, other crew members lounged in the warm tropic sun, as memories of frostbite, chilblains and Cape Horn weather gradually faded and the *Celticburn* plowed northward at a steady clip, pushed on by trade winds that finally petered out just below the Line.

To the crew and passengers on a modern steamer, traversing equatorial waters, the doldrums, with its dead calms, light fluctuating winds and torrential rains, is just part of the trip, but to the skippers of the wind ships, each yearning for a record passage, every day or week spent idly rising and falling on the ocean swell was tragedy, time lost never to be regained.

We did not fare too bad, however; it took us only ten days to drift and dribble far enough north to catch the northeast trades. One week later, on November 7, we sighted Cape San Lucas on the tip of the Lower California peninsula.

Our destination was halfway up the gulf, opposite Guaymas, but against head winds it took three weeks of almost constant tacking in ever-narrowing waters to sail a miserable three hundred miles.

On November 28, five and a half months after leaving Hamburg, we dropped anchor in Santa Rosalia harbor. Next morning we were stripping off hatch covers making ready to load coke into lighters which were already attaching themselves to the ship's sides like leeches. Stripped to the waist, we shoveled coke into iron buckets from six in the morning until six at night, and that is how it would be for many weeks.

A score of square-rigged ships of all nationalities swung at anchor in the harbor, most of them loaded, as we were, with coke from Europe or coal from Australia consigned to the copper smelters that were Santa Rosalia's principal reason for existence.

On Sunday we were given shore leave and allowed to draw one peso for spending money. No doubt the Old Man thought one dollar "Mex" was enough to squander on wine, women and song.

The town was a collection of squalid houses scattered out behind a row of cheap saloons, so after the first look around there was little for a hundred foreign seamen to do but congregate in the bars and drink or fight among themselves. One peso was not much for a spree, but the native brew of *pisco* was cheap, though vile, with a taste like gasoline and almost as explosive. A straight drink cost only *cinco centavos* and half a dozen shots were enough to drive a man loco, so by midafternoon most of the sailors were either down and out, dizzy on their feet or sojourning in the town calaboose.

I went ashore several Sundays, used my lone peso with discretion and always reported back to the ship on time, so there was no reason to think that New Year's Day would turn out different from any other day ashore.

It appeared, however, that New Year's was the one day when the smelters closed down and the town took a real holiday. Furthermore, in anticipation of trouble with the mobs of seamen on leave, scores of Santa Rosalia's more rugged citizens were sworn in as special guardians of the peace for that day.

Frenchy, Tony, Sarky and I were ashore early and after a first round of drinks I conceived a brilliant idea. The sea lawyer was at it again! We would pool our pesos and buy *pisco* by the bottle instead of by the drink. Elimination of the middleman, or bartender, would provide double the liquor for our money.

As the day wore on, bottles were passed with increased frequency until all became well oiled, and even the natives took on a rosy hue. At the height of the festivities I happened to pop my dizzy head out of a saloon door just as two policemen arrested a seaman for making friendly passes at one of the town girls.

To one whose ivory dome, flooded with the fumes of Mexican firewater, was now pulsing and throbbing like the pleats of an accordion at an Italian picnic, the arrest of a fellow seafarer became a grave matter that called for prompt and sympathetic action.

I shouted to the noisy mob at the bar that police were giving a shipmate the heave-ho and as the crowd of drunks surged into the street, I started running toward the officers now leading our martyred friend to the hoosegow a block away.

Screeching police whistles sounded from all sides and soon scores of Mexicans began converging on the crowd of running sailors, who suddenly became smart, reversed themselves and made for the saloons again, leaving me racing far out in front and very much alone.

Too dizzy to notice the police closing in around me or that I was the only sailor not going in the opposite direction, I had almost reached my fellow victim when the Commandante of Police, a tiny fellow with a gray goatee, came charging at me on horseback. As he reached for me, I grabbed his leg and almost dragged him from the saddle and then the vanguard of police arrived. Something smashed into my face and then the lights went out!

My next recollection was of being dragged uphill at the end of a rawhide rope, the other end being attached to the Commandante's saddle horn. At the top of the hill the rope was released and I was picked up by police, tossed bodily through the jail door and landed with a crash on a concrete floor. The door clanged shut, and I passed out again.

It was growing dark when I revived to find that I was in a large room with only brick walls and a corrugated tin roof. The windows and doors were of iron bars. Several drunken Mexicans lay around in a stupor and the sailor whose arrest had started my trouble sat on the floor in a far corner.

A crowd of excited natives outside the barred door were pushing each other around trying to look inside. The only loose object in the room was a slop bucket. I picked it up and threw it at the grinning faces, contents and all. Then I picked up the bucket and threw it at the lights high on the walls, smashing each in turn. Just then the police appeared at the barred door with a fire hose. The stream hit with such force that I turned a complete somersault before being smashed against the wall, where I slid to the floor and passed out again.

I woke in pitch-black darkness. Voices argued and cursed in Spanish and occasional fights broke out around me. Once, someone stepped directly on me, but I could only groan and lay there, scared almost speechless and afraid to utter a protest in English. My entire body felt bruised and swollen. Piecing things together, I realized I was in a mighty bad fix. My concern at the moment was that a half-drunken peon might stick a knife in my ribs. When daylight came I was half frozen and still badly scared, especially when bleary-eyed Mexicans began eyeing me curiously, probably wondering how many *centavos* I had in my jeans.

Soon a crowd appeared at the barred door, jabbering in broken English and pointing at my feet. Then I realized they were bidding for my shoes. I hoped that someone from the ship would appear and bail me out of jail, but if not, I was indeed in a mess, so I accepted ten pesos for my only pair of good shoes.

There was more spirited bidding for my fine wool sweater. Pure white, it was a nice job when I came ashore, but striped with bright red gore, it now looked like a barber's pole, so I let it go for six pesos. Several hours later the door clanged and we prisoners were herded into wagons and hauled to court.

According to testimony, I had suddenly run from a saloon with a crowd of sailors chasing after me, but when the police appeared the sailors turned and ran away. When the interpreter asked me if that was so, I solemnly nodded my head. The judge seemed convinced. He pointed to the empty sheath on my belt, and said something.

The interpreter explained that I had been fined twenty pesos for carrying a knife. I shelled out my sixteen pesos and turned my pockets inside out. Then the judge and the interpreter went into a huddle and decided to accept what I had and I was freed.

When I boarded the ship I was ordered to report to the Old Man. Captain Davis seemed startled at my appearance and directed me to a mirror. What I saw was actually gruesome. My face was raw and swollen and streaked with dried gore and grime. It looked like the mask of a hobgoblin on Halloween night. With the remark that any words of his could hardly add to my punishment, the Skipper sent me forward to meditate over my sins.

* 21 *

ONE NIGHT in January, Captain Davis received a courtesy call from a Captain Neilson of the American barkentine *Wrestler*, then discharging lumber about a half mile from our anchorage. While the two jovial skippers were enjoying each other's company, the *Wrestler's* second mate, a Mr. Barry, strolled forward and mingled with the *Celticburn's* crew. Casually inquiring if any Yankees were aboard, he was directed to me and, after a short conversation, made an offer.

He said the *Wrestler* had nearly finished discharging cargo and in another week would sail for Aberdeen, Washington. There had been trouble with the crew; two men had been discharged, and he, Barry, was authorized by Captain Neilson to sign up two other men at the American scale of thirty-five dollars a month.

He frankly admitted that if we should be apprehended in Mexico after jumping ship, we might be placed in irons and returned to England as deserters. However, he had formerly been a member of the Canadian Northwest Mounted Police and felt sure he could smuggle us aboard the *Wrestler* just before sailing.

I was greatly excited. This offered my one and only chance to jump ship and get back to the States, as we already knew the *Celticburn* had received orders to proceed to Sydney in ballast. I accepted the offer, agreed to provide a second man and arranged to meet Mr. Barry ashore on Sunday to complete the details.

Frenchy was my choice and he readily agreed to go with me but insisted on Tony's going too. On Sunday morning we were in the ship's small boat ready to cast off and head for the wharf when I was suddenly ordered back aboard the *Celticburn*.

Fearing that our plans had leaked out, I went aft and faced Captain Davis with shaky knees, only to learn that shore leave had been refused because of my trouble with the police on New Year's Day.

After sulking aboard ship all day, I made one of those sudden decisions that often got me into trouble. I just had to see Barry and the only way was to swim to the *Wrestler* after dark. That night I waited until I was sure everyone had turned in, then sneaked up on the forecastlehead and prepared for the long swim.

Only a few days earlier I had received newspapers in the mail from my old aunt down in Virginia. They carried graphic accounts of Chicago's Iroquois Theater disaster, and I thought they would be appreciated by Mr. Barry and the *Wrestler's* crew.

Slipping off my shirt and trousers, I wrapped them around the papers into a compact bundle, then lashed it on top of my head with my belt, which I drew tight under my chin. Dropping over the ship's bow, I clambered down the chains, eased myself into the water and, with the package nicely balanced on my head, struck out for the *Wrestler's* riding lights barely visible in the gloom.

All went well until I had almost reached the ship and something scraped lightly against my naked body. It was only then that I remembered with a sick feeling in my stomach the many times I had watched sharks lazily circling the *Celticburn* waiting for scraps and refuse tossed overboard by the cook. I became panicky, floundered wildly and in the excitement momentarily slipped below the surface. The package, saturated with water, slipped back over my head and the belt tightened against my windpipe. Using one hand to keep afloat, I worked frantically with the other trying to free myself of the weight dragging me down, then lapsed into unconsciousness. I experienced all of the agony, every symptom and sensation, that is a part of slow strangulation and drowning.

To all intents and purposes I had gone through the motions and was finished; yet it was my fortune to survive, even though I had passed beyond knowing or caring how or why.

Out of what seemed a nightmarish dream, I slowly emerged to find the soggy flesh that was my body being violently manhandled by strong hands, as salt water and bile were forced through my clenched teeth and free air once again entered my lungs. The blur of faces and unfamiliar objects gradually took shape. I realized that through some miracle I was still alive, and then I learned how lucky I really was.

When I went into my tailspin only a short distance from the *Wrestler*, one of the crew had just mounted the forecastlehead for a smoke before turning in. The harbor water was so full of phosphorescence that objects in the water could clearly be seen even in the darkness. My struggles splashed liquid sparks in all directions. Seeing the commotion, the seaman first thought it a battle between sharks and other fish; then recognizing a human figure in the water, he shouted an alarm, plunged in and towed my unconscious body to the ship where others hauled us aboard.

Since I came out of my debacle in one piece it was probably not caused by a shark, but that did not lessen the fright. After hot drinks and warm clothes, I explained to Mr. Barry about

Frenchy and Tony. It was agreed that Frenchy and I would sign articles at regular pay and Tony would be allowed to work his passage.

As the *Wrestler* would discharge its last lumber the next day, Barry would have his boat under the *Celticburn's* bow at midnight to row us to the *Wrestler*, where we would be stowed away until the barkentine was headed well down the gulf.

It sounded fine to me. Barry then rowed me back to my ship with oars muffled and left me climbing up the *Celticburn's* chains for the last time.

Late the next night we sneaked our dunnage bags out of the forecastle and were huddled in the shadows far forward when a moving light appeared on the *Wrestler*. When the small boat had quietly drifted under our bow, I began climbing down the chains and was startled to find Johnny, one of the apprentices, straddling the bobstay just above the water. He had learned that something was up and insisted on going too.

When Barry counted off four of us, including a fifteen-year-old boy, he was furious, but neither threats nor coaxing would move Johnny. If left behind, he would give the alarm. Barry glumly rowed us over to our new ship.

At daylight the sound of the clanking windlass let near-by ships know the *Wrestler* was shortening cable in preparation for getting under way. Captain Neilson, with his binoculars trained on the *Celticburn*, saw a boat put off and head in our direction.

In anticipation of a visit Mr. Barry had already made plans of his own. A trough had been laid between the canvas folds of the large spanker, and in it we four refugees took our place, lying end to end. Folds of canvas were then drawn up around us, leaving breathing spaces not visible from the deck. Except for a slight bulkiness the huge spanker looked no different from other furled sails when Mates Douglass and Thomas came aboard.

Captain Neilson expressed sympathetic surprise at the news that four crew members had taken French leave and offered to let them search his ship for stowaways. After searching the hold, the lazaret, the sail locker, forecastle, and even the muddy chain locker, the nonplused officers took a look in the cabin as a mere matter of form. There was a large bulge under a blanket in Mr. Barry's own berth; Mr. Thomas gave the blanket a jerk and presto!—there lay four dunnage bags in one of which was a striking likeness of Frenchy—tight pants, bow tie, bowler hat and handlebar mustache included. How our Mr. Barry happened to pull such a boner was never explained, but the searchers, with the law on their side, seized the bags, dumped them into their own boat and hurried back to report their find to Captain Davis.

Soon the *Celticburn's* longboat, furiously propelled by six sweating oarsmen, with a boiling-mad skipper sitting stiffly in the stern sheets, headed toward shore and probably the Mexican police headquarters.

A strong offshore breeze was blowing and long before Captain Davis stormed ashore, Captain Neilson had enough canvas on the *Wrestler* to give her a head start down the gulf, while the anchors still swung from the catheads. Many anxious glances were cast astern, but no smoke appeared on the horizon indicating a chase. Probably it was much too early in the morning for the Mexican police to bestir themselves on behalf of the British skipper.

The nearest I ever came to being buried alive was the four hours I spent laced tightly in that canvas shroud. Nervous and restless, unable to move hand or foot or even to breathe freely through the small slit in the sail, I suffered such agony that it would have been a relief to be discovered and taken back to the ship to answer for desertion.

Still shaky from the nerve-racking experience, we then learned that the dunnage bags with our every single possession had been taken away. I had already computed my money loss. Deducting the month's advance note in Liverpool, plus my few shillings drawn in Hamburg and Santa Rosalia, I had forfeited pay for seven months of hard work. My total worldly goods consisted of a pair of dungarees and a singlet. I hoped the new venture would make up for what I had left behind.

As only Frenchy and I were on the ship's articles, we agreed to divide our pay with Tony and Johnny. None of the three had ever been in America, and Johnny, in particular, was wildly excited at the prospect, but I had my regrets when I realized for the first time that Johnny, having been taken from an orphanage, was actually a ward of the British Government and the *Celticburn* captain was under bond for his safe return to England, "barring acts of God."

The *Wrestler*, running before a stiff fair wind, rounded Cape San Lucas on the second night out, and in twenty-four days, all told, made the run of eighteen hundred miles to Grays Harbor, where we received our discharge on February 17, 1904. After dividing less than sixty dollars' pay between the four of us and paying a fee to join the Sailors' Union of the Pacific, there was little left, so I accepted a berth on the three-masted schooner *Fanny Dutard*, bound for San Pedro with lumber.

After being shipmates with Frenchy, Tony and Johnny for nearly a year, and mainly responsible for their leaving the *Celticburn*, I can now dispose of them in a few lines. Frenchy worked for a while as a longshoreman, then built himself a shack on the river in Aberdeen, Washington, and became a salmon fisherman. I met him there several times in later years.

Tony shipped to San Francisco, registered at the Sailors' Union hiring hall and the following morning was found dead in his bed in a sailors' lodginghouse on East Street. According to the coroner's report to the union, Tony apparently blew out the gas before going to bed—whether drunk or sober was not known.

Johnny shipped as a cabin boy on the four-master *R. C. Slade,* bound for San Pedro, promising to meet me there. When I arrived in Pedro, I learned that the *Slade* had beaten us in by two days, so after work I went aboard and learned that Johnny was missing. During a dispute in the cabin, Johnny had bopped the skipper in the eye and then had walked ashore and disappeared. I never heard of him again.

As the *Slade* was to sail for Grays Harbor again, I left my ship and signed on her, reaching Aberdeen about a month later. Shortly afterward, the Union Hall blackboard announced that the four-masted tops'l schooner *Watson A. West,* loading lumber for Cape Town, South Africa, would sign on a crew. Like many an old salt who threatened to "quit the bloody sea and buy a farm," I had sworn never to round the Horn again, but when I learned that Cape Town was only the first leg of a voyage that would completely circle the globe, two of us, George Cainan and I, agreed to sign up and become shipmates for the long voyage.

Working cargo by day and patronizing Aberdeen's dance halls by night, we led a hectic existence, often stumbling aboard ship barely in time to change clothes and start "humping" lumber. Nursing oversized hangovers, we mumbled good resolutions through ten hours of sweat and strain while manhandling heavy timbers, sometimes in pouring rain; but when the six-o'clock whistle blew, the world again took on a rosy hue as we hurried ashore to keep our social engagements with the short-skirted belles of the Casino and the Eagle Dance Hall.

Sunday morning was less exciting, but no doubt more beneficial, as we hied ourselves over to the Finnish colony to steam the week's accumulation of applejack out of our systems. Clothed only in gooseflesh and a smile, we entered a small hut, each carrying a bucket of water and a tin cup. On the outside was a huge fireplace. Burning logs heated the back wall until the opposite side in the hut fairly glowed. Against the red-hot rocks we tossed cupfuls of water which brought forth clouds of vapor, thus providing an excellent steam bath for ten cents. The effect was little different from today's steam baths in swanky clubs, but the machinery was unique, not the least interesting part being a ruddy-faced Finnish lady who popped her head in the door at regular intervals as she replenished our water supply with no sign of embarrassment. It was a nice old Finnish custom.

Soon the ship was loaded and ready to be towed across the Grays Harbor bar at high tide, so the crew went ashore for a farewell night of whoopee before sailing. The local saloonkeepers knew that within a year the ship would be back in the home port with a crew itching to spend their accumulated earnings. Consequently, on the night before departure for a foreign port, it was customary for the saloonkeepers to hand each member of the crew a "farewell" pint on the house.

We staggered aboard ship at daybreak to find that rough water at the bar made it unsafe to attempt the crossing with such a heavily laden ship. That night we surprised our saloonkeeper friend by showing up for more "farewell" bottles. Then to the dismay of our benefactors, we continued to report for our quota of "bottled good will" on five more nights before we finally crossed the bar and headed out to sea.

Besides Captain Ludwig Sorenson, two mates, and the cook, there were only four able seamen in each watch, all living in the forward deckhouse, which, incidentally, was completely walled in and covered by the deckload and accessible only by climbing down to its sliding door over protruding ends of lumber. Unlike the great British square-riggers, life aboard the schooner was very informal. However, working ship from the flat top of the high deckload, without guardrails, when one false step on a dark night could mean a sudden drop and disappearance into the sea, was quite awkward at first, but we soon got our bearings and began to enjoy sailing along on a floating pile of lumber.

After a few days of fair weather we picked up the trade winds and, surprisingly enough, logged eight to ten knots an hour day after day, until we almost reached the Equator before running out of wind, thirty days after leaving Aberdeen.

Since we lacked the strict discipline of a larger ship and enjoyed better food and living quarters, the twelve days of calms, rains and variable winds experienced while edging our way through the quiet doldrums passed much quicker than they did on previous voyages. Then too, in light fluctuating winds, the schooner's fore and aft sails were far easier to handle than the heavy yards and numerous sails of square-rigged ships.

From the poop deck of the *Watson A West,* sharks were more noticeable than usual, perhaps because we were so low in the water, with the main deck actually awash. They nosed lazily around the ship patiently waiting for handouts. The skipper gave us permission to go fishing.

A two-inch rope was run through a block fastened to the spanker gaff. To this was attached a short length of chain, and a large shark hook was baited with a three-pound chunk of salt pork. While all hands stood by, there was a sudden flash of silver as a big fellow turned over, exposing his belly, and then he swallowed bait and hook, churning the water into foam as half a dozen men tagged onto the line and hauled him above the surface. Slacking away just enough to lower half of his fourteen-foot length onto the deckload, George Cainan chopped his great tail nearly off with one blow of an ax. Then we cut loose and allowed him to drop overside. There was a tremendous commotion in the water, but we were never sure whether he was attacked and eaten by his mates or merely trying to locate his missing tail. Later, a seventeen-footer was hauled aboard and allowed to hang until he could be laid out on deck and examined with safety. The post-mortem revealed numerous tin cans, an old shoe, wads of paper, pieces of cloth, and a paint brush. We severed his tail and nailed it to the end of the jib boom.

Of the eight seamen forward, only one besides Cainan and me had been around the Horn before, and as we left the warm weather behind and the wind blew stronger and the seas rolled higher, they asked many questions. Having made the passage in both directions, I could offer one slight ray of consolation: the prevailing winds were westerly, as a rule; therefore, the storms, terrific as they were, would help to blow us around the Horn and toward our eventual destination.

However, I asked myself a question. How would this sluggish, floating pile of lumber keep intact and afloat in those antarctic storms? If a great square-rigger with a tight iron hull like the *Belfast* just managed to keep ahead of those rolling mountains and caverns of stormy waters, how could this big fore-and-aft schooner with a leaky wooden hull, half a million feet of lumber lashed to her decks and the very deck itself practically awash in calm seas be expected to survive? If one of those smashing seas should tear a chunk of lumber from under those chain lashings and the deckload start to disintegrate on one side, what could prevent her from capsizing? Nothing. I gave up worrying about it.

By late August—winter in those latitudes—we were in the "deep forties" battling an endless succession of gales. At times the winds reached such hurricane force that Captain Sorenson, rather than risk being swamped by following seas, reduced sail to a mere triangle of storm canvas, lashed the wheel hard down and, with the ship's head to the wind, lay "hove to." All hands huddled aft watching solid seas break over the weather bow, hurdle the great deckload, race along its flat top and cataract over its side, while we hoped and prayed the chain lashings would hold.

After one siege of two days and nights, we found that the continuous pounding of the ship's bows into the smashing seas had torn the jibs out of their gaskets, leaving us with no head sails still standing except the lone fore-topmast stays'l. After hauling the ship around to run before the wind and the seas that rolled up under her stern, six of us made our way over the slippery fo'c'sle and out on the jib boom. There we managed to hang on for what seemed ages, bending new jibs while the plunging jib boom reared high into the skies one instant and in the next doused us deep beneath icy seas.

As we drove south and slightly east our difficulties multiplied. The added weight of the water-soaked lumber caused the ship to settle until the deck itself was several inches below the water. Soundings in the pump well indicated she was leaking far more than usual, so two men were assigned to work continuously at the pumps, to be relieved every two hours.

When running before the wind under shortened sail, her stern frequently failed to rise in time, and then a great green roller would break over the poop deck, crush the helmsman against the wheel and continue along the length of the deck-load until the wind picked up the spent remainder and whirled it over the bows. At other times, both ship and deck cargo would almost disappear under a deluge, then slowly emerge with solid water streaming over their sides like Niagara. At such times the helmsman was lashed to his wheel-box and the deck officer took refuge with the watch on top of the lumber, ready to leap into the rigging ahead of boarding seas.

With two men at the pumps and one man at the wheel, it was no longer possible to dismiss a watch for the usual four hours below, so all hands were ordered to stand by fully clothed and be ready to turn to at all hours. Sleep must come in catnaps between the hauling of ropes, the handling of canvas, a trick at the wheel or lookout and a spell at the pumps. Despite wind, wave and weather, despite lack of sleep, aching bones and bodies covered with salt-water boils under wet steamy clothing, each of us climbed down into a pit between protruding ends of lumber and took a backbreaking spell at the pumps for one hour out of every four. Water swirled about our feet and tons of it cascaded over our heads through the opening above. There was no complaining. Our lives depended on keeping ahead of the water pouring into the bilges of the ship.

Besides the danger of being water-logged, our greatest fear was that a particularly vicious sea might tear out one side of the deckload, causing the top-heavy ship to capsize. Every hour, night and day, the chain lashings and turnbuckles were carefully inspected and tightened. To us, those chains seemed like a bond that held the ship's body and soul together. We had standing orders to release the remaining chains if a boarding sea should smash away enough of the deckload to cause a severe list. In such a case, however, I doubt if we could have cut loose in time to prevent capsizing.

For days we ran before westerly gales, "cracking on" with enough sail to try to outrun the seas that followed and smashed over the after rails. Without a break in the overcast, we never glimpsed sun, moon or stars long enough to determine the ship's position, so Captain Sorenson set a course by dead reckoning. With all hands nervously on the lookout for Diego Ramirez to the south, we continued to drive east before an icy gale without once sighting land. On September 2, almost exactly a year since we had passed it in the *Celticburn* on the voyage out, we rounded the Horn for my third and last time.

If I seem to have dwelt extra long on those three passages around Old Cape Stiff there is reason enough for it. Before the turn of the century and even for a few years after, thousands of ships and multitudes of men made the same voyage with varying degrees of fortune, depending upon weather and circumstance, so there was nothing particularly novel about it in those days. But with the opening of the Panama Canal and the passage of time, the wind ships disappeared one by one and voyages around the tip of the South American continent became less frequent.

Ocean raiders in World War I sent many a fine ship like the *William P. Frye* to the bottom while their white wings still fluttered in the breeze. Each year since has taken its toll in one way or another until today none is left except a lonesome few that have been converted into floating museums or training ships. Occasionally one of these makes a trip around the Horn for photographic or some other purpose, but it would be far-fetched indeed to compare such voyages with the routine ones made in the old square-riggers.

No chanteys are needed on training ships to synchronize a pull on the braces or to lift a tops'l yard. At a command forty youngsters merely tag onto a halyard and walk the yard into place. Another two score can lay out on a yardarm and smother the great sail with sheer weight. All are well clothed and well fed.

Compare this with the sixteen or eighteen half-starved and ill-clothed nondescripts on a twenty-five-hundred-ton, four-masted square-rigger of forty or fifty years ago. Today the winds and the waters below Cape Horn are no better and no worse than they were in the times mentioned here. There are the same blinding snowstorms, the same hurtling seas, the same dull sunless skies, the hail, the sleet and the floating ice floes. It will always be so.

But the noble ships that sailed and battled their erratic course through those storms are no longer there, and will never be there again. Except for training ships and photographic expeditions, Cape Horn and all that it used to mean to the old-timer is as extinct as the dodo. Not that I or those others who so often swore they would "buy a farm and quit the bloody sea" would ever want to go back. Or would we?

* 22 *

PUSHED ALONG by strong fair winds and rolling seas alike, we rounded into the South Atlantic and cut far enough north to sight the Falkland Islands and check our position. This time I had a fine view of both islands, one much larger than the other but, curiously, both of the same general shape.

En route to Europe, we would have headed north, with each day bringing us nearer to flying-fish weather, but now we would remain in the "roaring forties" and stormy weather for a few weeks longer, while running down five thousand miles of "easting."

By noon of September 29 we had sighted Cape Agulhas on the tip of the South African coast and late that evening dropped anchor in Table Bay. It was a dark moonless night, but ashore the rows of street lights rising tier on tier against the shadowy slope of the great mountain, like flashing jewels against a velvet background, were a welcome sight after three and a half months at sea on a floating lumber pile.

And how we enjoyed that first night's sleep with no interlude of backbreaking labor at the pumps. I scrambled out on deck early next morning to get a first look at the town and the scores of ships with tall masts that dotted the waters of Table Bay.

Beyond the city, towering four thousand feet high and cutting the skyline with a jagged horizontal front two miles in length, was the sheer precipice of Table Mountain, called the most conspicuous landmark in the world. At times filmy clouds seemed just barely to cover its long flat top like a lacy white tablecloth.

Later in the day we were jostled into our dock by a fussy

little tug and soon were swinging slingloads of lumber to the pier, where native longshoremen loaded it onto flatcars. They were coal black and all wore nondescript, castoff clothing. Some were bare to the waist, wearing only trousers. Others wore a pair of sloppy shoes, a straw hat and a loin cloth—nothing else.

Cape Town was a study in contrasts. Although modern in many respects, with its Tivoli Theater, its Grand Hotel and its electrically driven trams, it was not unusual to see teams of sixteen bullocks plodding down Adderly Street, drawing creaky "wagons" nearly twenty feet long, their wheels and sides still caked with mud from the far-off veldt.

As the oxen lumbered along the cobbled street, the drivers, mostly bearded Boers, stood upright, cracking their long whips around the ears of the patient beasts, while on either side walked native Kaffirs, or "boys," prodding here and there, intent on keeping the leaders' mind on their work.

These lumbering vehicles, the front half piled high with produce, the rear portion a tent supplying living quarters for the whole family, were the principal means of transportation from inaccessible parts of the interior as far away as the banks of the Zambezi. Their destination was the Saturday Market, a public square devoted to free trade. Here they sold or auctioned off their loads of skins or agricultural products, and with the proceeds they bartered for scarce goods needed on lonesome farms many miles from civilization.

The market lot was rimmed with tents from which ebony-hued Kaffir and Zulu medicine men dispensed black magic and voodooism. In open kraals, fuzzy-headed Bushmen from the back country offered their wares, mostly Basuto shields, Matabele assagais, Mashona headdresses of leopard skin and Zulu snuff spoons made of bone. Piles of half-cured lion, tiger, leopard, hyena and silver jackal skins, spread out under the African sun, gave out an aroma distinctively their own.

There were piles of ostrich and emu eggs, and cages of slithering reptiles, chattering monkeys and gorgeously plumed birds. There were displays of "everlasting" silver leaves, plentiful in South Africa but said to grow in no other place in all the world. As soft as velvet, they last a lifetime and never fade or crumble. With an eye to the future, however, my personal preference ran to gorgeous ostrich feathers.

With rare foresight I laid in a stock of sixteen-inch plumes, packed them in sealed mailing tubes and, after returning to the States, found them useful in furthering diplomatic relations with the charming dance-hall hostesses of Aberdeen and San Francisco's Barbary Coast.

On the first week end after docking, instead of doing the pubs, I lowered myself in the esteem of my shipmates by going upcountry on a sight-seeing trip to visit Groote Schuur, at Rondebosch, home of the late Cecil Rhodes. After three and a half months at sea, I was anxious to see shade trees and green lawn again. Especially interesting was Rhodes's home itself, which had been converted into a national museum to house his famous collection of South African exhibits.

The next week end, however, was less quiet and peaceful. On Saturday night I, George Cainan, Mike Dugan and a shipmate, known only as Black Jack, made the rounds and sometime after midnight found ourselves in a crowded water-front pub. Dropping a tickey (threepence) in an electric piano, I proceeded to render "The Holy City" for the edification of what I mistook to be an admiring audience. The last loud "Hosannah" was still reverberating through the rafters when suddenly I realized that the place was in an uproar with fists, bottles and furniture flying in all directions.

In no time it was every man for himself, as tipsy sailors fell to the floor or dived beneath tables to escape the barrage. I received a sharp clip behind the ear that spun me around like a whirling dervish, and then recovered my balance just as a bottle crashed against the skull of Black Jack, dropping him to the floor where he lay motionless, his head a mass of gore.

Cainan and I each took an arm and dragged him outside as whistles sounded and police rushed the place. The two of us hoisted Black Jack to our shoulders and hustled for the *Watson West* nearly two miles away. Dugan overtook us and with his help we delivered Black Jack aboard the ship, where he regained consciousness, and then roared like a lion while the mate drew his lacerated scalp together with a dozen stitches.

Other crew members who had reported aboard just before us were equally indignant on learning that a shipmate had been mauled by "lime juicers." Soon a quart bottle appeared, and after that was properly attended to, it was unanimously decided to invade two British ships tied up to the quay just ahead. Eight of us, including the cook for good measure, boarded the nearest ship, entered the dimly lit forecastle, dragged several sleeping seamen on deck and tossed them into Table Bay.

On the next ship we walked smack into the bedraggled victims previously tossed overboard, reinforced by shipmates. In the scuffle that followed, Cainan and I, Dugan and the cook, all found ourselves in the bay, swimming for our own lives. We made the *Watson West*, clambered up the fore chains and were shedding our wet clothes when police arrived and carted us off to jail. Captain Sorenson let us sweat it out over the week end; then on Monday morning he paid a fine of two pounds each, charging it against our wages.

On October 21, 1904, the ship sailed in ballast for Newcastle, Australia. South Africa was suffering a severe depression as an aftermath of the Boer War. Thousands were out of work, including members of Pawnee Bill's Wild West Show that had recently gone broke and disbanded. Jobless men from the Yankee show were taking every possible chance to get out of Africa, so before departure, vessels anchored in Table Bay long enough to search for stowaways.

Captain Sorenson was particularly careful because a stowaway landing in Australia would subject the ship to a fine. Two woebegone-looking specimens were flushed out of the forepeak and rowed ashore. As the ship's gig was lifted aboard, we could still observe the two drooping figures on the quay as the *Watson West* headed for Cape Agulhas and the open sea. Five days later a sick-looking individual left his hiding place and listened to a tongue lashing from a very mad skipper, who threatened to put him ashore at Port Elizabeth. The Old Man finally agreed to let him work passage to America on his promise not to set foot ashore in Australia. He kept that pledge. A faded entry in my little notebook gives his name and very unusual address as John Kloot, Binnehaven, Handelsterren, Keet, D.D. Rotterdam.

Cape Town and Newcastle being in almost identical latitudes, our course was now due east, with nothing between but seven thousand miles of lonesome blue water. For fourteen days and nights we never once saw sun, moon or stars. Then, as if to compensate for the monotony of steady winds and leaden overcast, the clouds broke away one night, just as we sailed into a veritable sea of fire.

The phenomenon of phosphorescence is common enough in tropical seas, but on that night it appeared more brilliant and in greater quantities than I had ever seen it before. From horizon to horizon the ocean seemed to glow with a weird bluish light as though covered with a film of burning alcohol. As the foamy crests of the waves broke, they shattered into tiny sparks that shone like thousands of lightning bugs.

Captain Sorenson, who had suddenly popped his head above the companionway, explained phosphorescence as a jellylike form of marine animal life, almost invisible to the naked eye. We were still in the midst of it when the watch went below at eight bells, but when we reported on deck again, it was all behind us. There was more of it from time to time, but never again did it appear so fantastic.

Several days later a small-sized typhoon caught up with us, whipping the sea into a smother of foam and driving the ship before the blast at a terrific rate, though we had hurriedly stripped her down almost to bare poles. With a sound like a million banshees wailing at the wake of the All-Highest, the wind shrieked and moaned through the straining rigging while the seas grew higher and rolled up behind us so fast that the fleeing ship seemed fairly to leap from the crest of one sea to another, entirely missing the hollows between. Since the ship was light in ballast and riding high in the water, the skipper chose to run before the gale rather than attempt to heave to.

Suddenly the gale dropped to a light breeze, and before we could run up enough canvas to steady her, the ship fell off into the trough of the heavy seas and began to roll and wallow until the tips of her masts described an arc of fully forty-five degrees. And then it happened.

There was a lurch to port that almost rolled her over. The main sheet parted, freeing the great boom, which swung far to leeward and, with a sickening crash, broke squarely in two. After getting the ship under control, we managed to splice the boom by binding scantlings completely around it with heavy wire lashings. It looked like a gigantic leg put up in splints, but at least it would serve until we could reach port.

Two days later, when we sighted the volcanic peak of New Amsterdam Island jutting half a mile above the shimmering sea, there was considerable excitement as we half expected Captain Sorenson would put in for repairs, but the Old Man had other ideas and sailed right on without changing course. With a fair wind we sailed more than four thousand miles of easting in two weeks under a heavy leaden pall that seldom broke long enough to show even a glimpse of the sky.

Logging as high as three hundred miles in twenty-four hours, and sailing a course almost entirely by dead reckoning, we picked up Cape Leeuwin off the western tip of Australia, and a few nights later passed through Bass Strait. We skirted the end of a narrow finger of land so close that my imagination pictured a glow in the skies to the north as a reflection of the lights of Melbourne, less than a hundred miles distant. Passing Sydney Head the next afternoon, Captain Sorenson accepted a tow up the Hunter River to Newcastle, where we tied up at the coal bunkers on December 5, only six weeks out of Cape Town. Within a few hours, coal, consigned to Mahukona in the Hawaiian Islands, was streaming into the ship's hold. We, the crew, had the privilege of participating in this function by shoveling coal from seven in the morning until six at night.

On the first Saturday night George, Mike and I hurriedly washed the accumulated coal dust from behind our ears, shook out our shore clothes, drew twenty shillings each and took a train for Sydney, sixty miles away.

In a small lane behind George Street we found a joint called the Hole in the Wall. It must have been a one-way hole because we never emerged until early morning, in the meanwhile loading up with a brew called "She-oak." This drink, mild enough in its early stages, possessed some of the qualities of a delayed-action bomb.

Its aftereffects first became evident when, on returning to our ship at Newcastle, Mike, unable to distinguish between a gangplank and a vacuum, stepped blithely into the space between the ship and the dock and landed in a cargo net. In an attempt at rescue George lost his balance and fell head first on top of Mike; whereupon the two of them just gave up and went to sleep.

In complete forgetfulness of George and Mike sleeping comfortably in their net like oversized spiders in a web, I owlishly surveyed several sawhorses on deck which supported a large timber. Carpenters had been shaping it into a new main boom. Call it playfulness or just plain cussedness, I removed the chocks that held the massive log in place and watched bug-eyed as it rolled to the deck with a crash that shivered every timber in the vessel's hulk. The noise rumbled throughout the ship like rolling thunder. Every soul aboard rushed on deck in a state of undress, fearing an earthquake or a collision. In the van was the skipper, his long shirttails flaring in the morning breeze. Mike and George slept through the excitement, but before being locked up in the after cabin for safe keeping, I mentioned their plight to the Old Man, who broke up their slumber with a rescue squad.

There were other trips to Sydney when we enjoyed the hospitality of The Blue Anchor, the Bells of Shandon and the Marble Bar. In Newcastle we frequented Mother Hall's and the Black Diamond Tavern. One unforgettable character was Nellie Norman, a middle-aged barmaid at O'Connell's Hotel on Bolton Street. Nellie was part owner of the place and fairy godmother to men who sailed the sea. She fed and housed them when broke, and got them out of jail when in trouble.

Her greatest charm was a nautical vocabulary of such technical accuracy that we wondered if she had not at some time worn trousers and served a hitch before the mast. While nonchalantly scraping an overflow of suds into the scuppers, she would break out with a line of salty cuss words that would have shamed old Long John Silver. As she took special interest in me because of my apparent youth, I wrote her later from America and received a warmly worded reply. Mention of her name to shipmates in the years that followed revealed that Nellie of Newcastle was known and respected wherever seamen met to exchange yarns.

* 23 *

ON DECEMBER 22 we sailed for Mahukona, loaded so deeply with coal that the decks were almost awash, but this time our course lay through tropical seas with only moderate winds and warm weather ahead. In three weeks we passed Suva of the Fiji Island group, and three days later we crossed the international date line and gained a day. Day after day we basked half naked in the warm sun, while the skipper craned his neck seeking stray puffs of wind. Then one night the last bright star of the Southern Cross failed to appear above the horizon and we knew we were far enough north of the line to expect a little wind soon. It came on schedule and on March 9 we dropped our mudhook in Mahukona Bay, seventy-seven days out of Newcastle.

Soon we were back at the old job, shoveling coal from daylight to dark. In the ship's hold we loaded huge buckets, which were swung overside and dumped into lighters, reminiscent of Santa Rosalia.

Mahukona harbor was a natural aquarium. There seemed no limit to the number of strange-looking specimens always on parade just below the ship's rail. Flotillas of nautiluses (Portuguese men-of-war), spreading delicate, shell-like sails, glided along before the light breeze like a squadron of small ships. There were unwelcome specimens too—sharks lazily nosing their way below the staging caused a panicky withdrawal of dangling bare feet.

Mahukona was only a small village, so our shore visits were few and brief. On my first trip to town I purchased a bunch of bananas for twenty-five cents and began nursing an idea. When the coal was nearly discharged, George and I asked permission of Captain Sorenson to hang one hundred bunches of green bananas from the deck beams in the ship's hold. It had been estimated that the run to Grays Harbor would take about three weeks, just about time enough for the bananas to ripen for sale to the Aberdeen merchants at a price of one dollar a bunch.

The captain gave his consent, the load of bananas was delivered and George and I found ourselves in the banana business. Shortly after leaving port, the wind dropped to a mere whisper. For a week the booms rolled and jerked back and forth, the sails hung straight down and the hot sun beat down on the deck just above our fast-ripening fruit. Soon our bananas took on a nasty yellow tinge and we began to consume a few advanced numbers.

By the end of the third week we had served fried bananas, baked bananas and banana fritters, and Grays Harbor was still far away. The Old Man was sympathetic and allowed a day or two more to pass before making a reconnaissance tour below decks, where he found overripe fruit dropping like manna from heaven. He decreed that the entire mess must be scuttled forthwith. The blended aroma of bilge water and banana oil was a shade too much. On April 26 we crossed Grays Harbor bar and competed the globe-girdling voyage of twenty-five thousand miles in less than a year.

After deduction of money advanced, I was paid off with $272, more money than I had ever before possessed. Aberdeen was a hectic place, catering to sailors, longshoremen, loggers and mill hands. Saloons stood shoulder to shoulder, making it mighty convenient to stagger from one to the other. The bright-light district beyond the railroad tracks was a miniature Barbary Coast of dance halls, expensive parlor houses, cheap "cribs" and even a "bull pen" where eager ladies sat in windows and beckoned.

My favorite hangout was the Eagle Dance Hall, which featured good music and hostesses who, if not good, were at least good-looking. After each short dance you led your partner to the bar and ordered two bourbons. The lady swallowed her shot of straight liquor with a grimace, even though you both knew it was only cold tea. As a bonus, however, the bartender tossed her a brass check worth ten cents, which added up to a respectable total by closing time, especially on Saturday nights when the loggers and lumberjacks came to town and danced the schottische and two-step without even changing their hobnailed boots.

After being paid off, my first stop was Sailors' Union Hall to pay up back dues and sign the hiring-hall register, which put me in line for a future berth. Holding out $22 for current expenses, I placed the balance of my pay, $250, in an envelope, sealed it, signed my name across the flap and watched Billy Gohl, the union agent, place it in the safe. With funds in pocket, money in the safe and ideas in my head, I set out to see the town, which meant the Eagle Dance Hall. In those days the bartender placed a bottle in front of you and you helped yourself. At first I poured short ones. As the evening lengthened, so did the drinks.

About noon the next day I awoke in the back room of the Tom and Sam saloon. A doctor was working me over and the boys stood around conversing in low tones as if at Finnegan's Wake. It seems that I had been found standing upright, fast asleep, leaning against the railroad trestle opposite the Eagle Dance Hall. Rain was falling heavily, and I was soaked through, but the bourbon was stronger than the elements and I survived.

When my throbbing temples had been brought under control, I presented myself to Agent Billy Gohl at Union Hall and asked to draw some money. He riffled through several envelopes and said none bore my name. When I insisted, he said I had returned and claimed the money the night before. I complained to the police, who refused to take any action. As a half-year's wages was at stake. I shipped to San Francisco on the schooner *Alumna* and appealed to Andrew Furuseth, secretary of the Sailors' Union of the Pacific.

A fair and honorable man, Furuseth was friendly and sympathetic, but his attitude was that the union agent's word was as good as mine in a court of law, and no action would be taken without more evidence.

It seemed hopeless but I decided to take one more crack at Agent Gohl. I shipped north in the bark *Vidette,* an ancient old tub that had seen better days. The passage took a full month and we almost did not get there at all. Besides eight A.B.'s, two mates and a cook, the captain's wife and two young kids were aboard. Perhaps the family was planning on a nice summer vacation.

Anyhow, after battling adverse winds for three weeks, the *Vidette* ran into a nasty storm and was driven north of Cape Flattery, where we lost the fores'l, tops'ls and t'gans'ls and barely escaped piling up on the rocks. Our gallant old bark rolled and rocked so badly that we thought surely she would capsize or lose her sticks; and if she had, no one would have cared because the captain, his wife and kids, the mates and nearly every man forward became deathly seasick.

When we stepped ashore at Aberdeen on June 16, we almost kissed the ground. Years later, in San Francisco Bay, I saw a familiar-looking old hulk with stumped masts. The name on her stern was *Vidette.* The ancient old craft had become a coal barge thirty years too late.

Back in Aberdeen, I called once more on Mr. Gohl. There were accusations, denials and threats. Several hangers-on took up his side of the argument, and soon I felt myself being propelled down the long, steep flight of stairs that led to the plank sidewalk below. Other attempts to collect proved equally futile.*

With my savings gone, I went to work on the dock as a longshoreman, loading lumber on the four-masted schooner *Alert*. Things went well until one morning after a hard night I reported for work in a slightly befogged condition and began stowing lumber in the hold of the *Alert* without the formality of shedding my "going ashore" clothes except to hang my coat and vest on the protruding end of a two-by-four.

Ten hours and several headaches later, I realized that coat and vest had been nicely stowed away in the hold behind several tiers of lumber. In the vest pocket was my only trinket of value, a very good watch. By the time the ship was loaded, I had solved my problem.

The *Alert* was bound for Guaymas, opposite Santa Rosalia. Identification as a deserter from the *Celticburn* could mean a free trip back to England. Still, I wanted to retrieve my coat and watch, so I signed on for the trip.

In Guaymas on Sunday one went to the Plaza de Toros. One could sit in the *sombra* (shade) for ten pesos or in the *sol* (sun) for two pesos. Sun or shade, inside the jammed arena it is red hot and the crowd swelters, but the heat goes unnoticed be-

---

* In the summer of 1910, E. S. Erickson, San Francisco agent for the Sailors' Union, informed me that Billy Gohl had been arrested, tried and convicted in Aberdeen for the murder of a seaman. Recently, when these pages were begun, I requested a check of the Chehalis County Court records for accuracy. The old files revealed that Billy was sentenced to life imprisonment at Walla Walla penitentiary on May 24, 1910, for the murder of one Charles Hadberg, whose body was found floating in near-by Indian Creek on December 23, 1909.

Evidence introduced at the trial indicated that he was also responsible for the death of many others, mostly seamen, whose erratic mode of living made it easy to explain their disappearance. A later check-up at Walla Walla revealed that he went berserk as a result of the stabbing and death of a cell mate and died in the State Institution for the Insane at Medical Lake, Washington.

cause the crowd is waiting for blood. Perhaps a couple of horses will be turned inside out, or even the matador.

A bugle sounds, gates open and here comes the parade: *chulos* (picadors on horseback); banderilleros with their colorful barbs; the matador himself, strutting in all his magnificence; even the team of flea-bitten nags whose part in the pageant will be that of removing the unfortunate bull's carcass from the arena.

The ring is cleared. Again the gate opens, this time for business. A slightly puzzled bull paws the ground. *Chulos* taunt him by waving their capes, then dodge nimbly behind the barriers. The matador appears. The bull leaves his other tormentors to rush at him. The magnificent figure moves only slightly, extending his heavy cape toward the furious animal who thunders past. Back he comes as the great man flicks his cape, executes a couple of graceful twists, turns his back and deliberately walks away while the bull rushes headlong across the arena frothing at the mouth.

Two picadors enter on padded, blindfolded horses. They carry long lances and as the bull rushes forward, a picador jabs his lance into the flesh below the backbone, holding him at bay, and the frenzied crowd screams.

The horses, though unable to see, know something is going on. They shiver and tremble. And well they might. An instant later the bull disengages himself, makes a wild rush toward a horse and literally disembowels him. Now the crowd, already in a frenzy, almost has its money's worth, but it still hopes for the worst.

Exit picadors, and bring on a banderillero, holding a dart in each hand high above his head. The bull charges. The banderillero skips aside, leans over and jabs both barbs into the animal's shoulders.

The bull is now a slobbering, crazy beast, and the shouting mob is ready for the kill. Out steps the matador again, this time with only a small red cape and a long slender sword that will mean sudden death (if the matador is lucky). The maddened bull stamps with rage, sees a flash of red cape and rushes straight at his tormentor. For a fraction of a second the man appears doomed. His arm goes up; a sword flashes above the animal's horns and its point punctures a vital spot. The bull drops, just a quivering thing.

The crowd goes loco. Hats sail into the ring, the band blares out, the matador makes an obeisance before his adoring public, or his favorite lady love, and proudly struts from the arena.

It was a great day today, but not always so. Sometimes that last quick sword thrust fails to reach a vital spot. Then the crippled bull hobbles around the arena while the bloodthirsty crowd registers slight disapproval by throwing cushions and beer bottles at the unhappy toreador.

After one such performance you are ready to turn Guaymas back to the *chulos,* the *espadas* and, yes, to the butchers, for tomorrow the markets will bulge with freshly stocked beef, and sometimes horsemeat as well.

* 24 *

IN A FEW DAYS the cargo was discharged, I had retrieved a mildewed coat and a badly rusted watch from the ship's hold and the *Alert* was scooting down the gulf on a fast passage that carried us around Cape San Lucas in two days and back to Grays Harbor by mid-September.

As we warped the *Alert* into her berth at Hoquiam, I heard a shout from a big four-master just astern of us, and there was George Cainan, my erstwhile partner in the banana business. As his ship, the *Dauntless,* loaded and ready for sea, was short one hand, I signed on her next morning; so George and I became shipmates once again, this time bound for San Pedro.

American in the Rough

Early in November we were back in Aberdeen, where George and I, with two shipmates, Oscar Swendsen and Teddy Turner, planned to "shack" for a few weeks. "Shacking" was a practice followed by groups of sailors to kill time ashore and thus avoid some of the winter gales in northern waters.

Each of us deposited twenty-five dollars in the kitty, with Teddy as banker. A month's rent was paid for a decrepit old shack on the river bank, and the balance was deposited as credit with the butcher and grocer to be drawn upon as needed.

Thus, having collectively assured ourselves of food and lodging, we could squander our surplus funds on winebibbing, taxi dancing, and "alley-catting," each according to his likes, with no fear of having to sign on the first outward-bounder.

We took turns at cooking and light housekeeping, and for a while "the goose hung high." Then, as our credit with the butcher and grocer slowly evaporated, choice cuts of meat and crisp, fresh vegetables gave way to shank bones and withered leftovers, until finally there was only the old stand-by, mulligan stew, as the standard dish.

By the third week the thinning contents of the community stewpan had deteriorated to one part solids and nine parts river water, as Oscar, the cook, sampling the evening meal for taste, licked his chops and murmured, "I'll stir in lots of pepper and salt to make it stro-o-ng." It was then that Teddy and I sounded the tocsin and came to the rescue.

The town's only theatrical offering was provided by a small theater where movies were supplemented by song slides and a single vaudeville act. After trying unsuccessfully to dislodge the local singer, I worked up a blackface skit with Teddy, and, after numerous rehearsals, our act was hired on a trial basis at three dollars a night.

Just in case one wonders why the act was accepted at all, I blush to reveal a hidden clause in the deal which provided that Teddy and I must plaster the Sailors' Union premises and environs with handbills announcing the show to our seafaring friends.

We made good by delivering a fair sprinkling of water-front characters at each performance, where the claquers applauded noisily during the act, and then abruptly left to seek more refined entertainment in the "parlor houses" across the tracks. However, the end justified the means, as the weeks' earnings restored our credit with the tradesmen and once again the mulligan pot boiled merrily.

In December of 1905 Congress enacted a law which provided that officers on all American seagoing ships must be citizens. As Americans then sailing the high seas were almost nonexistent, I suddenly found myself on the receiving line, with offers of a second mate's berth, plus a bonus for signing on.

Thus, in less than four years, after being unceremoniously dumped aboard the *Belfast* in San Francisco Bay, I tossed my dunnage bag into the second mate's cabin on a big four-master, the *Forester*, already loaded and ready for sea.

Next morning we were towed across the bar in a high wind and heavy sea. I was "standing by" on the forecastlehead, when suddenly, with a jar that shook the vessel from stern to stern, the *Forester* hit the bar.

A tremendous sea rolled over the bow, sweeping me along with it, until I brought up against the overhanging deckload with a force that nearly tore me apart. As the water drained off, I lay helpless, almost impaled on the protruding ends of lumber, until two seamen scrambled inboard from the pitching jib boom and hauled me aft for first aid.

The tug drew alongside and I was placed aboard. Then the *Forester* hoisted sail and headed south, leaving me to be taken to the Hoquiam Hospital for needed repairs. My first berth as a ship's officer had lasted just twenty-four hours.

I celebrated New Year's Day, 1906, trussed up in a hospital bed. Though badly bruised, no bones were broken, and in another week I was en route to San Francisco as second mate of the *A. B. Johnson,* a four-master owned by the firm of Hind, Rolph and Company.

More than a decade later, on June 8, 1917, during World War I, the *A. B. Johnson* was to be sent to the bottom of the South Pacific in Lat. 3 degrees N., Long. 150 degrees W., by the German raider *Seeadler,* commanded by Count Felix von Luckner. Just two days later, only a few miles from where the *Johnson* went down, Von Luckner also encountered my old ship, the *R. C. Slade,* sending her to the bottom as well.

Another ten years passed, and on July 7, 1927, the German good-will ship *Vaterland,* built with pennies contributed by German school children, sailed into San Francisco Bay, commanded by that same Count Felix von Luckner. That evening the Royal Order of Jesters, of which I was the directing head, were guests aboard the *Vaterland.* In the master's cabin I sat with Von Luckner and Sunny Jim Rolph, then mayor of San Francisco, later governor of California. Von Luckner had just performed his favorite stunt of tearing a telephone directory in half with bare hands, when I took a post-card picture of the *A. B. Johnson* from my pocket and asked him if he had ever seen the ship before. Greatly agitated, he stared at the picture and excitedly exclaimed, "I sunk 'dot' ship!"

Jim Rolph took the picture from Von Luckner, looked at it and quietly added, "Yes, and I owned that ship."

My next meeting with the Count would be many years later. It was at the Dutch Treat Club in New York early in December of 1951. Bob Considine was my host.

As I passed the speakers' table my eyes popped wide when I beheld Count Felix von Luckner, now seventy-nine, and back in this country from his native Germany after nearly twenty-five years.

At our table Considine handed a hurriedly written note to Ed Murrow, and Ed passed it up to Toastmaster Lowell Thomas.

Thomas turned to the guest speaker and said, "I want the Count to hear this—just below is an old friend of yours who served on a couple of ships sunk by you when you were raiding in the Pacific."

The Count jumped from the platform and embraced me fervently while tears streamed from his eyes.

Several weeks later I received a letter from him which concluded by asking if his old friend Captain Haldor Smith of the *R. C. Slade* was still alive. It was signed "Felix, Sea Devil and Pirate."

The same evening at a Shrine Meeting a fellow member said, "Mr. Coffman, I'm Gustav Fath. I read the Considine story. Is Captain Haldor Smith still alive? I sailed with him on the *R. C. Slade*."

"Well, Gus," said I, hauling out Von Luckner's letter, "two inquiries about the same fellow on the same day deserve an answer, so I'll get busy."

Inquiry developed that the firms owning the *Slade* and the *Johnson* had folded years ago. However, from the Masters, Mates and Pilots Association I learned that the skipper was still going strong, though past eighty.

At his home I said, "Captain, I have a message for you from your old friend Count Felix von Luckner."

"What, that old fraud!" he exploded. "He sunk my ship, then invited me to sit with him at Town Hall while he bragged about it! Did you say you sailed out of Aberdeen?"

"For many years," I replied.

"Then you must have known Billy Gohl, the Sailors' Union agent," he said.

"I certainly did," said I. "Billy Gohl robbed me of a year's wages from the *Watson A. West* back in 1905."

"Well," said Captain Smith, "I helped convict him of murder!"

"More power to you," I said; "tell me about it."

"It was this way," said the skipper. "I left Aberdeen with a load of lumber and had hardly dropped anchor in Santa Rosalia Bay when a telegram came from the chief of police of Aberdeen asking me to hold John Klingenberg, my donkeyman [winch driver], as an accessory to murder.

"Maybe John smelled a rat. Anyway, he asked to be paid off right away. I couldn't discharge cargo without a donkeyman, so I refused, but I offered to pay him off when the last stick of lumber went over the side. He agreed.

"When the last slingload dropped on the lighter alongside, he packed his dunnage bag and came aft for his money. I had it counted out and ready.

" 'Well, John,' said I, 'I hate to lose a good donkeyman, but a deal's a deal, so let's have a little farewell drink on it.'

"John downed a stiff shot of rum and soon keeled over, dead to the world. He never knew what hit him. I had added a few drops of chloral just for good measure. When he woke up we were well down the gulf and headed for Aberdeen.

"When John got around to asking what happened, I told him he'd better get his heart examined if he couldn't stand a jolt of liquor. When we crossed Grays Harbor bar a couple of weeks later the Aberdeen police were there with the welcome sign.

"At the trial John turned state's evidence and got off with a light sentence, while Billy Gohl took the whole rap for murder, and got life at Walla Walla." [Incidentally, Billy Gohl's wife, Ada, a former dance-hall girl, was the sister of Jessie and Frank James, the old-time bandits.]

"With more than twenty murders charged against him he was lucky at that," said I, "and but for the grace of God I might have been one of the twenty. Now, what about Von Luckner and the sinking of the *Slade?*"

"Okay," said the skipper. "War or no war, Von Luckner was a pirate, though pleasant enough when things were going his way. Go through what I went through; see your ship fired on and sunk; watch scores of armed men swarm over a little French sloop and take possession; be marooned on a little coral atoll only five feet above the sea, with all of the boats purposely stove in; go through all that and tell me if he was anything less than a pirate!

"Well, we cleared from Sydney on April 26 with copra for San Francisco. Then on June 17 the lookout reported a full-rigged ship astern. I went aloft and took a look. She was hull down, but coming up fast, too fast for sail only. Soon she was hull up on the horizon. Then came a flash of gunfire and a shell dropped two miles astern. The officer on watch came up.

" 'What does she want?' he asked.

" 'Well,' said I, 'I can tell you this much, she's not saluting.'

"Soon shells were skipping and bouncing on the sea around us. We hove to, and she ceased fire. It was dark when the ship came abreast, six ship-lengths away. Orders were shouted to clew up the sails. They were German voices. I knew our goose was cooked. They put out a motorboat and in a few minutes the *R. C. Slade* was a prize of the German raider *Seeadler*. The first act of the prize crew was to fall to on my Scotch whisky.

"Aboard the *Seeadler* I was greeted by an old friend, Captain Petersen of the American schooner *A. B. Johnson,* and his crew of nine men. Their ship had been captured and sent to the bottom by the raider just three days earlier.

"Standing at the rail facing our ship at daybreak, we saw a thrilling sight: the Stars and Stripes were still flying above the *Slade* in the early morning breeze. The sight also drew an outburst of *Donnerwetters* from the raider's crew and shouted commands from Von Luckner. In the excitement and darkness of the night before, the flag had been overlooked and the prize crew had slept beneath American colors.

"It was not pleasant to stand by and watch the tall masts of my ship blown skyward with dynamite bombs, or to watch her burst into flame when hundreds of gallons of petrol were poured over her cargo of copra. It was farewell to my command and I retired in weariness and rage.

"On July 8 I came upon another old acquaintance, the American schooner *Manila*. She was plunging along under full sail in squally weather when the *Seeadler* picked her up and gave chase. It was nearly dusk and Von Luckner thought he had surely lost her when the heavy clouds opened up and a beam of light fell full upon her, heading directly toward the *Seeadler*. Shells had been fired in her direction and Captain Southard had taken the gun flashes for distress signals. What a surprise for her crew of ten.

"The *Manila* was light, so a bomb was placed in her vitals. There was a sharp detonation, a puff of smoke, a white ridge of surging water and that was all.

"After eight months at sea with sixty-eight restless crew members, Von Luckner decided to run south to the little coral island of Mopeha, give the men a run ashore, rid himself of the twenty-nine of us who were prisoners and then put back around the Horn for the Atlantic and home.

"The Germans knew little about the islands of the Pacific. They asked our advice: which was the safest approach; how did the tides run; where was the best anchorage; what winds could be expected. We American captains had a weather eye out to do them harm, but must use care.

"As we approached the atoll and neared the narrow channel, two motorboats took soundings. When the ship edged in, the navigating officer got excited and yelled, 'Let go.' Down went the heavy anchor. The anchor hit the edge of a coral shelf and bounced off into deep water. It never reached the bottom because there *was* no bottom. The cable paid out a hundred and five fathoms before it stopped with a jolt that almost tore the hawse pipe out.

"For four solid hours they heaved at the capstan in relays and when at last the anchor appeared, the stock was broken off. No seaman worthy of the name would have used that broken anchor again, yet the Germans did.

"Once more the Count asked for advice. I told him to go in as close as possible, drop anchor and run a wire cable to the rocks ashore.

"'Are you sure it's safe?' he asked.

"'Absolutely,' I said. 'I know these islands. There's a steady trade wind blowing year in and year out, and what with the anchor and that cable ashore and those trade winds, the ship will be as safe as in drydock.'

"But I knew that the trade wind dies out, especially in the neighborhood of land. He didn't. So the *Seeadler* was left trailing before the trade wind, without sufficient swinging room.

"Next morning half the crew and we American officers were taken ashore for a picnic. Suddenly we heard the boom of the *Seeadler's* guns. We turned back and found her stern pounding on the rocks, the big swells pushing her higher every minute.

"Once back on board, Von Luckner took the bridge and signaled for the Diesels to start. The brass propellers just ground the coral into pink mud and soon the blades were battered and useless. There was nothing to be done but abandon ship and move the stores ashore.

"The first thing they tackled was the booze, including scores of cases of champagne taken from French ships in the Atlantic. Some of the sailors broached casks of rum and soon most of them were reeling. Three forgotten prisoners were in the ship's brig below decks, with sea water almost up to their necks. We got them out just in time.

"The provisions taken ashore were stacked on low ground.

That night they were partially destroyed by the incoming high tide. We found four Kanakas on the island left there by French concessionaires to gather copra. With the ship's canvas we set up a tent village.

"Augmenting stores saved from the high tide were coconuts, fish and turtles, thousands of eggs from sea fowl and four pigs belonging to the Kanakas. On August 23 Von Luckner fitted up a motor sloop with a machine gun, rifles, hand grenades and supplies. Selecting three officers and a seaman who had bragged of being on the firing squad that shot Nurse Edith Cavell in Belgium, he put out to sea.

"Their avowed purpose was to be picked up by a merchant ship, take charge by force and then return to Mopeha for the *Seeadler's* big guns and the balance of the raider's crew. [They were captured near Suva of the Fiji Islands on September 22 and interned in New Zealand until the end of the war.]

"On September 5 the little French trading schooner *Lutece* put into Mopeha to pick up the Kanakas. The heavily armed Germans overpowered the crew, took possession of the *Lutece* and sailed away leaving only the Kanakas and Americans marooned on the atoll. [On October 4 the *Lutece* entered the harbor at Easter Island, a possession of Chile, hit a rock and foundered. No lives were lost. The Germans remained in Chile on the loose until war's end.]

"Before leaving Mopeha the Germans smashed all of the *Seeadler's* boats, but one dinghy, though badly stove in, looked promising, so I went to work. Unbeknown to the Germans I had secreted tools, row locks and nails, and in two days I had her pretty seaworthy.

"Then a nasty situation developed. Papeete was only 250 miles to the north, but it meant head winds all the way, whereas Pago Pago was a thousand miles south, but with favorable winds I felt we could make a quick run of it. Things reached a crisis and after engaging in fisticuffs with some of the men I stepped aside in favor of Captain Southard of the *Manila,* who picked four Kanakas for a crew and set out for Papeete.

"Nine days later they returned with the boat barely afloat and the legs of the natives horribly swollen, so I took charge. In two days I had the boat in shape again and shoved off with my second mate, the second mate of the *Manila* and one seaman from the *Manila.* This was on September 19.

"The entire ten days run to Pago Pago was in squally weather with a heavy cross sea running. We divided into two watches. One man steered while the other bailed. The twenty-two-foot boat leaked badly and the cross seas kept pitching water into her.

"Our food was mostly crackers plus coffee, but what a problem to heat that coffee. Our only stove was a paint burner, like a plumber's blowtorch. One man held the coffeepot while the other used the torch. At the same time the boat pitched and tossed wildly.

"On the morning of the tenth day when we sailed into the little harbor of Pago Pago a gunboat turned its guns on us, while on the hills above, under flying American flags, men scurried about the big guns in a businesslike manner.

"At the dock we were searched while rumors flew that we were some of Von Luckner's pirates. We were then placed in Fitafita Barracks and not allowed to communicate with anyone until our stories were checked.

"I took my best suit from a waterproof bag, put it on, and we were taken before the port authorities for further questioning. A naval officer pointed to my Shrine pin and said, 'Where did you steal that?'

" 'That pin belongs to me, sir,' I answered. 'I am a member of Islam Temple in San Francisco.'

" 'By Joe, so am I,' he said and shook hands with me.

"After that formality the first place I made for was the petty officers' mess and ham and eggs—with nary a cracker, and coffee not made with a paint burner. We were treated fine and our boat was raffled off for the Red Cross. By the time we boarded a ship for San Francisco we learned that relief ships had rescued all of the people from Mopeha.

"So the *R. C. Slade* is stricken from the Shipping Register, and the *Seeadler* too, thanks to bad anchorage and *other things*, and here I am none the worse for wear, but not at all wishful for another spell of the same weather."

"What a story!" said I. "But I didn't know you were a Shriner; I'm a Past Potentate of Islam Temple."

"Don't I know it," he chuckled. "I was there last meeting when you made your report. Don't you remember? I won a turkey."

That was the same night when Gustav Fath asked me if Captain Smith were still alive; and the three of us were under the same roof!

Two months after listening to Captain Smith's interesting story I was lunching at Queen's Surf in Honolulu with Underwood's chairman, Philip D. Wagoner, and his friends Mr. and Mrs. Robert G. Calder, of Pawling, N. Y. As the breakers boomed in just below us the conversation turned to ships and the sea.

I described the December reunion at the Dutch Treat Club. When I had finished, Mrs. Calder cast a puzzled glance at her husband and remarked, "Now we know who the man was."

It then developed that Lowell Thomas and Count von Luckner had been dinner guests of the Calders on the week end following the Dutch Treat affair, and Lowell Thomas had related the incident in detail, but could not recall the name of the Count's seafaring friend of so many years ago. And so ends the Von Luckner story.

Leaving the *Johnson* in San Francisco, I broke away from the sea temporarily and found work at the Union Iron Works. An American-Hawaiian freighter was under construction and as huge derricks swung steel plates into position, it was my job to clamp the numbered sections together with temporary bolts, making them ready for the riveting machines. During the usual lay-offs I hung around Sailors' Union Hall, frequently chatting with old Andrew Furuseth, whose one objective in life was to try and better the lot of the common sailor.

Andy was an emancipator of men's rights rather than a labor leader. He consistently refused to accept increased pay for his work as secretary of the Sailors' Union, insisting that he wanted no more than the men themselves received. He spent his own money in their behalf, lived in squalid quarters in Washington while personally lobbying for the rights of seamen. He frequently appeared before Congress to plead for legislation that would correct some of the abuses of the time, when wages were low, hours long and living conditions pitiful.

Though under fifty when I first knew him, his face looked old and wrinkled, almost mummified, and his stooped shoulders seemed to sag under the woes of those to whom he dedicated his long and useful life. During those years he lived utterly alone in a ramshackle place on Steuart Street, from the vicinity of which so many miserable men had been shanghaiied.

Born a Norwegian, Andy sailed before the mast for many years before arriving on the Coast in a British bark from Calcutta. He continued as secretary of the Sailors' Union of the Pacific until 1934, and when he passed away in 1938 at the age of eighty-three, he was still head of the International Seaman's Federation.

Ably assisting Andy in those early days were Walter McArthur, editor of the *Coast Seaman's Journal*, and Paul Sharrenberg, both alive and active in the cause of labor at this writing.

Opposite San Francisco's Ferry Building and just a short block from his old union headquarters on East Street stands a bronze bust of Furuseth. Carved into the monument are the

words spoken by him when threatened with arrest during a
water-front dispute:

YOU CAN PUT ME IN JAIL, BUT YOU CANNOT PUT ME IN
NARROWER QUARTERS THAN, AS A SEAMAN, I HAVE ALWAYS
HAD: YOU CANNOT GIVE ME COARSER FOOD THAN I HAVE
ALWAYS EATEN: YOU CANNOT MAKE ME LONELIER THAN I
HAVE ALWAYS BEEN.

IV

25

I SETTLED DOWN in a small furnished room at 47 Tehama Street.
When layoffs at the Union Iron Works became too frequent, I
found extra work with song slides on Saturday and Sunday
nights at the Empire Nickelodeon on Market Street. This
brought my total earnings to about ten dollars a week.

After paying for room and meals, the balance added up to
quarters, dimes and nickels, but in those days small change
had purchasing power. A nickel was good for a man-sized
steam beer at the Fiesta or Zinkand's Café or an oversized mug
at the Ale House on Montgomery, with free lunch to boot. A
movie cost a nickel, and if you were a commuter, five cents
would pay your ferry fare not only across the bay but all the
way up Oakland Creek to the foot of Broadway.

It cost only a dime to enjoy good vaudeville from the balcony
at the Orpheum, to view melodrama from the gallery at the Central Theater or even to see Little Egypt do her famous muscle
dance at the Midway Plaisance on Market Street. Half a dollar
would buy a six-course French dinner with red wine at Bergez
Frank's Old Poodle Dog, provided, of course, you did not covet
an upstairs parlor with "trimmings." And later in the evening
for a quarter you could hear Madame Luisa Tetrazzini sing in
grand opera at Doc Leahy's Old Tivoli Theater.

Though low in funds, I had time to spare, so I was quite content to admire San Francisco's swanky *maisons de joie* from a
respectable distance, but I vowed that some day I should come
to know them better. The curtained booths of Marchand's, Del-
monico's and the Maison Dorée were not for one who labored
nine hours a day at the Iron Works for a wage of $1.50. Neither

were the elegant third-floor hideaways of the Pup and the Old Poodle Dog where a discreet patron could relax, French menu in hand and a French madame on his knee.

Leaving the Dodie Valencias, the Jessie Haymans, the Tessie Walls and other tenderloin socialites to those who could afford the better things of life, I skipped the Powell-Eddy-O'Farrell Street innkeepers, and instead, patroled a beat that led from my bunkhouse on Tehama Street straight out Kearny to Pacific, and sometimes back via Dupont.

There was Morton Street (now dignified Maiden Lane). Lining its southern exposure were groups of "cribs," each chummy cubbyhole of a window framing the animated features of a painted French doll. Here and there was a drawn shade, the "busy" signal.

Commercial Street was a busy alley between Dupont and Kearny. Crowds on promenade milled up one side of the street and down the other. Curiosity seekers, eyes right, absorbed atmosphere. Others, not so curious, hesitated long enough to cast an appraising eye over the rows of painted, grimacing faces before side-stepping into a dim-lit doorway. In Bartlett Alley, skirting Chinatown, slant-eyed beauties in gorgeously embroidered kimonas eagerly awaited the "drop-in" trade.

Hinckley and Pinckley alleys were reserved mostly for ladies of color. Further along was the So Different, where Lew Purcell's three-piece Negro orchestra (clarinet, trombone and snare drum) gave out with such rhythm the very walls of the place seemed to pulse and sway in sympathy with the weird jungle beat.

Pacific Street. One short block. Kearny on the west. Montgomery on the east. Here, on both sides of the narrow street, leaning shoulder to shoulder as if for moral support, music and raucous sound belching from every inviting doorway, stood the Hippodrome, Thalia, the Cave, Coppa's Neptune, Fat Dougherty's, Parente's, the Midway—familiar names, synonymous with the name and fame of old San Francisco itself. Here was your Barbary Coast; here—your Terrific Street.

I walked that beat on the night of April 17, 1906. I also walked it later. Many times. But somehow, after that night, it never seemed the same again.

The earthquake of April 18, 1906, occurring as it did shortly after five in the morning when most of San Francisco's 400,000 inhabitants were sound asleep, was so terrifying in its violence that every person able to scramble out of bed took to the open spaces in varying stages of undress and waited nervously for what might happen next. The first shock, variously estimated at from forty-five to sixty-five seconds, was soon followed by another, and then as smoke billowed into the skies on every side, the panic was on.

Thousands excitedly milled up and down the streets while others watched the growing conflagrations from the crowded tops of Nob, Telegraph, Russian and Rincon hills. Soon a trickle of refugees, laden with bundles, bird cages, baby carriages and even trunks, began moving toward the water front.

Later the boom of dynamite could be heard as structures in the path of the flames were blown to bits. Then the thin lines heading down Market Street swelled to solid masses of people treading on each other's heels in a mad rush to board the overcrowded ferries and leave the burning city behind.

Of 200,000 people residing in the burned area, particularly the transients in hotels, fully half of them left town during the first twenty-four hours, some to return later, many to settle elsewhere. As for me, with neither kith nor kin to worry about, I was caught up by the excitement and remained not only while the city was reduced to smoking rubble but during the first months of reconstruction as well.

Any eyewitness account would naturally be colored by the

manner in which events affected the life and fortunes of the individual concerned. What follows, therefore, is merely an account of personal experiences and is in no sense an attempt to relate the story of the earthquake and fire as a whole.

Number 47 Tehama Street, an ancient two-story brick building, was located about two blocks below the Palace Hotel. From economic necessity rather than choice I had acquired a roommate, Alex Granby, part-time musician. We shared what had once been a front parlor, separated from the dining room by a pair of creaky folding doors.

Our section of town was not without its own excitement on the evening of April 17. It was the second night of the opera season, with Caruso singing the lead in *Carmen*, and though the neighborhood around the Opera House on Mission Street had grown shabby over the years, this was one occasion when high-toned society from Nob and Russian hills did not mind crossing "south of the Slot," into the near slums to see and hear not only the great Caruso but Sembrich, Eames, Fremstad, Scotti and Dippel.

Recalling my spear-carrying nights at Coney Island, I wandered over to have a look at the town's best people as they alighted from their elegant carriages and paraded into the Opera House under the admiring gaze of the people from Minna and Third streets and near-by Skid Row.

Then, while the enthralled audience relaxed under the spell of Caruso's first and last performance in San Francisco, I strolled as usual out Kearny to Pacific Street where the throng pushing through the swinging doors of Coppa's and Cowboy Mag's and Spanish Kitty's sought entertainment less refined but more in keeping with the purse of the common man.

I still have a vivid recollection of that last night of the old San Francisco: of blaring music and brilliant lights in the Barbary Coast dance halls; of dark alleys and lurching drunks; of fist fights and the rap of a copper's night stick on the pavement;

of skullcaps and bland, inscrutable faces peering from dim-lighted hallways on Dupont Street; of Hinckley and Pinckley alleys; of business as usual and tomorrow just another day.

It was past midnight when I reached my room and as Alex had not yet come back, I turned in and fell asleep and was only dimly aware of his crawling into bed some time later.

Suddenly I became conscious of a deep rumble that seemed to reverberate from the earth below the building, followed by a nightmarish feeling of being violently shaken from side to side as if by giant hands.

For an instant I imagined myself aboard ship with sails aback, slatting against masts and yards, and wind and sea pounding the vessel. Then, as my eyes popped wide in the dim light, I realized that the great folding doors next to my bed were shaking with an unearthly clatter, while directly above, the big glass chandelier, its crystals tinkling merrily, was swaying wildly from side to side, threatening to let go any instant and bash our skulls.

Like two jacks-in-the-box, Alex and I sat bolt upright, then rolled out of bed and sprawled on the floor as an ornamental lamp slithered from a table and splashed between us in a shower of glass and kerosene oil. As I scrambled to my bare feet my two highly prized ostrich eggs rolled from the plate rail above and splattered on the floor. Even in the excitement I re-call feeling depressed over the loss of my souvenirs.

Alex never hesitated. Without stopping to dress, he reached the door in two leaps and rushed into the street barefoot, clad only in a nightshirt, and a very abbreviated one at that. Though panicky enough, I did take time to draw on my trousers before rushing to the street where excited crowds grew larger each moment as people poured through doorways and popped out of first-floor windows.

Shortly after reaching the street there was a second violent shock and a section of wall from No. 47 fell outward, sending the hysterical crowds into another panic. Unable to move around in my bare feet because of broken glass, I tied the sleeves of my shirt around my feet for protection, dashed into the house, picked up shoes and Alex's trousers, thrust a few cherished objects into a small bag and scurried back outside. Later I was thankful for having shoes on my feet, not to mention Alex's gratitude for saving his trousers.

In the crowd outside I located our landlord, Mr. Allen, with his wife, two small daughters and Emma, a girl of twenty. Clustered around a small trunk which they had managed to salvage, they were trying to calm another roomer, a Mrs. Johnson. She was in hysterics because her husband had disappeared after safely leaving the house. To please the weeping Mrs. Johnson, Alex and I volunteered to search for her husband.

Leaving my bag with them, we headed toward Mission Street where black smoke was already billowing high above the spires of St. Patrick's Church.

Toward Market Street the Claus Spreckels Building, tallest in the city, stood serene and apparently unharmed by the earthquake. Minutes later, wisps of smoke spiraled upward from the moonlike windows of its rounded dome, followed by tongues of greenish flame. Soon the entire sixteen-story monument became a golden glow.

Adding to the confusion and fright that had already gripped the people, a herd of steers being driven along the water front stampeded and raced the length of Mission Street, foam flying from their nostrils and tails straight in the air, imperiling everything in their path, while policemen took pot shots at their flying hides.

I looked around for Alex, but in the excitement he had disappeared, and I never saw him again. Weeks later I read his name among a list of convicted looters. Incidentally, looting began as early as noon of the first day when it became evident that nothing could save the downtown area. Display windows of large jewelry stores were the first victims. With all windows shattered by the earthquake, nothing stood between the loot and the looter except his conscience.

Like wild animals fleeing jungle fires, herds of frightened people converged into the downtown streets, then overflowed into parks and public squares, gazing fearfully at the rising columns of flame and smoke threatening to hem them in on every side. Market became a one-way street jam-packed with a mass of half-clad refugees who were carrying children in arms, bundles, baskets, bedding and trunks dragged over the cobbled streets. Weeping or laughing hysterically, or with drawn, set faces, they threaded their way through a maze of slow-moving automobiles, horse-drawn vehicles, pushcarts and wheelbarrows, all headed for the water front and safety.

Occasionally they made way for oncoming fire apparatus hurriedly ferried across the bay from Oakland. Clanging bells only added to the confusion and served no purpose because all water mains had been broken by the earthquake, leaving only the dynamiting of large buildings as a last desperate resort.

At the ferry gates the halted crowds milled and churned about, clawing at the iron grill work. When a ferry drew into the slip, they battled their way through narrow openings guarded by hurriedly drafted bluejackets.

Rumors were flying thick and fast.

"Los Angeles has been destroyed by a tidal wave!"

"The Cliff House has fallen into the sea!"

"Buildings have dropped through yawning crevices opened by the earthquake!"

"Freed inmates of jails and insane asylums are preying upon the people!"

"Looters are being shot on sight!"

"Forty people have perished in the collapse of the Valencia Hotel!"

Actually, only the last two were true.

Turning south along the docks, I reached the Harbor Hospital just in time to give a hand to unloading injured people from a horse-drawn ambulance, then climbed in with the driver and made several trips to pick up badly mangled people, including one man battered almost beyond recognition who passed out while our wagon bounced over the cobblestones.

Later, working among the ruins, I heard the boom of dynamite close by and learned that the Monadnock and Palace hotels were being blown up to prevent the fire from spreading. Until then I had completely forgotten the custodians of my little handbag, so I hurried over to Tehama Street and there they were, huddled around their trunk exactly where we had left them hours earlier. I vaguely wondered why I bothered with them. Maybe it was because Emma was a mighty good looker, but whatever the influence, I did see them safely through.

I bedded my party down in a water-front warehouse and then walked over to Market Street where the crowds were larger and even more excited than they had been earlier in the day. People were still streaming through the ferry gates and thousands drifted aimlessly, seeking friends or lost relatives. Messages written on bits of paper and cardboard were posted on the walls of the Ferry Building. Rewards were offered for information about missing people and in some cases photographs were posted.

The night scene was one of intense excitement and confusion. Only a few blocks distant, the triangular area north of Market, between Kearny and California streets, was burning fiercely. As the flames shot upward, they were reflected in the sky, turning night into day and emphasizing the extent of the growing disaster.

Martial law had been declared, with General Frederick Funston in charge. Under him were fifteen hundred soldiers from the Presidio, detachments of Marines and bluejackets from Mare Island, members of the National Guard and a thousand citizens hastily sworn in as special police officers, but all of these were hardly adequate to police the fire lines and cope with nearly half a million frightened people.

A proclamation was issued by Mayor Eugene E. Schmitz, the first paragraph of which read:

THE FEDERAL TROOPS, MEMBERS OF REGULAR POLICE AND ALL SPECIAL POLICE OFFICERS HAVE BEEN AUTHORIZED TO KILL ANY AND ALL PERSONS FOUND ENGAGED IN LOOTING OR THE COMMISSION OF ANY CRIME.

Shortly after midnight I watched a fireman manipulating a salt-water hose and agreed to hold the nozzle a few minutes while he hunted for a sandwich. Hours later, when daylight came, I was still at my station, so I asked another bystander for relief while I, also, "went for a sandwich."

As the fire began eating its way into the sailors' boardinghouse district around Steuart Street, water-front bums began breaking into the saloons. Many drank themselves into a stupor and fell asleep in doorways directly in the path of the flames. Others, opening bottles taken from display windows, found themselves gulping swallows of putrid water, faked to look like whisky and gin.

On Thursday morning, barely twenty-four hours after the city started to burn, a consolidated newspaper, the *Examiner-Call-Chronicle,* which was printed in the Oakland *Tribune* plant, appeared with headlines: EARTHQUAKE AND FIRE—S.F. IN RUINS.

As if the worried citizens needed to be told! However, with news not only of the outside world but also the first authentic information of what went on in their own city now crumbling around them, copies were eagerly seized.

At the wharf, where I had left the Allen family, I learned that old Mrs. Johnson had disappeared. Several hours later she reappeared, sobbing hysterically, and said she had found the

burned body of her husband. It seemed incredible, but Emma
and I followed as she threaded her way through ruins on
Howard Street, where the fire, after leveling every flimsy building in its path the day before, had swept on and at that time
was several blocks south, eating its way toward the lumber
yards along Islais Creek.

The body claimed by Mrs. Johnson was one of four lying in
the middle of Howard Street, all within one block. All were
literally burned to a crisp, but the old woman threw herself
upon one, claiming to recognize a ring and bits of unburned
shirt cloth beneath the charred body. Emma and I were of no
help in identifying the remains but we comforted the old lady,
and, as it was not possible to move the body, we covered it over
with burned tin and led the disconsolate woman back to the
wharf. Incidentally, as all possible aid was needed for injured
persons, dead bodies were allowed to lie in the streets until the
fire was brought under control.

How four persons happened to burn to death within such a
small area was a mystery, unless shot as looters, which of itself
was unlikely because there was little to tempt looters in that
neighborhood.

On the way to the wharf I dropped behind and, raking among
the ruins of a burned cannery, retrieved a dozen cans of
salmon. The contents were so dry that they rattled in the cans,
but they served as food which we needed badly.

Shortly after dark I had settled down for a second helpless
night with the party when a detachment of soldiers arrived and
ordered all persons to vacate the wharf and board a steamer
about to leave for Vallejo, thirty miles distant. Mrs. Johnson
refused to leave the city because her husband lay dead in the
streets. The soldiers ordered the rest of us to go, after promising
to find a safer place for her.

Loading the trunk and packages on a two-wheeled coal cart,

we moved along and joined hundreds of other refugees boarding the Vallejo Steamship Company's *General Frisbie*.

* 26 *

As THE STEAMER backed slowly out into the bay, its screaming sirens adding to the din and confusion, I climbed to the upper deck where clusters of frightened men, women and children were staring with glazed eyes at the fantastic sight directly ahead: the sight of a beautiful city being completely gutted by fire, each familiar landmark a blazing torch as flame and billowing smoke belched from its windows. Monuments of steel and stone glowed like furnaces from the heat within.

To the south, below Mission Street, lay a belt of smoldering debris several blocks wide and fully two miles long, its ashes already darkening where the first day's holocaust had partially burned itself out. North of Market Street, between Van Ness Avenue and the water front, was a blazing cauldron of fire and ruin enclosing four square miles of the city's finest structures: its banks, stores, hotels and apartment houses; its towering office buildings; its exclusive clubs; its orphanages and hospitals; even its great spired cathedrals and synagogues, each blazing edifice part of a terrifying yet magnificent spectacle that seemed as unreal as a painted panorama at a county fair.

Crumbling into ashes were the colorful foreign colonies, world-famous restaurants and theaters, Nob Hill mansions and the gilded hideaways of the downtown tenderloin. Chinatown and the French Quarter were already gone, and only North Beach and the Barbary Coast would hold out for a scant twenty-four hours longer before they too would burn and crumble.

As the *General Frisbie* headed north through waters reddened by the reflection from leaping flames, our view of the burning city was mercifully blocked out by the steep walls of Telegraph Hill, which, so far, had escaped the flames. In the flickering ghostly light I glanced at the faces of the people around me, most of them leaving behind relatives, friends and personal possessions.

Some wept silently and others bawled like children, but most just stared grimly ahead through unseeing eyes. I had nothing to lose, not even a friend, but my insides were doing strange things. No human being could watch that dramatic scene without emotion.

Although it was near midnight when we reached Vallejo, the docks were crowded with people eager to help. After the injured were carried ashore and placed in ambulances, the rest of us were taken to a large public building where we received food and the first hot drinks since the quake. Women and children were then bedded down on cots and the men in pallets on the floor.

I retired with the others but was restless and unable to sleep after so much excitement. Mr. Allen and I agreed that I should return to San Francisco and search for Mrs. Johnson.

At the dock I learned that I must have a pass signed by the mayor of Vallejo before being allowed to board the steamer. After a lot of red tape and a promise to do relief work, I was given a Red Cross armband and a pass reading: "To Whom It May Concern: This gentleman is willing to do any duty assigned to him. Signed, J. J. Madigan, Mayor of Vallejo."

Long before the steamer reached upper San Francisco Bay, the rolling clouds of black smoke and the boom of exploding dynamite and heavy artillery were warning enough that the conflagration was raging worse than ever. I hurried over to the warehouse and learned from the guards that Mrs. Johnson with other refugees had been taken aboard the U. S. naval training ship *Marion*. Relieved of that worry, I presented my credentials to the staff at the Harbor Hospital and was put to work.

Then followed two full days and a night of nerve-racking labor with little time out for food or sleep. The injured arrived in an unending procession, some under their own power but most delivered by passing vehicles serving as temporary ambulances. With others I helped prepare cases for treatment, held arms and legs while splints were placed and bandages passed, took care of patients as they came out from under the ether, and topped it off by carrying stretcher cases to steamers, where we placed them in rows of cots for delivery to hospitals in near-by cities.

When the supply of anesthetics grew scarce, we were called upon to pinion squirming bodies on operating tables while surgeons cut, slashed, sewed and bandaged mangled bodies and set broken bones. Many medical men and city officials reported in and out, but I recall the names of three in particular, Drs. Magnus, Herzog and Diggins, who seemed always to be on the job.

When medical supplies became dangerously low, Dr. Diggins, a former ship's surgeon, volunteered to replenish the supply. Anchored in the bay opposite the hospital were a dozen great sailing ships owned by the Alaska Packers Company, all loaded with supplies and waiting only for crew and cannery hands to report before sailing for the Alaska salmon fisheries.

By law each carried a complete medicine chest. Also anchored in the bay was the U. S. cruiser *Boston.* (In April 1946, the *Boston,* after fifty-nine years of service, was sunk off the Farallones by the U. S. Navy.) Commandeering a big launch, Dr. Diggins embarked on a piratical career. He boarded the *Boston,* stated the emergency and was given a detachment of bluejackets under Chief Yeoman Friedman. Their first call was on the ship *Abbie Palmer,* where they seized the medicine chest, then visited the other ships in turn and gathered up enough supplies to meet the emergency.

Back at the hospital the fresh-water supply ran out, so the

doctor persuaded the captain of the Norwegian collier *Titania* to bring barrels of water ashore from his ship.

Scores of women and children camped on near-by piers and then rushed the hospital with cans and buckets seeking water; this gave the doctor still another idea. Commandeering two launches, he again boarded the Alaska Packers' ships and brought ashore enough provisions and clothing to half fill the waiting rooms of the Hatch Steamship Company, whose rooms he also took over without permission.

Saturday afternoon, after laboring thirty-six hours with little rest, I took a nap in the half-filled waiting room. A few hours later Dr. Diggins banged on the locked door and instructed me to open cases and get ready to hand out canned goods and ships' biscuits to the public. By the time Friedman's bluejackets had formed the crowd into an orderly line, I was passing out canned beans and ships' biscuits over an improvised counter.

Following instructions, I put up shelves and stocked them with cans, packages and sacks of food, ready for the next distribution. Next morning (Sunday) I received hundreds of loaves of bread and several forty-quart cans of milk from Vallejo.

Crowds quickly gathered and police were called to form lines. Each person was given a can of food and half a loaf of bread. Milk was reserved for women and children, but the anguish was great when many women were unable to produce a can or bottle. Some solved the problem by consuming a can of beans on the spot, using the empty tin to carry away a ladle of milk. At the next line-up, however, empty bean and meat cans were plentiful enough.

The biggest surprise came next morning when bulky packing cases arrived marked: "Santa Barbara Relief Committee." The crates contained hundreds of pounds of fried chicken, roast turkey, baked hams, sandwiches and hard-boiled eggs, contributed and pooled by community groups.

Other cases held scores of specially packed boxes and baskets contributed by families, many enclosing notes of sympathy and good cheer. The food was divided into parcels and handed out to the shuffling lines of refugees, along with the notes and messages, and since many included names and addresses, it is probable that some notes were eventually acknowledged.

Supplies, including fresh meat, vegetables, bread and milk, began arriving in larger quantities, so we set up a soup kitchen in an open lot directly across East Street, next door to Sailors' Union Hall, and used volunteer help to serve hot soup, stew and coffee to long lines of hungry people each morning and evening.

Next, with supplies in abundance and a voluntary staff of cooks at the soup kitchen, I cleaned up my own place and turned the front portion into a private dining room, intended for the use of the hospital staff. Then the word got around and soon our special guests included Mayor Eugene Schmitz, Police Chief Jerry Dinan, Coroner Walsh, Judge Thomas Graham and other city officials.

In the meantime, after the east side of Van Ness Avenue had been mowed down by dynamite and artillery fire, the conflagration had been brought temporarily under control by late Friday night. Then an isolated dynamite squad, anxious to prevent any further possibility of the flames leaping the wide boulevard, blew up a lone warehouse near the foot of Van Ness Avenue, possibly as a last defiant gesture.

As the burning embers flew sky high they were picked up and scattered by a freakish northwest wind, and soon another fire was eating its way through the last remaining unburned section.

Exploding oil from large storage tanks fed the flames which swept toward the wharves on the north and easterly toward the slopes of Telegraph Hill. It was then that hundreds of Italian residents, in desperation, rolled out barrel after barrel of red wine, smashed in the barrel heads and, using bucket brigades, drenched the shingled roofs with wine while hundreds of others beat off the encroaching flames with blankets and gunny sacks soaked in the juice of the grape.

Throughout the night the efforts of all available firemen, aided by soldiers, sailors and thousands of residents, were concentrated on fighting the new conflagration. On the water side fireboats continued all-out efforts to save the miles of docks and warehouses that had miraculously escaped during the first three days and nights of destruction.

By the following day (Saturday) when the battle was finally won, there was left in all downtown San Francisco only its water-front piers, a small collection of wooden houses perched on the slopes of Telegraph Hill, a small section of North Beach, including the colorful Meiggs and Fisherman's wharves, and occasional islands of buildings that happened to survive through freakish changes of winds.

After the first three days of terror and confusion some semblance of order was restored. Burned bodies had been gathered up from the streets and carted to a temporary morgue in Portsmouth Square opposite the destroyed Hall of Justice, and groups of men drafted by military authorities began searching still smoking ruins for others.

Although the fire was responsible for most of the city's destruction, the earthquake itself had also taken its toll. The seven-million-dollar City Hall was in ruins before the fire reached it. Two big ships in drydock had toppled over and one, the *City of Pueblo,* had been neatly cut in half by a pair of giant derricks.

And though the quake did not open any canyons in the streets large enough even for a midget to drop to the nether regions below, as suggested in the movies, some very wide cracks did appear over made ground which had been improperly filled in during the earlier years when the city suffered its growing pains.

On the fifth morning after the quake (Monday) while I was putting things in order in my storeroom, I tapped what I thought to be two barrels of vinegar and found instead that they contained gin. Both had been brought from the ship *Abbie Palmer* with other stores, and I now found myself in as much of a pickle as if I were immersed in one of the barrels because General Funston had issued orders for the arrest of anyone possessing alcohol.

Apparently others were in on the secret. The next night while asleep above the storeroom I heard suspicious sounds and dropped below to find the door wide open and two men rolling one of my precious kegs down the wharf. I was about to shout an alarm when I noticed that the men wore blue uniforms. Instead of making a fuss, I reported the matter to a Mr. Jack Bender, then in charge of the relief station. I was then loaned a revolver with instructions to use it only to scare off future intruders.

I moved my pallet downstairs and slept with one eye open. Sure enough, two nights later I had other callers. Toward morning there was a knock on the door and, thinking it might be someone from the Emergency, I asked who was there but heard only running footsteps. Sitting on the floor with my back against the gin barrel and my gun on my knee, I fell asleep and then awoke suddenly with the feeling that someone was standing just outside the door.

In the ghostly light of a flickering candle I stared with bulging eyes at a slowly turning doorknob and a key wobbling in its lock, as unseen hands directly in front of me unsuccessfully tried to dislodge it. In the deadly silence my spine tingled and I could feel my skin breaking out in a rash of goose pimples.

I tried to call out but the muscles of my throat tightened and vocal cords refused to function. Then, as the fumbling shifted from the door to the window fastenings just over my head, I came out of my panic, aimed high and let go with a rattle of musketry that sent my visitor on his way in a hurry and left me quaking in a cold sweat as people from the hospital pounded on the door to inquire what the shooting was all about.

Next day a helper moved in with me and, following instructions, we transferred the gin to gallon bottles and delivered most of them to the hospital, whether for professional use or otherwise we never knew.

Among my stores were two cases of syrup put up in one-pint tins with screw tops, each the shape of a small log cabin. I emptied them and filled them with gin. Luncheon guests from the City Hall and ex-shipmates across the street in Sailors' Union Hall were both grateful and surprised when they received presents of Log Cabin Syrup.

There were no more unofficial visits, but a few nights later an accident occurred that could have had disastrous consequences. While I was fussing with a kerosene lamp it exploded and covered my clothes and the surroundings with burning oil.

Near by were several cans of fresh milk. I fell to the floor while my partner deluged me with milk. We were badly frightened as orders were to use candles only and another fire might have done untold damage.

Throughout the entire city illumination was limited to candlelight; no fires for cooking or other purposes were allowed in homes in the unburned residential districts because chimneys were considered unsafe until officially inspected. In consequence, all cooking was done over campfires or on temporary stoves set up on the street curbs, some protected by canvas windbreaks as large as a kitchen.

Temporary shacks were thrown up everywhere, some singly, some in communities of several hundred. Smart-cracking signs were numerous, but the one I thought funnier than most read: EAT, DRINK, AND BE MERRY, FOR TOMORROW WE MAY GO TO OAKLAND.

Bringing order out of chaos, however, was not a matter of days and weeks but months, and troops continued to patrol the streets for ten weeks. Five hundred city blocks, comprising twenty-eight thousand of the city's largest buildings, had been turned into four square miles of charred and twisted ruins.

Yet by May 1 Market Street had not only been cleared of debris sufficiently to allow streetcars to bump along its full length, but the curbs on both sides of the street were lined by hucksters and pitchmen and trades people of every type, their places of business generally a pine board across two beer barrels.

In clouds of grime and stinging dust from the blackened ruins around them they loudly hawked silver from Shreves, porcelain cups from Chinatown, and Satsuma vases looted from the mansions of Nob Hill, or so you were told. These Market Street curb vendors, ranging from the gent who confided that he personally had raked his phony gems from the ashes of the Diamond Palace to the shirt-sleeved proprietors of outdoor soup kitchens and fresh-air barbershops, continued to do business for months after the fire. They were almost as interesting to sight-seeing visitors as the actual ruins.

In the vanguard of famous persons escorted among the "damndest, finest ruins" with all the pomp and ceremony of a visiting queen was Madame Sarah Bernhardt, who alternately wept and wondered at the sights unfolded.

Early in May all relief stations were consolidated, so I locked up my half-filled storeroom and visited the Allens in Vallejo. Returning the next day, I found shelves stripped bare. Even my blankets and personal things were gone. With cupboard bare my job was done, so I bid good-by to my friends at the hospital, particularly Dr. Diggins, who had just been arrested and charged with "piracy" for his part in raiding the Alaska Packers' ships of medical supplies and stores. (Later, when taken before Captain Badger of the U. S. Flagship *Chicago,* Dr.

Diggins was absolved of all blame and complimented for his actions during the emergency.)

* 27 *

I FOUND WORK on the docks as a stevedore and with a fellow worker took a furnished room in a private home on Noe Street. One day my friend mentioned that a brother was expected to arrive from Antwerp on the British bark *Celticburn*. I was quite surprised as I had heard that my old ship had been posted by Lloyd's of London as overdue on her passage from Santa Rosalia to Sydney.

Boarding her at Meiggs Wharf in the hope of recovering my lost belongings, I went forward and found young Hughes, an apprentice, to be the only member left of the old crew, except the mate, who had become Captain Douglass. I started for the wharf and met the skipper in the middle of the gangway. He was about to step politely aside, then blocked my path, gave me a searching look and exploded, "I know you. You're that damned Yankee!"

Shaking hands cordially enough, he said that we had caused untold trouble by leaving the *Celticburn* shorthanded in a foreign port and that Captain Davis had been heavily fined because of Johnny's desertion, he being a ward of the British Crown. He confided also that though sorry to lose the others, they were glad to be rid of me, the sea lawyer and troublemaker. When I asked for my dunnage bag, he chuckled with satisfaction and said all of our effects had been taken back to London and sold at auction by the Board of Trade, according to British maritime law.

Several nights later my stevedore friend found himself in an embarrassing situation. While alone in the house, our landlady's three little daughters found and confiscated the contents of a hidden bag belonging to him. We walked into the house to find them decked out in a bewildering array of necklaces, lavaliers, brooches, watches, rings and bracelets—the sort of cheap jewelry usually left overnight in display windows. His complexion turned a sickly yellow as he gathered up the loot, thrust it into his grip and made a hurried exit.

Evidently both he and Alex Granby had worked the jewelry-store beat while I was accumulating sardines, beans and crackers on Howard Street for my adopted family.

The incident must have reminded me of the Allens because I quit stevedoring and joined them in Vallejo, and for the next two months was an industrious young man indeed. As deck hand on a ferryboat carrying workers to and from Mare Island Navy Yard, I turned to at five in the morning, shoveled coal into the bunkers until seven, handled mooring lines at each end of the run until six in the evening, dined leisurely with girl friend Emma and her family until seven-thirty, then did a nightly stint with song slides at the little novelty theater until ten o'clock, after which, until five next morning, I was as free as a bird on the wing.

After weeks of such a lazy, carefree existence, it was little wonder that I deserted the town of Vallejo and signed as second mate of the four-master *King Cyrus.*

We made a fast and uneventful trip to Tacoma and back, and then, after fiddling around outside the heads for hours waiting for a towboat, the wind turned fair, so the skipper saved the towing fee by sailing in through the Golden Gate channel and down the bay to an anchorage off Mission Rock.

It was dusk and the night of October 20, exactly six months since the *General Frisbie* had backed away from a burning, dying city. Ashore, the flame and smoke were gone, but the scars were there—great dark voids from which jutted occasional lofty shells of twisted steel and concrete, silhouetted against the sky, each black-rimmed window seeming to stare into space like the empty sockets of gaunt grinning skeletons.

As second mate, it was my duty to stand anchor watch, so while our lookouts paced back and forth on the fo'c'slehead, singing out their half-hourly "All's Well," and foghorns blared out a warning to prowling ferryboats, I filled in the long night watches jotting down recollections of those days and nights when it seemed to me that San Francisco must surely be blotted out as a modern city.

I mailed the manuscript to my worried old aunt in Virginia. It was nearly thirty years before I laid eyes on it again. It is from those notes that the preceding chapter was written.

When the *King Cyrus* docked, I jumped to another ship, the *Balboa,* loaded redwood ties at Eureka and was paid off at San Pedro on December 1, 1906, just in time to sign as second mate on a seven-hundred-ton four-master, the *Lyman D. Foster,* thereby putting myself in line for a knockdown-and-dragout scrap. Discharge papers show the skipper's initials as D.J., but in deepwater circles he was better known as Crazy Kill-man, and crazy he certainly seemed to be.

On December 22 we lay to off Cape Flattery expectantly waiting for a tug that would tow us through the Juan de Fuca Strait and up Puget Sound to Bellingham. All night and most of the next forty-eight hours the Old Man paced up and down, spouting profanity and using his binoculars by the hour, searching for a cruising towboat. What the captain could not know was that no tug had been outside the cape for ten days because of a coal strike.

On Christmas Eve one of Cape Flattery's worst southeasters tore into us with hail, sleet and snow, driving the ship across the entrance to the strait and almost piling her up on the shores of Vancouver Island before we broke free and headed toward the open sea.

By then the captain's blood pressure had reached the explosive stage. It was my watch on deck. The helmsman was having a hard time of it, so I gave an occasional hand on the lee side of the wheel. The skipper was below in his bunk, watching the compass above his head, when the ship went slightly off course. Suddenly he came raging up the companionway. Leering in my face, he called me every dirty name he could think of. Just then the helmsman struck eight bells and the mate came on deck as another seaman relieved the wheel. I went below, shaking with excitement.

In my small cabin I removed oilskins and sea boots and then, on a hunch, sat on the edge of my bunk to await developments. Captain Killman clumped down the stairs and, standing directly in front of my door, began shouting all over again. Unnerved and enraged almost to the point of homicide, I slipped my fingers around the edge of the sliding door and, when the ship's stern rose high on the next wave, slammed the door back and threw myself at him. We crashed to the wet slimy deck, clawing and scratching, each trying to stay on top as the ship rolled and pitched in the heavy seas. Unable to stay on our feet long enough to get set for a solid punch, we turned it into a mauling and gouging wrestling match as the vessel lunged crazily, smashing us against jutting stanchions and wrapping our flailing arms and legs around the iron table supports.

Outside, the southeaster raged while the mate, shouting for help to man the wheel, alternately lent a hand to the struggling helmsman and peered down the half-open companionway trying to gauge the progress of the brawl going on below. Deciding to get into the fight at the risk of the ship's safety, he started down the ladder as a huge sea burst over the weather quarter, pinned the helmsman against the wheel and poured down through the open companionway, carrying the mate along with it.

When the tons of swirling water partially drained off, the captain lay draped around an iron stanchion, half strangled with sea water and barely conscious.

At change of watch the mate banged on my door and I struggled back on deck, wretched in body and in mind. It was Christmas morning, and as I huddled behind a flimsy windbreak against driving sleet and snow, I almost forgot the aches and pains of a badly battered body as I wondered about my doubtful status aboard ship. Although terribly provoked, I had been goaded into making the first pass and if the captain should press charges before the U. S. Shipping Commissioner, it would be his word against mine.

During the entire week after Christmas, while we lay hove to and then battled our way back to port on New Year's night, Captain Killman merely glared at me; he never spoke a word and excluded me from the cabin where he took his meals with the mate. I was fearful indeed, hardly knowing what to expect on reaching port.

On January 4, 1907, we were paid off at Bellingham. As the U. S. Shipping Commissioner filled in my discharge papers, Crazy Killman, sitting at his right, eyed the scratching pen as though fascinated. Then, in utter silence, while the mate and other crew members stood by, he drew a line through the word "Good" under character, ability and seamanship and substituted his own words instead. That document remains as a souvenir of a hard, stormy voyage and a tough old sea captain.

Happy at escaping a possible Federal prison term for assault and mutiny on the high seas, I decided to celebrate in San Francisco. I stowed away aboard the old passenger crate *Coos Bay* by merely taking a nap in the bunk of a former shipmate.

* 28 *

IN "THE CITY," as San Francisco was affectionately known among seafarers, I became a boarder at the Excelsior on East Street, which was run by George Larson and his son Willie. While the proprietors were not above shanghaiing a boarder occasionally when a fifty-dollar "advance note" was needed to cancel out an overdue board bill, most of them catered to old-timers who alternated between short spells ashore and round-trip voyages, mostly coastwise.

The homeward-bounder would burst through the swinging doors, toss his bag in a corner, order a round of drinks for the bleary-eyed hangers-on and then, under a little urging by Mr. Larson, he would settle for a "dead horse," as represented by a handful of IOUs tucked away in the back of the cash drawer. These would include mysterious rounds of drinks he could never remember ordering, but the sailorman's philosophy was easy come, easy go, and he could always wangle a farewell bottle before shoving off for Grays Harbor or Callao.

Some had the foresight to leave part of their pay with Mr. Larson before trying their luck on Pacific Street, but most, with conscience clear and credit re-established, shot the works on the first night ashore. After that they were guests of the Excelsior until their credit began to strain at the seams, whereupon the landlord would suggest a short sea voyage. In the interest of future good will he much preferred that his guests sign on voluntarily. However, should a little coaxing become necessary, Mr. Larson generally rose to the occasion.

Apparently my credit limit was two weeks because one morning Willie shoved an "advance note" in my hand and told me to sign at the spot marked X. Proving that I had learned a few things since a memorable day some five years before, I duly noted that the ship was British and the destination Antwerp, so I declined without thanks, whereupon Willie, whose hair was red and whose temper was short, dispossessed my roommate and me and put our few belongings in cold storage.

Broke and in debt, we decided to join the Navy, took the naval tug to Goat Island, passed the physical, and then, before signing up, received permission to go ashore for our dunnage bags, hoping to talk Larson into releasing them. At Sailors'

Union Hall my friend found a letter from home enclosing a twenty-dollar bill. Then and there Uncle Sam lost two promising recruits. On the following day Erickson, the union agent, shipped me as quartermaster on the steamer *Santa Rosa*.*

All went well for a matter of six months; then I ran across a former shipmate, Mortimer Swanson. Mortimer, a husky Swede, had quit the sea to become valet and masseur to Philadelphia Jack O'Brien, the fighter, and at that time was on loan to Tommy Burns, in training to defend his world's championship title against Bill Squires, champion of Australia. I had heard much of Squires while in the Land Down Under, and when I learned that my friend Mortimer was on the staff of the world's champion, I determined to see the fight which was set for July 4, 1907, at Colma, near San Francisco. As the *Santa Rosa* would be at sea on that day, I quit my job and purchased a ringside seat for the "battle of the century."

The streetcar men were on strike, so with several others I climbed aboard a rickety horse-drawn wagon and bounced over cobblestones for two hours, reaching the fight arena as the great epic was about to begin. My ringside seat was already occupied. The interloper refused to vacate, so an usher attempted to eject him just as the bell clanged to start the first round. I heard a sudden roar, looked around, and there on the canvas, being counted out, was Australia's pride and joy, Bill Squires. Needless to say, the disputed seat was quickly vacated. And while the bewildered Mr. Squires was being led from the scene, I battled the mob for the privilege of bouncing back to town in a homemade jaunting car.

Out of a job again, I gravitated to my former haunts. In little more than a year the Barbary Coast had been rejuvenated. Gaudy but flimsy buildings had already taken root over blackened ruins on Pacific Street, with only here and there a gaping space littered with debris and reminiscent of hectic days and

* Wrecked off Point Arguello on July 7, 1911.

nights of not so long ago. The still familiar names were there: Parente's, Fat Daugherty's, Spider Kelly's, the Montana, the California, the O.K., the Crutch, and Cowboy Mag's.

At the Thalia, newly revived by Mike Riley and Red Kelly, I found, as master of ceremonies, my old friend Frank Gardner, late of the Klondike and still later of Aberdeen's Eagle Dance Hall. Through Gardner I met the Hedges brothers, Freddy and Alvin, a pair of entertainers. They were heading for Gold-field, Nevada, then at its lurid best, or worst. Before the evening was over, I had wangled from them a card of introduction to the Palace Club in Reno.

At the Palace I was hired to sing with a three-piece orchestra under a character known as Cowboy Newman. High above the gambling tables was a platform enclosed by a guardrail, prob-ably to prevent orchestra members from interfering with the gambling by dropping into the spinning roulette wheel. The ceiling was low and when I stood up and tried to make myself heard above the noises around me, my dizzy noggin seemed to float in a mixture of stale tobacco smoke and the scent of body odors wafted upward from the perspiring throng below. It was not difficult to understand why the job was vacant, but I was in need of the pay, so I managed to hang on a week before con-tinuing south to Tonopah.

The casino, center of Tonopah's night life, was something to see. Half the size of a city block, it sported a large orchestra and a staff of pretty girls who served as dancing or drinking partners. They received a percentage on drinks served, plus substantial gratuities on occasion. They wore the usual thin silk blouse cut extremely low, skirts well above the knee and the always inter-esting black silk stockings held in place by fancy garters.

Except for the few off-shift gambling-house employees and the ever-present pimps and *maqueros,* who kept a watchful eye on their pretty meal tickets, practically all patrons of the casino were miners, spending their off-shift time under the bright lights instead of in the miserable shacks they called home. Their trousers were stuffed into the tops of high boots and few bothered to remove caps or helmets even while dancing.

Only seven years before, the spot which was Tonopah had been sand and sagebrush, marked only by a hidden spring known to a few hardy prospectors who lived and starved on the desert in the hope of some day stumbling on another Comstock Lode. According to legend, one Lazy Jim Butler, taking shelter behind a ledge for protection from a sandstorm, had idly chipped off a few pieces of rock. The specimens looked interesting, so he took them to an assayer friend who, in return for a half interest, found that the samples assayed several hundred dollars a ton, and the rush was on.

From a nucleus of the first dozen claim stakers, headed by Lazy Jim, Tonopah soon boasted a population of fifty thousand souls. A few months later in 1902 rich gold deposits were unearthed thirty miles to the south, and Goldfield was born. Its growth was even more spectacular, reaching twenty thousand population at its peak in 1907. Then Rhyolite burst into being like a skyrocket, boomed to a population of seven thousand in two years and in another year had completed the cycle back to the starting point: nothing.

Also reflected in the glamour and temporary prosperity of Goldfield and Tonopah were Rawhide, Bullfrog, and Searchlight, but after a short day in the sun each in turn took its place with Virginia City, Eureka, Austin, and other Nevada ghost towns. In midsummer of 1907 most of these boom towns were at their peak, particularly Goldfield.

Main Street, only a few blocks long, was lined on both sides with one-story gambling houses, restaurants and small shops. At the end of the street were dance halls and swanky "parlor houses," and beyond were the "cribs" and "bull pens" where red lights burned until dimmed by the rising desert sun.

On the four corners at Main Street and Crook Avenue were

the Northern, Palace, Mohawk and Hermitage. Farther along were the Oriental, Mint, Phoenix and Combination. Largest and best known was the famous Northern owned jointly by Tex Rickard, late of Nome, Alaska, and Ole Elliott, one of Goldfield's founders. Its bar was nearly a half block long and in the foreground were roulette, crap, blackjack and faro tables.

The Palm Grill was the best supper club in town, a kind of oasis in the desert, where fine foods brought from Reno in special iced chests were served along with the choicest of wines. Its patrons included the top mine and resort owners, the big-shot gamblers and visiting celebrities.

After several weeks working in the Hedges brothers' own club, I was boosted into a spot at the Palm and then I was really in the money. Working with only two musicians, one a pianist, the other a marvelous violinist known only as Julius, was to roam among the diners singing request numbers. Our fee was nine dollars, the union scale (paid each evening in cash), but the wage was insignificant compared to the harvest of tips which among us averaged from fifty to seventy-five silver dollars nightly.

Like all other places in town, however, the Palm had dice and roulette tables, and they gathered in the silver disks almost as fast as we earned them. Occasionally I made a killing but that only meant transferring operations to the dance halls down the line. Win or lose, I was always broke in the morning, but when night came there I was at the Palm, black trousers, white pongee silk shirt and fancy black tie, mingling with people whose names made news.

And Goldfield did have its share of names. Three of them, Tasker L. Oddie, George Nixon, and Key Pittman, became United States Senators, and a fourth, Nixon's partner, George Wingfield, later became Nevada's most influential banker. Frank Golden of Reno, Tom Kendal, founder of the Tonopah Club, and Ole Elliott were part and parcel of the town, and

Death Valley Scotty loved to change large bills into silver dollars and toss them into the crowds.

Broadway was represented by Nat Goodwin, Edna Goodrich and Lew Dockstader. The Gans-Nelson world's championship fight not only put Goldfield on the map but started its promoter, Tex Rickard, on the way to fame and the management of New York's Madison Square Garden.

The Goldfield of 1907 was wild, woolly and glamorous. It was prosperous to a fabulous degree and the question naturally arises, From whence came the flow of gold that supported the elaborate gambling palaces and other wide-open spots? True, the gold came from the Jumbo, the Red Top, the Mohawk and other mining properties near by, but under normal conditions the take from the mines would funnel out of the community through regular banking channels.

Part of the answer was what is known as "high grading," which meant that literally tons of rich ore were smuggled out of the mines piecemeal by individual miners willing to work for low wages while illegally augmenting their regular earnings many times over.

Small amounts of selected ore were brought out in pockets, lunch pails and even special canvas belts worn next to the skin. Shift foremen as well as the mine owners knew what was going on and tried to control it, but with leases due to expire on specified dates and time very much the essence, they could not afford trouble with the miners which might involve possible shutdowns. They had no choice but to work the mines night and day while still under lease and allow the miners to share in the haul, until finally it was a question as to who profited most, the owner or the miner.

With the mines working three shifts daily, and the miners unloading their "high grade" profits on the town, with bartenders and gambling-house employees earning twelve dollars a shift, Goldfield boomed and "the goose hung high."

In the fall of 1907, however, the golden bubble burst when the Mine Owners Association decided that enough was plenty and ordered "change rooms"; under the eyes of watchers the men were required to change clothes after each shift. The miners went on strike. The IWW moved in and began organizing various labor groups and caused more disturbances.

Then came the 1907 panic that hit Goldfield along with the rest of the nation. When the mine owners began using "clearinghouse certificates" to pay off miners who were digging out a million dollars in gold each month, the miners struck once again.

Violence broke out and at the request of Nevada's Governor Sparks, President Theodore Roosevelt ordered troops to Goldfield under General Frederick Funston. When the strike was called off and troops withdrawn in March of 1908, most of the town's color and glamour had faded. "High grading" was at an end, gambling houses began to fold and Goldfield subsided into just another mining town.

Tex Rickard sold his half of the famous Northern and with Nat Goodwin, the actor, and George Graham Rice, well-known promoter, started the town of Rawhide. From nothing, Rawhide doubled its population each week or so until at the end of three months it boasted ten thousand souls. Soon there were dance halls, gambling houses, and even churches. Rawhide actually produced a million dollars in gold and many times that in beautifully lithographed mining certificates, but a few months later it was only a name and a memory.

Goldfield settled down after its troubles of 1907-8 and though less colorful than in the golden days of "high grading," produced nearly one hundred million in gold before the mines finally closed in 1919. Swept by fire in 1923 and deserted by its few remaining inhabitants, it stands today just a scar on the desert. Gone are the Northern, the Mohawk, the Palm. Gone are the silk-shirted entertainers, the stony-eyed faro lookouts, the Wingfields and Nixons, the Goldens and Pittmans.

As for me, my finish as an entertainer and the partial eclipse of Goldfield occurred about the same time. Alone in a small shack on the outskirts of town, I was stricken with fever late in October of 1907, lay unconscious and delirious for several days and almost passed out without benefit of physician or clergy before a searching party from the Palm decided my prolonged absence must be due to something more serious than a hangover. By November I had recovered sufficiently to leave for the Coast, incidentally on borrowed funds despite all of the easy money that had come my way.

∗ 29 ∗

ONCE AGAIN I turned to the sea, this time as able seaman on the passenger steamer *Roanoke,*∗ but left her a few months later to become first mate on the *Ethel Zane,* a three-master. While on this voyage Captain William Tornstrom reminded me that the day of the sailing ship was passing and advised me to put in a year or two in steam and then try for a master's license. Accordingly, I shifted to the steam-schooner trade.

Besides working ship at sea, sailors were also required to work cargo while in port, so in order to get the most out of the men the skippers of these lumber *droghers* became experts at timing.

After stowing lumber all day in a northern port we put to sea about dark, took our trick at the wheel or lookout and always managed to dock in San Francisco early enough to turn to for a full day's work. After a quick meal and an evening on Pacific Street, we rolled into our bunks about daylight, turned to

∗ The *Roanoke* was wrecked several years later off Eureka with forty-five lives lost.

again at seven, and before dark that night were again headed out through the Golden Gate.

My ship, the *Grace Dollar*, sometimes loaded at what was known as an "outside port." Instead of tying up at the dock in a protected harbor, the ship was made fast to floating buoys in the open sea a few hundred yards offshore.

Heavy hawsers from bow and stern passed through rings on the buoys, and in cases of a sudden blow the lines were slipped, allowing the ship to put safely to sea. From a point high on the hillside a cable was brought down to the moored vessel and made fast to a shorter cable stretched between the ship's two masts. Slingloads of lumber traveled on this cable from a temporary rail terminal on the hill down to the floating ship.

On my second trip, while moored opposite Albion, California, I met with an accident that practically ended my seafaring career. As slingloads of redwood ties were dropped through the hatchways down in the ship's hold, we crew members stowed them in tiers reaching to the deckbeams above. A heavy ground swell caused the ship to lurch badly, and as the starboard side rose high, a dozen ties broke loose and crashed over me, the only casualty.

I was hoisted on deck bleeding like a stuck pig and with a broken right leg. Moorings were slipped and the ship raced to San Francisco where I was taken to the Marine Hospital. Broken bones were set and other injuries attended to under Dr. Alanson Weeks, but it was months before I was discharged on November 2, 1908, still hobbling on crutches.

The accident stopped me in more ways than one. During the weeks of convalescence in the hospital the hours were lightened by visits from my girl friend, Miss Edythe L. Deu Vaul. Possibly the crutches interfered with my usual speed, or maybe we were inspired by the romantic surroundings, but in any event we became engaged while sitting on a hilltop overlooking a graveyard where rows of white headstones marked the last resting places of men who went to sea in ships.

On leaving the hospital I decided to make one final voyage to acquire a nest egg before marrying. By a coincidence the berth I landed was second mate on the same old barkentine *Wrestler* on which I had left Santa Rosalia after deserting from the *Celticburn* years before.

We loaded in Astoria, Oregon, discharged cargo in San Pedro and had returned north to Portland when Captain Björnstrom received orders to load lumber for Callao, Peru. I was tempted to make just one more offshore voyage, when I received word from my future wife to come back or else. I took the hint.

In San Francisco it was June; we were on our honeymoon and in my pockets were two hundred dollars. We rented a beautiful apartment that even boasted a piano. I spent half of my nest egg the first week and half of our remaining funds the next week. The sailor was in the saddle again.

Nearly broke, I wandered from place to place looking for work. We rented a wretched room on McAllister Street for $1.25 a week and cut our meals to fifty cents a day. Each morning I scanned the advertisements hoping someone might have a job that only a sailor could do, such as painting flagpoles or smokestacks. To my troubled wife I broached the possibility of making one more sea voyage, then learned to my consternation that a baby was expected in the spring. I gave up the idea.

The greatest obstacle to securing employment was lack of a union card. Each morning I trudged several miles over the Fillmore Street hills to the Labor Temple on Fourteenth Street and pleaded with the agent of the Laborers' Union for a job, any job. He was nice enough about it and promised to give me a chance if jobs came in and no union men were available.

I canvassed the city but had no luck except to earn an occasional quarter or half dollar doing odd jobs. When a break did come it was indirectly brought about by a tragic accident.

American in the Rough

At that time, in the year 1909, it was the practice of certain companies employing large groups of laborers to pay off, not in cash, but by a time check that must either be held several weeks until maturity date or discounted for cash. This dubious practice was brought sharply to public attention in San Francisco when a laborer employed by a construction company, after being handed such a check, demanded cash and when refused shot and killed a young woman cashier.

As a result of the scandal members of labor unions refused to accept work on such jobs. When a call came for laborers to do pick and shovel work on Brannan Street, the agent refused to send union men but told me about it. With nothing to lose, I reported and was put to work digging sewer trenches. Such work is hard at best, but we were digging down through debris left from the fire of 1906 and the going was tough. When I swung my pick from shoulder height, it crashed against slabs of asphalt or concrete and the impact sent sharp pains through every part of my body. By five o'clock I felt as groggy as a prize fighter saved by the bell. The work lasted six days. Instead of the time check expected, I was given twelve dollars in cash and told to report on another job next morning. Climbing the stairway to our room, carrying the first good food we had been able to buy for weeks, I felt like shouting from sheer happiness.

There would still be times in my life when poverty and want would be too close for comfort, but in looking back I think the turning point came after that first day on Brannan Street when I dragged my weary feet home, shoved my pick and shovel under the bed and slept like a dead man after earning my first real money in several months.

My next job was excavation work for the new St. Luke's Church at Van Ness and Clay Streets, and on Thanksgiving Eve when I was handed six dollars for three days' work and told to report back again, my cup of happiness overflowed. We

237

purchased a regular holiday feast at a near-by delicatessen and paid up a little more back rent. It was indeed Thanksgiving for us.

Next morning while busy shoveling sand, I saw bad news show up in the person of the fat walking delegate of the Laborers' Union with a demand for a fifteen-dollar initiation fee. I compromised by agreeing to pay two dollars each week and received a temporary union card. A week later I was hired by the C. J. Lindgren Company for work on the new ten-story Y.M.C.A. building.

I was first put to work stripping lumber from concrete forms, but when the foreman learned that I was a former sailor able to splice ropes and wires and rig tackles, I was transferred to a rigging crew working on the iron beams far above the street. It was our task to rig up tackles and to haul lumber and other materials to the upper floors. High up in the air we scurried back and forth, walking the two-inch steel beams, balancing lengths of lumber like tightrope walkers performing under the big top. It was exciting, almost like being back aboard ship. In fact, when the noonday whistle sounded it was my daily custom to step off into space and slide eight or ten stories down the rope falls to the sidewalk below. Just a throwback to the old sailing days.

Large groups of men were laid off and rehired from time to time, depending upon availability of materials, but my work as a handyman kept me on the job during the entire construction period, except for a few weeks when I was transferred to work on the new Olympic Club building under construction by the same contractor.

Although my pay was only eleven dollars for a five-and-a-half-day week, we prospered and soon were able to move into a furnished three-room cottage perched high on the side of Twin Peaks, where preparations were made for the next big event. On April 4, 1910, came the big day and a son, Robert, was born. He was a large, fine child, apparently strong and healthy, but eleven days later he suddenly passed away, and our months of planning dissolved like thin air.

After nearly a year on the Y.M.C.A building my next contribution to the architectural beauty of San Francisco was on the new Hall of Justice, where I carried sacks of cement on my shoulder, not for days, not for weeks, but for months. I would pick up a hundred-pound sack, toss it over my shoulder, walk up a series of runways to the floors above, drop it and return for another. Our city, San Francisco, has a well-built Hall of Justice. I should know.

In May of 1911 when the new Y.M.C.A. had been open to the public for several months, I applied to Chief Engineer Phillips for the job of elevator operator. He was anxious to help, but no operators were needed. Suddenly he remarked, "They are looking for a swimming instructor here. You were a sailor. Why not apply?"

First, it struck me as ridiculous; then something clicked inside. Why not, indeed. What have I to lose?

Mr. Phillips was all for arranging an immediate interview which could have had only one result. Instead, at my suggestion, the time was set for the following day.

First, I purchased a Spalding textbook titled *The Art of Swimming* and spent hours soaking up technical information on the crawl, trudgeon and breast stroke. Then followed a visit to Professor John A. Jackson at Lurline Baths, who, for the modest fee of three dollars, undertook to make an expert of me in three hours. At home, later, I spent more hours balanced on my stomach over a stool, perfecting the hand and foot movements which Professor Jackson had taught me. After a few hours' sleep I was up and at the exercises again, topping them off with more hours of book learning.

By the time I was ushered into the presence of the general secretary, Noel C. Jacks, and the physical director, H. M. Strickler, I had almost convinced myself that I was good. Mr. Jacks opened the interview by stating that the man they were seeking must have the quality of leadership, not only in the physical sense but in the spiritual sense as well; he must love little boys; he must have led a righteous and just life; and—oh, yes—he must be able to teach swimming not only to individuals but to large groups as well. The salary would be seventy-five dollars a month. Did I feel that I could qualify?

With a few mental reservations I readily admitted possessing the necessary qualifications, explained how fond I was of little boys and then opened up with a barrage of conversation describing the various swimming strokes, including techniques for training young and old, single, double, and in herds. As a final wallop, I drew a chair into the middle of the room, balanced myself on it and demonstrated the arm and leg action that I had acquired practically overnight from Professor Jackson and the Spalding textbook. They were quite impressed and, to my relief, did not ask for an actual demonstration in the pool below. They suggested a probationary period of three months. The following morning I was installed in a small office alongside the pool, with a businesslike desk, a telephone and a sign over the door which read: PROFESSOR COFFMAN, SWIMMING INSTRUCTOR.

In such fashion came about the simple transition whereby he who had worked only with his hands would henceforth work with his noodle. Decked out in snappy swimming trunks, I was able to dispel any doubt that might have arisen over the "new professor's" prowess in the water, when it was noted that my arms and chest were elaborately embroidered with tattooed designs, indicating that I was perfectly at home in aquatic surroundings. However, the worst was yet to come. I had the job; now to hold it.

Using my first day on the job to scout the layout, I noted that when the gym class was dismissed some sixty young sprouts from eight to twelve years of age stampeded pell-mell down several flights of back stairs, discarding gym shorts en route, and plunged directly into the pool, attired in nature's own bathing suit. After half an hour of splashing and shrieking, they were cleared out of the pool and sent on their way. I confess to feeling a bit panicky at the prospect of changing their routine.

When the time came to take over, I was slightly nervous, especially when several upstairs officials showed up as spectators. Soon there was a muffled roar and a minute later the mass of naked humanity catapulted down the stairs, where they were intercepted and lined up against the wall facing the pool.

In a short talk I explained that they would be taught to swim the famous Australian crawl, that each boy had it within himself to become a champion and that special prizes would be awarded each boy who perfected the stroke. Then, with sixty pairs of startled eyes focused upon me, I balanced my midriff over a piano stool and went into the movements of the crawl stroke.

Body balanced in a perfectly flat position, head and chest fairly high, eyes level with the body, arm reaching over arm, hand engaging the imaginary water in a downward and backward press, with elbow slightly tilted. Next, the rhythmic drive of the legs with six up and down beats to each full cycle of left and right arms.

Actually, the demonstration, while impressive, was quite easy to master after hours of practice, and I had a hunch the kids would be eager to try it. Soon I had sixty boys balanced over a long row of benches, going first through the arm drill, then the leg drill, after which they were dismissed with instructions to practice at home on a chair. I felt satisfied with my first effort, as did the "Y" officials.

The second lesson was a duplication of the first, but I had a surprise for the third. After ten minutes of land drill devoted to synchronizing the arm and leg action, the class slid into the pool and practiced the leg movement only, while stretched full

length in the water and with fingers lightly clutching the overflow gutter. Then with a pair of water wings placed under the
stomach of each to add confidence, they were instructed to
shove off and put arm and leg practice into actual use. Soon
dozens of water wings were being discarded when they found
themselves able to use the balanced crawl stroke without aid.
After another couple of lessons only a few of the most timid
were reluctant to discard the water wings and these soon qualified after a little individual attention. In less than thirty days
the "professor" was being interviewed by the press for the first
time in his life, and large picture layouts were published in
the local papers, featuring mass teaching of swimming at the
Y.M.C.A.

With the boys' classes well under way, Physical Director
Strickler suggested that I apply for a sanction to hold the annual
swimming championships of the Pacific A.A.U. With well-
feigned enthusiasm I agreed that it was a splendid idea. I had
never heard of the A.A.U. nor witnessed a swimming meet, but
with a little help from the Olympic Club's famous coach, Syd
Cavill, not to mention my Spalding guide, sanction was granted
to hold the championships on August 11, 1911.

Besides having to master the mechanics of conducting an
event of such importance, for which, incidentally, there would
be a substantial admission fee, I realized with some misgivings
that I was expected to produce a representative team to com-
pete against the club swimmers, whose roster included J. Scott
Leary, national record holder; William McWood, Coast champion; and Walter Pomeroy and George Bond who were soon to
gain fame as the first to swim the Golden Gate.

Keeping an eagle eye on the most promising of the "Y's"
older boys, I began haunting the Lurline and Sutro Baths
hoping to pick up some outside talent. Then I heard of two
high-school swimmers, Ernest M. Smith of Lowell and Lincoln

V. Johnson of Cogswell. Both were wary about signing up with an unknown coach, but I won them over. Among my best prospects was a husky youngster named Christofer Theophilous; later he became known as Jim Londos, world's champion wrestler.

The Pacific A.A.U. championships were held before a packed gallery and with surprising results. My boys took most of the honors. Later, Johnson was to be accorded a special tryout for America's Olympic Games team; Bab Small was to be the first to defeat the celebrated Duke Kahanamoku, and Ernie Smith, now a well-known sportscaster, was to become the Pacific Coast champion. Apparently I had qualified well within the ninety-day probationary period.

Said the *Chronicle:*

"There was great joy in the Y.M.C.A. last evening when the swimming teams defeated the strong sextet of the Olympic Club. W. M. Coffman, swimming coach, expressed his pleasure by jumping into the pool, clothes and all. Syd Cavill, Olympic coach, felt like jumping in himself, but having on his best suit, refrained."

In January of 1913, when presenting a bang-up show, including back stroke and breast stroke events for the first time in California, I experimented a little further by presenting a hundred-yard dash exclusively for ladies. This immediately brought forth a mighty roar from the national A.A.U. secretary, James E. Sullivan, who wired from New York to ask what the heck I meant by featuring races for women, who at that time were not recognized by the Amateur Athletic Union.

My aquatic promotions had drawn hundreds of spectators and had also made a substantial profit for the Y.M.C.A. Recalling the tremendous crowds at the Redondo Beach Natatorium, it occurred to me that even greater audiences could be attracted to Sutro Baths at the ocean beach. Sutro, the largest indoor baths in the world, was built almost entirely of glass, and the largest of its seven tanks was 75 feet wide by 300 feet long, with seats for seventy-five hundred spectators.

Calling upon Dr. Emma L. Merritt, executrix of the Sutro Estate, I offered to promote the most ambitious aquatic event ever staged in the West. I explained that Duke Kahanamoku had emerged from the Stockholm Olympiad as the most spectacular swimmer the world had ever seen and that with Duke as the key attraction, Sutro Baths could be filled to capacity for the first time and gain world-wide publicity as well. I offered to serve without compensation. On my promise to hold the total expense under four thousand dollars, I was told to go ahead on my first big promotion that would either make or break me.

Having no contacts in Honolulu, I wrote directly to Duke and offered full expenses for himself and a trainer. The invitation was accepted by William J. Rawlins, president of Honolulu's Hui Nalu Club. Then, I announced that Honolulu's Chamber of Commerce would send not only Duke but a total of fourteen Hawaiians.

The newspapers devoted entire pages to the event.

On July 4, crowds stormed Sutro Baths, filling the seventy-five hundred seats and all standing-room space. As was expected, Duke won the 50, the 200, and the 440, setting new Pacific Coast records in each. My breast-stroke swimmer, Guy de Villepion, an unknown, broke the American fifty-yard record. Next day, before another sellout crowd, the sensational Duke swam the fastest hundred yards ever recorded. Wrote Ed Kneas in the *Chronicle* of July 6: "The meet was a record breaker and followers of swimming have never witnessed anything to compare with it. All credit goes to W. M. Coffman of the Y.M.C.A. who worked night and day to put it over."

I had indeed worked night and day on it. Receipts over expenses amounted to thousands of dollars, and I was mildly expectant that my efforts would be rewarded, but the executrix

of the Sutro Estate never offered me a thin dime. With her, a
bargain was a bargain. I had agreed to serve for nothing and
that's how it would be. However, my superiors considered it
good advertising for the Y.M.C.A. and rewarded me with my
first increase, raising my salary to eighty-five dollars a month.

Being now in the money, I purchased a cheap lot at
379 Rolph Street, paying installments of ten dollars a month.
For ten dollars I purchased a set of plans and then negotiated
installment contracts for lumber and millwork, cement, hard-
ware, plaster, plumbing, paint and electrical work. These obli-
gations totaled fifty dollars a month, leaving little enough for
rent, food and incidentals, and God help us in case of illness or
accident.

Under the guidance of the carpenter who sold me the building plans, I made the wooden forms, mixed and poured the concrete foundations and laid the rough flooring. Then followed
three weeks of sawing the studding, roof rafters, girders, and
ceiling joists into proper lengths as provided for in the specifi-
cations.

On the fourth Sunday, with one helper, I put the entire skel-
eton framework together, after which, with only the assistance
of Edythe, my wife, I shingled the roof and closed in the four
sides with weather boarding. Window and door frames were
installed, window sashes were fitted into position, front and
back doors were hung, and by the first of September 1913, almost before the plaster was dry, we moved our few pieces of
furniture into the house.

It was like camping out, but from then on I could work on
the interior at all hours, day or night. More important still,
there was no more rent to pay.

* 30 *

AFTER SUCH a highly successful aquatic show at Sutro Baths, Dr. Emma Merritt suggested that I repeat it on July 4-5, 1914, on a much larger scale. I agreed on condition that I receive all profits from the printed program.

While Duke Kahanamoku undoubtedly was the world's outstanding *individual* swimmer, I knew that the Illinois Athletic Club of Chicago had assembled the greatest all-round team in America. Financial terms were soon agreed to by William Bachrach, the coach who later developed champion swimmer Johnny Weissmuller.

Early in 1914 I was called to the office of the general secretary, Ralph C. Goodwin, and to my surprise was greeted by Dr. Merritt. The executrix of the Sutro Estate, it seems, was there to offer me the management of the big baths at a salary double that which I was then receiving. In a daze I heard Mr. Goodwin explaining to the good doctor that while I was in duty bound to remain with the Y.M.C.A. for another year, having just received a *ten-dollar* advance in salary, he, the general secretary, would not stand in my way. Rather he would suggest that I take an indefinite leave of absence while remaining in charge of the "Y" swimming department, with a substitute* to carry on until such time as I should elect to resume my duties or remain away permanently. (As that understanding was later put in writing, I presume that I am still privileged to call myself "Professor," despite not having used my little office alongside the pool for some thirty years.)

* The vacated position was taken over by Mr. George Lineer, now swimming expert of the S. F. *Chronicle*.

As anticipated, the three-day tournament proved a terrific success; it attracted nearly twenty thousand spectators, who left the baths well satisfied after watching California's Ludy Langer defeat Kahanamoku in the half-mile and later defeat the equally great Perry McGilvray in a sensational quarter-mile battle that established a new world's record. They also saw Duke defeat McGilvray by a matter of inches in the furlong and then lead Raithel to the tape in the hundred. Hebner set a new American record for the back stroke, and McDermott did the same in the breast stroke. Raithel, Hebner, Vosburgh and Mott proved themselves America's fastest quartet in the relay.

With the big show now only a matter for the record books, I settled down to the new job. Heretofore, my dealings with Dr. Merritt had been only on a casual basis, but now as my new boss, I found the seventy-year-old daughter of the fabulous Adolph Sutro to be a remarkable character in her own right.

Prussian-born Adolph Sutro had reached California in 1851 just after the discovery of gold. A mining engineer, rather than a miner, he staked no claims and dug no gold, but when the famous Comstock property in Virginia City became unworkable because of the constant seepage of water into its vitals, Sutro, the engineer, worked out a tunneling project which eventually changed the Comstock Lode from a liability to a multimillion-dollar asset. In the process he battled the powerful William Sharon and other bonanza kings in the courts, fought the silver lobby in Washington and, at times, even participated in gang fights with the men who worked in the mines. Then, penniless, after establishing his legal rights, he was forced to borrow the necessary funds in Europe to complete the project.

With his share of the profits he proceeded to buy up land grants involving thousands of acres of sand dunes as well as miles of bay frontage extending completely around Land's End in San Francisco, to and including the high ground on which the Cliff House now stands. He fenced in several acres of wooded land on a prominent eminence overlooking the Pacific Ocean (now Sutro Heights, owned by the city), built himself a mansion on its crest, imported a shipload of beautiful statuary which he placed along the shaded footpaths and in his sunken gardens and there he lived like a feudal prince of old.

Far below, he could see the ocean waves pounding against the rocky cliffs at Land's End, sending spray high in the air. Being an engineer as well as a dreamer, he resolved to harness that falling spray by building a great concrete catch-basin at the edge of the rocks from which the sea water could drain into a settling pool. Then it could be channeled into a set of tanks enclosed in glass and become the largest indoor baths in the world.

He built several breakwaters and watched each disappear into the ocean before his problem was finally solved. When completed, the vast institution had six pools kept at varying temperatures ranging from an ice-cold fresh-water plunge to the mammoth tank of unheated sea water that flowed in by gravity from the outside catch basin.

Above, great laminated trusses of curved wood resting on steel columns supported acres of corrugated glass panes tinted in various colors. These were imported from Europe. Its glassed-in roof and sides gave the appearance of an enormous conservatory, and the effect was heightened by giant palm trees that grew fifty feet high in terraced spaces on either side of the wide main stairways.

Far above the tanks, on the main entrance floor, was a museum housing exhibits from the Mid-Winter Fair of 1898. After spending fully a million dollars on his pet project, Sutro, in order to bring the public to the baths, built his own steam railway from downtown San Francisco over a scenic route skirting the cliffs to its terminal at the very entrance to the baths.

Elected mayor, Adolph Sutro apparently gave the city an excellent administration, but during his incumbency his personal reputation was tarnished by gossip that he furnished large sums of money for the defense of Theodore Durrant, then on trial for the murder of Blanche Lamont and Minnie Williams in the bell tower of Emanuel Baptist Church.

When it became known that Durrant's mother had at one time served as housekeeper for Mr. Sutro, there was speculation of a possible close relationship between the man on trial for murder and the city's chief executive; but nothing came of the rumors and in due time Durrant was convicted and executed.

During my three years of close association with her, not only did Dr. Merritt glory in the name and achievements of her father, believing that he could do no wrong, but she also believed so implicitly in the works he had left behind that no material changes were allowed to be made in the physical layout of either the baths or the Cliff House.

From the beginning the baths had been an expensive hobby, losing a fortune annually, and in her special office on the Heights we engaged in many bitter quarrels, particularly when I continued to advocate throwing out the musty old museum and replacing it with money-making concessions. This included freezing the big tank to accomodate ice skating, hockey, and bathing under the same roof. (All of this has since been done, but, alas, the good doctor was not there to see it.)

Despite the quarrels, however, on evenings when the baths were kept open, I was always a special dinner guest in the home on the Heights. The setting never changed. At one end of the long table sat Dr. Emma, a very gracious hostess. At the other end sat her husband, Dr. George. Servants tiptoed in and out serving the finest of foods to all except Dr. Emma. In front of her they placed a large bowl of nuts on which she complacently munched throughout the meal.

On those occasions business was seldom discussed, and it was then that she liked to talk of her beloved father. When "good nights" were said, however, the truce was off. Next morning she invariably popped through the turnstiles at seven and went directly to her dressing room. The vision that emerged a few minutes later was something that made one instinctively cover his eyes. Her scrawny figure was draped from head to toe in a chic little number that would have shriveled a scarcecrow with envy. Proceeding to the big tank, she would back down the ladder, rung by rung, until the water reached her earrings; then she would strike out with a snappy breast stroke for a few yards, climb out of the tank and scurry back to her little nest like a frightened bird.

At eight o'clock her secretary, Miss Johnson, would show up with notebook and poised pencil, and the daily inspection tour was on. Upstairs and down, through dressing rooms, men's and women's toilets, laundry, engine room and finally into the very bowels of the building, examining concrete foundations and testing steel piers, the doctor dictated and Miss Johnson took notes in shorthand.

There was only one flaw in Dr. Emma's system. Miss Johnson simply could not keep up to date on the doctor's voluminous dictation, with the result that each day a messenger from the Heights would hand me a batch of neatly typed slips from which it might be noted that on a day three weeks past green slime was observed on the bottom step of stairway two, tank five.

The informative notes went quickly into the waste basket, but the doctor had done her duty and we were both happy.

Although the long irregular hours and the strain of dealing with such an eccentric character were very trying, the new job had its compensations. Not only did the difference in earnings enable me to meet long-overdue bills, but when our first daughter, Virginia, was born on July 30, 1914, bringing additional problems of financing, we found ourselves completely solvent for a change, which was something just short of miraculous.

When plans began smoking up for the Panama Pacific International Exposition in 1915, I was one of a group selected by the president, Charles C. Moore, to present a suitable aquatic program. Then through a shift in control I suddenly found myself in full charge. I soon convinced the exposition management and A.A.U. authorities that a show of such magnitude should be held in the fully equipped Sutro Natatorium rather than in the open waters of the Yacht Harbor.

Coast and local contests were disposed of early in the month and then we squared away for the great events of the World's Fair. Contestants included the Illinois Athletic Club's Hebner, McGilvray, Raithel and McDermott; New York Athletic Club's Joe Wheatley, Bud Goodwin, Arthur McAleenan and Al Downs; Kahanamoku, Stubby Kruger and others from Hawaii; Smith, Johnson and Resleure of San Francisco; Langer of Los Angeles; Laubis of St. Louis; Fereday of New Orleans; and the up-and-coming Norman Ross of Portland, Oregon.

Before an almost hysterical audience that jam-packed every foot of space in the big natatorium, Duke defeated all comers in both the 50 and the 220, swam neck and neck in a dead heat with Raithel in the 100 and then, when a swim-off was ordered, won by inches in new world's record time. Hebner cracked the world's record in winning the back stroke. McDermott did likewise in the breast stroke, Ludy Langer defeated both McGilvray and Joe Wheatley in a roaring 500 yards and, to top it off, the Illinois Athletic Club set a new world's record in winning the relay.

Never before or since have I witnessed such sensational competition, and I include events of the Tenth Olympiad held seventeen years later in Los Angeles, events in which I had a special interest as assistant manager of the American swimming team.

With the exposition over, I was glad to forget competition and resume my duties in and around the baths, where things were always happening to keep life from getting too dull. Either the lifeguards would be using the pulmotor on some matron who forgot to close her mouth when going down the third time, or Miss Hazel Laugenour, the outdoor athlete, would be making another attempt to swim around the Seal Rocks, or further down the beach, the mounted officer, Arthur Dolan, would be riding his horse into the surf and using his famous lasso to haul out another would-be suicide.

Or perhaps something very unusual would happen, such as the morning I was seeking the manager of the Cliff House. Climbing a ladder leaning against the building, I found him chasing the Filipino cook across the roof top. The trembling cook had a carving knife in his hand, but it was hardly adequate against the butcher's cleaver carried by the man chasing him.

Perhaps my sudden appearance saved the cook's life and the irate manager's neck. Shortly afterward, this sweet-tempered character, since gone to his reward, gave up his lease of the Cliff House to manage two of America's most famous hotels. Nice guy!

Then there was the time we were publicly accused of stealing the famous Seal Rocks! Under certain weather conditions turbulent seas smashed sections of the glass in our west wall, so we decided to build a concrete breakwater between the baths and the nearest rock. Work had proceeded openly for several weeks when suddenly newspapers reported in headlines that "someone, either in the dead of night, or in the heart of a fog, is craftily building a bridge to an island in the Pacific Ocean."

There was a great hullabaloo while the city's Park Commission and the U. S. Surveyor General promised to investigate the rights of the Sutro Estate. Nothing came of it, however, but in the meantime, further damage from the waves was averted and at last reports the breakwater is still there.

Early in 1916 I began to think of holding a big meet on our traditional Fourth of July. The Amateur Athletic Union had enfranchised women athletes in November of 1914, but as yet no swimmer had clearly established a right to the hundred-yard national title.

There were many claimants, particularly Olga Dorffner of Philadelphia, Claire Galligan of New Rochelle, and Dorothy Burns of Los Angeles. Honolulu had its Bernice Lane, and San Francisco its Frances Cowells and Dorothy Becker. I guaranteed to pay the expenses of all major claimants and was awarded the affair by the A.A.U.

My troubles were many, including a serious squabble with Dr. Merritt, who insisted that the contestants wear racing suits equipped with concealing skirts, but A.A.U. rules won over modesty so presumably the dear lady watched the race through smoked glasses.

Miss Olga Dorffner established a new American record in winning over Claire Galligan with Dorothy Burns third. As most of the girls looked well in sleek racing suits, the news services gave us tremendous national publicity. Nearly five thousand spectators turned out to see what proved to be the last big-time swimming event held in San Francisco for many a year.

By then I was getting fed up both with the baths and its fussy owner, and after the birth of my second daughter, Donnie, on August 9, 1916, I began looking around for a way to better myself.

I answered an advertisement wherein a nationally known office equipment company offered an attractive proposition to salesmen who could qualify. To me, office equipment meant typewriters or adding machines, either of which I was willing to tackle, but I was completely flabbergasted to learn that the product was bookkeeping machines, something I had never even remotely heard of.

Mr. Wilkinson, the gentleman in the Monadnock Building who interviewed me, explained that his marvelous machines required little actual selling as they could do practically everything in a business office. With a writing surface "as flat as the desk used by the old-fashioned pen bookkeeper" it was only necessary to clamp ledger sheets and monthly statements in the machine, punch the necessary figures into its computing mechanism and presto the work was done and the books in balance. And now, what line had I been selling, and could he see my references, please?

Well, there was the letter from Captain Björnstrom of the *Wrestler* certifying to my character and seamanship, and one signed by the Y.M.C.A.'s president, Mr. Henry J. McCoy, praising my fitness as a teacher of young men. The bewildered Mr. Wilkinson scratched his head and suggested that I return next day for the answer.

Years later I learned that after a prolonged huddle between Mr. Wilkinson and his superior, Mr. F. F. Wright, they awarded me an A for ambition and an X for being an ex-sheepherder, sailor, and bathhouse manager. They decided to gamble seventy-five dollars of the company's money on a thirty-day trial, so on December 15, 1917, I receipted for a stack of textbooks on the complicated subject of bookkeeping machines and became a sales representative for the Elliott Fisher Company of Harrisburg, Pennsylvania.

It will never be my privilege to know whether I might have selected a finer firm to represent or a better product to sell. The company of my choice in the year 1917 in due time became an integral part of the great Underwood Corporation of today, and during the nearly forty years that have intervened I have known no other employer.

The word "employer" is synonymous with the name of Mr. Philip D. Wagoner, the man who became the company's president about the time this cub salesman was hired, and whose genius has guided its affairs smoothly and safely through several great mergers until today the Underwood Corporation stands pre-eminent in its field: the world's largest manufacturer of typewriters and other office equipment. Today, Mr. Philip D. Wagoner is chairman of Underwood's board of directors and I am proud to call him my friend.

There was another whom, because of his great tolerance and understanding and the love he bore his fellow men, I learned to look up to as a guide, an inspiration and a true and faithful friend. Frederick Fullerton Wright was the finest man I have ever known. No words, however carefully chosen, can say more. He fulfilled his mission and departed more than a decade ago, but to me the memory of him today is as vivid as on that morning in 1917 when he offered his hand and ushered a bewildered man into a new way of life.

Had I deliberately searched for a complicated way of earning a living, I doubt if I could have found anything more confusing or difficult than the work I had chosen. I was soon to learn that my task involved not merely the sale of a machine but rather the working out of accounting systems to which the machine could be adapted efficiently and with economy. Accounting problems, simple enough to a trained bookkeeper, hardly fitted in with my badly neglected educational background, and when I boned through the stuffy textbooks for answers, I wound up completely baffled and ready to throw in the sponge. Only my pride and the panicky realization that a man of thirty-four could not afford to change jobs too often kept me from quitting under fire.

Among other worries, I faced the serious problem of feeding and clothing a family of four on a guarantee of only seventy-five dollars a month. I owned an Overland sedan, but in the interest of economy used trolleys for transportation, occasionally paying a dime to ride in a jitney bus. Suddenly I saw the light and applied for a license as a jitney bus driver. In this manner I augmented my income by several dollars each day, carrying passengers for hire before nine each morning and after six each evening.

When summer came I made a deal with Mr. Bert York of Oakland's Idora Park. I would promote swimming meets in the Idora pool on Sundays at ten dollars each. I would also write and direct all swimming publicity, to be paid for at the rate of twenty-five cents per column inch. He agreed.

Selecting the prettiest of the girl swimmers, I dressed them in the sheerest of silk racing suits and engineered layouts of pictures in the Sunday papers, running up my space rates to a considerable sum.

By mere chance, after an exchange of correspondence with Australian athletic authorities concerning bringing Miss Fanny Durack, world's swimming champion, to America, a Mr. William Unmack and I became the innocent parties in a crossfire of charges and countercharges, mostly humorous, between Marion Salazar, sports editor of the *Bulletin,* and the *Call's* Scoop Gleeson. This filled columns of space, on which I naturally collected space rates from Idora Park until Manager York facetiously offered to trade jobs with me. With this extra money, augmented by occasional commissions from sales made with the help of more experienced men in the office, I struggled through the year 1918.

It took a long time to lick those confounded textbooks and to coax the right answers out of one of those damned machines, but by July 1, 1919, I had earned the right to attend the company's first convention at Harrisburg, and at year's end I received an engraved certificate from the president, Philip D. Wagoner, entitling me to membership in the exclusive All-Star Salesman's Club of 1919.

There were other All-Star honors, and then in July 1922 I was placed in charge of the company's San Francisco operations. Determined to make good on the new job, I became active in civic and business organizations, assuming the top office in several.

In the meantime, our little family needed more elbowroom, so in 1923 we sold the house on Rolph Street and used the proceeds to acquire a beautiful home in Westwood Park. Our fine new plans failed to work out, however, because shortly afterward, the health of my daughter Virginia, turned bad and on the advice of our doctor, Edythe and the two girls took up temporary residence in a milder climate at Long Beach, California.

✶ 31 ✶

THE FIRST East-West All Star football game, conceived as a ten-thousand-dollar venture, actually cost three times that amount and caused its sponsors many jittery days and nights before the thrilling spectacle unfolded itself at old Ewing Field on December 26, 1925, but it was acclaimed a grand success by twenty thousand spectators.

The All Star idea was new, the advance sale was pitifully small and a wet day would have meant disaster. Providentially, however, the sun shone brightly, the people responded and, as a result, the San Francisco Shriners Hospital for Crippled Children received a check for twenty-five thousand dollars.

Thus was born the first of a series of colorful classics that, because of its always brilliant contest of strength and skill, its parade of name players, its glittering pageantry and its appeal as a strictly charitable enterprise, has survived and prospered for thirty consecutive years.

The roster of college luminaries who have played in past games exceeds twelve hundred and includes such familiar names as Clark Hinkle of Bucknell; Horrell, Riegels and Muller of California; Ace Parker and George McAfee of Duke; Garbisch and Galiffa of Army; Ingram of Navy; Bill Dudley of Virginia and Herman Hickman of Tennessee; Tom Harmon and Bill Hewitt of Michigan; Orsi and Fortman of Colgate; Lloyd Yoder of Carnegie Tech; Swiacki and Kusserow of Columbia; Chub Peabody of Harvard; Larry Kelley of Yale and Dick Kazmaier of Princeton; Nowack of Illinois; De Correvont of Northwestern and Isbell of Purdue; Pihos and Hoernschmeyer of Indiana; Lujack, Connor, Lattner and Hart of Notre

Dame; Doak Walker and Kyle Rote of Southern Methodist; Kutner and Bechtol of Texas and Buck Bailey and Monte Moncrief of Texas A & M; Frankie Albert, Chuck Taylor, Hamp Pool and Bobby Garrett of Stanford; Nagurski, Joesting and Soltau of Minnesota; Bob MacLeod, Myles Lane and Mutt Ray of Dartmouth; Jack Jacobs of Oklahoma; George Stirnweiss of North Carolina; and Jug Girard of Wisconsin.

Tom Fears and Bob Waterfield of U.C.L.A.; Jeff Cravath and Don Doll of U.S.C.; Arnie Weinmeister and Hugh McElhenny of Washington; Reagan and Savitsky of Penn.; Ray Richards and George Sauer of Nebraska; Jim Barber and Ollie Matson of U.S.F.; Ray Morse of Oregon; Percy Locey of Oregon State; Herman Wedemeyer of St. Mary's; Alyn Beals of Santa Clara and Bob Kennedy of Washington State.

Pingel and Coleman of Michigan State; Johnny Bright of Drake; Vic Janowicz of Ohio State; Willis Glassgow of Iowa; Dutch Clark of Colorado; Shephard of Maryland; Bausch of Kansas; LeBaron of College of the Pacific; and a thousand others whose names made football history.

The Shrine is a fraternal organization and its activities are many. Once each year prior to 1925 an aging group of its members met a similar group of steam-room athletes representing the lodge of Elks in an "earth-shaking struggle" on the diamond, the net proceeds from which went into their respective charity funds.

Thus it was not surprising when my friend E. Jack Spaulding conceived the idea of organizing a similar group of Shriners to meet all comers on the football gridiron. The idea seemed a good one, until it was realized that the bruising game of football might prove a bit too strenuous for doctors, lawyers and business tycoons whose girths had grown slightly out of bounds since leaving the college campus.

As an alternate suggestion, Mr. Spaulding proposed that the Shrine sponsor a plan to put the late Walter Camp's All-America idea into actual practice by matching two teams of football stars on the playing field instead of between the covers of a widely circulated magazine. The suggestion was enthusiastically received by Islam Temple's Potentate, H. K. McKevitt, and in due time the sum of ten thousand dollars was voted to defray the cost of the game. It was decreed that all profits should go to the San Francisco Shriners Hospital for Crippled Children.

Starting with the key members of California's famous Wonder Team as a nucleus (A. B. "Pesky" Sprott; Harold "Brick" Muller, George "Fat" Latham and Charlie Erb), Spaulding formed his West Committee by adding the names of O. E. "Babe" Hollingbery, C. D. Woods, J. R. Hickey, Dr. Albert Boles, J. R. Klawans, Chris Bauer, Bart Macomber and A. C. Kienley. Navy Bill Ingram, then head football coach at Indiana University, agreed to assemble and bring to San Francisco a group of top-ranking Eastern football stars to meet a similar team from the West.

From the beginning it was decided that the proposed East-West game should be conducted on a strictly amateur basis. There would be no paid promoters, and all coaches and players would be asked to serve without pay. With this assurance, Pacific Coast Conference officials granted a special dispensation, allowing students to play in the game without penalty.

With the matter of West team personnel settled, and positive assurance that Eastern representative Bill Ingram would turn up in due time with a carload of top-name players, there was a lull for several weeks during which apparently no effort was made to organize working committees or to ballyhoo an event that was already showing signs of costing several times the amount originally voted.

Since 1918 I had passed up all connection with athletics in order to establish myself firmly in business. With that accomplished, I had again become active as swimming commissioner of the Olympic Club's athletic committee and had also agreed to serve as chairman of a group to entertain the visiting East-West players on arrival. That was my only connection with the proposed East-West game until a well-remembered Sunday when I joined Potentate McKevitt and Jack Spaulding at the Lakeside Country Club.

Potentate McKevitt settled down in an easy chair and asked the chairman of his football committee how things were coming for the big game.

Jack replied that both teams would be in the pink and that everything was just fine.

"But," protested the much worried Mr. McKevitt, "how about the committees, the publicity, the advance sale? What is it going to cost?"

Jack was quite vague about actual plans but still sure that everything would be all right.

By then, Mr. McKevitt had got mad. Very mad.

The budget was ten thousand dollars. Apparently expenses were going to be several times that amount. The publicity was almost nil. The advance sale ditto. Even assuming that the two All Star teams would actually materialize, everything else must start from scratch. And only four weeks to go! The Potentate's temperature had reached the boiling point. Finally, I volunteered to work up an organization and get things started. We excused ourselves, hurried home and there worked for hours on committee assignments, putting down one little name after another.

I do not recall then or ever being delegated any real authority in connection with that first game. Things had to be done and done quickly, so I just moved in and took charge. Financial commitments were checked and trimmed wherever possible. We soon had an effective publicity setup. Speakers made talks at public gatherings. Posters advertising the game appeared on donated billboards. Trucks equipped with blaring loud-speakers traveled the downtown streets, and volunteer workers hawked football tickets.

As a publicity stunt, California's Brick Muller volunteered to catch a football dropped from the twenty-third floor of the new Telephone building. In a noon-hour mob so dense he could barely free his arms, Brick caught the ball on the fourth try. We used every known form of ballyhoo and soon public interest began to perk up.

Pesky Sprott, Fat Latham and Babe Hollingbery had been chosen to coach the West team. With a line-up that included Muller, Imlay, Erb, Nisbet, Carlson and Horrell of California; Cleaveland, Campbell, Shipkey and Patrick of Stanford; Carrothers, Brown and Avery of the Olympic Club; Shields and Mautz of Oregon; Locey of Oregon State; Bradshaw of Nevada; John Vesser of Idaho; Needles of Santa Clara; Hickey and Bryan of Washington; and an unbranded maverick named Buck Bailey from far-off Texas A & M, the West looked formidable enough to meet any aggregation that Bill Ingram might deliver from the East.

And right there appeared the worst pain in the neck I had experienced thus far. With the West line-up already announced and newspapermen screaming for the East roster, our eastern representative remained utterly unresponsive, while I fussed and fumed and bombarded him with telegrams begging for names, names. But no replies came back. When I asked, "How come?" I was told that Navy Bill never wrote letters or answered telegrams while coaching football.

With that we had to be content until one morning while eagerly scanning a sports page, I read a news dispatch from Chicago stating that Bill Ingram, coach of Indiana University, accompanied by a team of football stars, had entrained for San Francisco to engage in a charity football contest. I copied down the names one by one and only then was I sure there *would* be an East-West game.

Navy Bill's methods may have been exasperating, but when he arrived on December 15, he delivered the cream of the year's football crop. There were only eighteen besides himself, but three of them—Ed Garbisch of West Point, Lavern Dilweg of Marquette, and Ed Slaughter of Michigan—still hold places on the football writers' consensus of all-time All-Americans who have played in thirty East-West games.

Led by a gaily uniformed Shrine band, East and West players, each in an open auto with his name emblazoned on its sides, were paraded to the City Hall to receive a typical welcome from the city's mayor, Sunny Jim Rolph.

Besides Garbisch, Dilweg and Slaughter, the East squad included Utteritz and Edwards of Michigan; Marks and Fisher of Indiana; Sloan of Drake; Wyckoff of Georgia Tech; Jones of Florida; Chase of Pitt; Martineau of Minnesota; Davis of West Virginia; Reese of Vanderbilt; Powell of Davis-Elkins; Fry of Iowa; Hutchinson of Nebraska; and Farwick of West Point.

Even when both teams were on hand ready to play, there were gloomy predictions that the affair would prove a "bust." There were requests from important people that names be kept out of the printed program and one official demand that this jittery executive secretary remain on call in his office instead of meeting the arriving East team at Reno, as planned. Rain was a constant threat, especially on the eve of the game.

I cannot speak for the rest of the town's populace, but with the also jittery Mr. McKevitt very much in mind, "the condemned man ate a hearty meal and spent the intervening hours, clothed in goose pimples, his elbows resting on a window sill, while he stared at alternating patches of rain clouds and blue sky until the dawn mercifully came."

As the record will show, the Lord did provide. The rains stayed away, the sun came out and with it the crowds. Charity's cornucopia was filled to overflowing, and soon the cry was heard: "I knew it all the time. Let's do it again."

As for the football game, won by the West with the score of 6 to 0, newspaper writers called it a "classic" then and still do after these many years. And among those who so described it in syndicated news articles were Warren W. Brown of Chicago's *Herald-Examiner,* Walter Eckersall, football's best-known All-American, who came West to referee the game, and Damon Runyon, who wrote, "They were mythical teams breathed to life; made real. It takes this California to make dreams come true." Said Navy Bill Ingram, "I looked upon the two greatest ends I have seen in my time. One was Muller. The other was Dilweg." The teams were evenly matched with one slight difference. That difference was Brick Muller, who leaped high in the air to snag a pass thrown by Tut Imlay and ran fifteen yards for the only score, with Larry Marks of Indiana clinging to his back.

Runyon and Eckersall, incidentally, sat in at our committee meetings, offered constructive suggestions and shared in the game souvenirs awarded players and coaches. The record would not be complete without mention of other writers who adopted that first East-West game as their very own, and by their works made a strong contribution to the cause of crippled children.

Faded newspaper files revealed these still familiar names: Harry B. Smith, Ed R. Hughes, William Leiser, Prescott Sullivan, Edgar ("Scoop") Gleeson, Pat Frayne, George J. Davis, Tom Laird, Brick Morse, Franklin B. Morse, Vic Klee, Eddie Murphy, Ernest M. Smith, Al Santoro, and Harry Hayward.

Gross receipts were $55,158; expenses ran slightly more than $30,000. The book was officially closed on that initial East-West game when a check for an even $25,000 was gratefully accepted by Mr. John D. McGilvray, chairman of the Shrine Hospital's board of governors.

* 32 *

As an aftermath of the first game, newspaper editorials complimented the Shrine and urged that plans be started at once to perpetuate such a worthy enterprise. Before leaving for home, Bill Ingram agreed to return the following year with another group of players and Babe Hollingbery agreed to do likewise for the West. It was decided to play a second East-West game on January 1, 1927.

The Shrine duly elected its new set of officers for the ensuing year, and now there was no lack of volunteers ready and willing to put on a bigger and better show. There were loud demands for California's Memorial Stadium seating eighty-five thousand people, but the boys finally settled for the new Kezar Municipal Stadium which would accommodate a modest thirty-five thousand fans.

Having acquired a bit of experience the hard way while directing the first game, I assumed that I would continue in charge. With the preliminaries settled, I returned to my business and also knuckled down to the task of developing swimming and water polo teams for the Olympic Club, having become its swimming commissioner.

In April I took an eleven-man team to Chicago where, in the Illinois Athletic Club's pool, our Olympic Club water polo team successfully defended its national championship against the best of the East.

The next East-West game was coming up, and plans had to be made. A few days before the game my old friend Christy Walsh arrived in town and when we came out of a huddle, it had been agreed that Christy's protégé, "The King of Swat," would kick off at the ball game. Our hopes for a crowded stadium failed to materialize, even though the weather was fine. When the grinning Babe Ruth slammed his mighty toe against the ball, only to see it dribble feebly down the field, the stands were less than half filled.

Anything that happened on the field, however, was anti-climactic when it was discovered that Bill Ingram, the East coach, was missing. When excited newspapermen interrogated Johnny Beckett, Ingram's assistant, Johnny casually mentioned that in anticipation of being appointed at the Naval Academy, Bill Ingram was in Pasadena scouting the teams playing in the Rose Bowl. Under Assistant Coach Beckett the East played a fine ball game, taking the lead of three points in the second quarter, when Rauber booted a field goal from the West's twelve-yard line.

With both teams playing a tight defensive game, that three-point lead was good only until two Montana pals went into action. From deep in East territory Wild Bill Kelly of Montana State College tossed a long pass which Russ Sweet caught in mid-field. Being a ten-second track man as well as a football player, Russ led a pack of would-be tacklers fifty yards to a touchdown. The extra point was kicked and the West won its second game, 7 to 3.

Losing by such a close score was no help to Bill Ingram, and for a while the local press had a field day at his expense, but fortunately he was not on hand to gather the clippings and in due time his new appointment was announced by the Naval Academy.

I was far from happy myself. After the unqualified success of the first game, the second effort was a definite letdown, and I felt partly to blame for many of the things that had happened. From twenty thousand, the attendance had dropped to half that number. Expenses had gotten entirely out of hand and had increased over the first game by $9,000. As a result, profits to the hospital dropped from $25,000 to a mere $8,666, and a wet day would have wrecked the enterprise, probably for all time. In the first game many busybodies had merely fluttered around the edges for fear of being identified with a failure. In the second affair everybody tried to get into the act, causing untold confusion. Instead of waiting around to be fired, I decided to step out as soon as final reports were compiled.

In due time there was another election, another Potentate and another huddle. Asked by the new top man, Julian D. Harries, to reconsider, I agreed to do so, but I insisted upon full authority to revamp all committees, to make necessary changes in coaching staffs, to authorize all expenditures and, finally, to originate and sign every check, in order to avoid any misunderstanding concerning financial commitments.

Though the authority of Potentate Harries expired with his term of office, those conditions have not been altered in thirty years, nor has there been any major disagreement over policy during that time.

Despite his apparent eccentricities, Bill Ingram was a fine fellow and a good football coach, and I was not overlooking the important fact that if he had not brought an outstanding team West in 1925, there would have been no first East-West game and no contribution of twenty-five thousand dollars to the cause of crippled children.

Accordingly, I let the coaching situation simmer for several months before going East for a conference with Ingram. He indicated that he would like to continue as East coach, but reminded me that he was then a naval officer subject to orders and could not give positive assurance that he would be available. We then agreed that it was advisable to select some other coach who would be free to plan ahead.

American in the Rough

I chose Andy Kerr, head coach at Washington and Jefferson College. As a coach at Stanford in 1925, Andy had observed the first East-West game, and he was keenly interested in work for crippled children. Realizing the importance of having top players from the Big Ten Conference, we invited Dick Hanley, head coach at Northwestern University, to serve with Andy. The ideal combination of Kerr and Hanley continued for ten years until Hanley retired from collegiate football. Andy Kerr is still head man for the East after serving for twenty-eight consecutive years.

The first team assembled by Kerr and Hanley looked unbeatable. It was led by the great Herb Joesting of Minnesota; Notre Dame's Elmer Wynne and Chile Walsh; Nebraska's Glen Presnell and Ray Randels; Bruce Caldwell of Yale and Myles Lane of Dartmouth. But again the wily Babe Hollingbery was ready. This time he had four wild-eyed Texans—Rags Matthews of Texas Christian; Joel Hunt and Joe Sikes of Texas A & M; and Gerald Mann of Southern Methodist—who put on their own show, scoring two touchdowns and a safety for sixteen points in the first two minutes of play.

The East then took charge, marched sixty-one yards in nine plays, with Bruce Caldwell roaring over for a touchdown; but the final score was West 16, East 6. The crowd numbered thirty thousand; gross receipts were up $21,000; expense was down $5,000 and the net of $35,079 exceeded the combined profit of the first two games.

Having seen the Municipal Stadium filled almost to its thirty-five thousand capacity in the third East-West game, the city fathers took heed and enlarged Kezar to accommodate sixty thousand persons. That was opportune planning, because on December 28, 1928, fifty-five thousand football fans poured through the gates for the fourth game and watched a collection of Easterners mow down the West by a score of 20 to 0. The score in dollars was better still. Gross receipts were $108,848, expense, $50,348, and the Shrine Hospital's share reached a high of $58,500.

It is not my plan to describe in detail the twenty-nine games that have already become football history. However, at this time I am going off the deep end with the comment that the East team of 1930 was the greatest squad ever to play in the series. Salute Jack Cannon of Notre Dame; Willis Glassgow of Iowa; Frosty Peters of Illinois; and Minnesota's powerhouse of football, the great Bronko Nagurski.

Early on New Year's morning Coaches Kerr and Hanley had sworn that Jack Cannon would decorate the bench throughout the game. Jack had broken training on New Year's Eve. They inferred that no man in Jack's rundown condition had any business on a football field. Maybe so, but Jack talked himself into the game early in the first quarter and from then on it was Cannon here, there and everywhere. He smeared West plays time after time, and whenever a swarm of players untangled themselves, there was the grinning Jack Cannon at the bottom of the heap, hugging the ball. Whenever the East needed power, there was always Nagurski, the old Bronko himself, backed up by the plunging Willis Glassgow. When extra points were needed, Frosty Peters gave lessons in the lost art of drop-kicking.

In the second quarter, with the score East 6, West 0, the ball lay near the side lines, forty-four yards out. Frosty coolly picked up the pigskin and drop-kicked it neatly between the goal posts. Just before the gun ended the game, East was in possession of the ball on the West's twenty-yard line. Once again Frosty Peters nonchalantly scooped up the ball, drop-kicked it squarely between the goal posts and the game ended East 19, West 7.

Sixty thousand football fans wiped the perspiration from their collective brows and slowly moved out of the stadium muttering to themselves. The box score in dollars was gross receipts, $114,440; expense, $54,440; Shriners Hospital for Crippled Children, $60,000.

Promotion of a special event such as the East-West classic once each year might seem routine to the outsider, but actually there are things to be done and decisions to be made throughout the entire twelve months between games. That there has never been a slow or uninteresting game during its thirty-year history undoubtedly accounts for the automatic sellout of the stadium's sixty-two thousand capacity months in advance of the event.

Even in its earlier stages, the East-West game had achieved nation-wide recognition as a gridiron contest featuring the most publicized names in college football. Over the years, however, a pattern of pageantry has been developed to such proportions as to challenge the game itself in spectator appeal. For pomp and ceremony, music, color and sheer delight to the eye, nothing approaching the East-West show can be seen in any stadium in the nation.

Beginning in 1925 as a modest display of marching units, it has developed over the years into a mighty spectacle featuring 4,200 colorfully uniformed participants, including 1,200 musicians, 1,000 color bearers carrying 800 flags in mass formation, and scores of individual units representing Shrine Temples, Army, Navy, Marines, Coast Guard, Land and Sea Scouts, Chinese and even Scottish bagpipers.

Seated in order of marching formation in the two ends of the stadium, two separate groups of 2,100 participants rise at the half-time signal, move directly forward on the gridiron, fan out to the side-line stripe, march to the opposite goal line, reverse and countermarch, each glittering uniform and each fluttering flag contributing its small part. The stadium's green carpet is converted into a kaleidoscopic vision of color, music and patriotic fervor never to be forgotten over the years.

Suddenly all movement ceases, followed by a breathless silence; the silver tip of a tall pole rears skyward; the Stars and Stripes slowly ascends and 60,000 voices join in a chant of Allegiance to the Flag. A baton is raised and 1,200 musicians join in playing our national anthem as 60,000 souls stand at attention. Spines tingle and goose pimples break out afresh. A bugle sounds. The spell is broken as thousands break ranks, and the floor of the great oval momentarily takes on the hue of a gigantic magic carpet. Gradually the two halves of the procession unwind and head toward their respective stations as twenty-two gridiron gladiators take possession, and the play goes on.

* 33 *

PROMOTION of those first East-West games involved much time, not to mention keeping the Olympic Club's swimming and water polo teams at the top of the heap, nationally.

I had now been with Elliott-Fisher Company ten years, five as manager, when my outfit suddenly merged with the Sundstrand Adding Machine Company of Rockford, Illinois, under the trade name of General Office Equipment Corporation.

For a while my business future was in doubt. The Sundstrand manager, Mr. Edgar Jessup, was one of the smartest men in the office equipment field. He later became president of the Marchant Calculating Machine Company. I received the appointment. It meant learning an entirely new line of machines as well as hiring and training additional sales and service personnel.

One year later, with the affairs of the new company under control, I was elected president of the Pacific Association of the Amateur Athletic Union and had just assumed the duties of the office when Frankie Campbell, a heavyweight boxer, died on August 25, 1930, as a result of meeting Max Baer in the prize ring.

The grand jury investigated and sent a written report to California's Governor, C. C. Young, reflecting upon the integrity of the State Athletic Commission and its licensees.

The Governor then appointed a board of inquiry including Harry Brand and Charles Hutson of Los Angeles, John Sinclair and this writer of San Francisco, with the director of State Veterans' Affairs, Allen Bixby of Sacramento, as chairman. The board also had the services of the Honorable Leon French, deputy attorney general, as counsel.

Meetings were held throughout the state. Commission members, fight promoters, managers of boxers and wrestlers, seconds, boxing inspectors, and newspaper writers were subpoenaed and questioned under oath, and as a result two thousand pages of testimony were turned over to the Governor's office.

The report finally was released. It said, among other things, that connivance existed between managers and boxers with the end in view of arranging the outcome of contests; that many contests were staged where one boxer, or the other, would feign injury, or in boxing parlance—"take a dive"; that there was little doubt that in many instances a manager, in order to match a boxer under his charge, has had to agree that his boxer would be the loser; and that in some cases a fight manager controlled both boxers in the same match. Testimony also revealed that practically all wrestling matches were hippodrome exhibitions, instead of contests.

In conclusion, the board of inquiry recommended that the Governor accept the resignation of one commissioner, previously submitted, that a second commissioner not be reappointed and that the third be commended. New appointees were Dr. Harry Martin of Beverly Hills and newspaperman Bob Edgren of Pacific Grove. Later I declined a similar appointment by the Governor, James Rolph, Jr.

For diversified activity, wacky situations, headaches and downright hard work the year 1932 was tops. In December of 1930, my company had become part of another merger, this time with the Underwood Typewriter Company. For more than a year, however, both companies had continued as separate operating units.

Now in 1932, and to continue for many months, would come the actual consolidation of properties and the merger of field and office personnel. This transition began in April, catching me in the midst of numerous outside activities to which I had committed myself.

Los Angeles had been awarded the Tenth Olympiad. As president of the Pacific Amateur Athletic Union (fourth term), my official duties involved not only fund-raising for the American Olympic Committee and over-all supervising of the Olympic Boxing and Track and Field Trials but also working as assistant manager of the American swimming team and as chairman of the British Empire-United States Games to be held in San Francisco on August 14, immediately following the close of the Olympics in Los Angeles.

It also happened that the National Shrine Convention had been awarded to San Francisco. As an officer of Islam Temple, to become its Potentate in three years, it had fallen to my lot to organize and direct some twenty different entertainment committees.

Budgets totaling $200,000 had been approved plus an additional $50,000 for a glamorous spectacle, a so-called Hollywood Electrical Motion Picture Pageant, which under a special committee was expected to produce at least $125,000. For this event, Mr. Frank Murphy, chief electrical engineer of Warner Brothers, would produce a dozen marvelous floats, and Mr. Norman Manning would deliver a score of famous movie stars.

All was serene until the convention directors heard a rumor
that the Motion Picture Producers Association had turned
thumbs down on the project. The Shrine directors then voted
to send Mr. George J. Hatfield and me to Hollywood to determine the exact situation.

After conferring with Louis B. Mayer of M-G-M, Winfield
Sheehan of Fox, Joe Schenck and Harold Lloyd of United Artists, and the Will Hays Office, our report to the directors was
short and not too sweet. Frank Murphy and Norman Manning
were both out, and $5,000 of the pageant budget had been
spent with no tangible results.

The minutes of the meeting of the board of directors, June
15, 1932, reveal that "Directors Hatfield and Coffman reported on the Hollywood Conference, stating that all plans
were at a standstill and that entries of floats and movie stars
were problematical. Director Coffman stated that if the directors desired him to take over the project, he would expect to be
given full power to enter into contracts, with authority to spend
the remaining $45,000 according to his best judgment. It was
moved that Director Coffman proceed with plans as outlined."

Well there it was. Along with business reorganization plans,
the A.A.U., the Olympic Games and British Empire Games, I
was now in the movie business with $45,000 to spend and just
six weeks to get the job done. For the first time I really felt
panicky. Three days later, in Hollywood, I signed contracts to
build thirteen gorgeous floats and spent an added $5,000 for
rental of special studio generators.

While these creations were an essential part of the big show,
the real rat race was just beginning. Each morning I flew to
Hollywood in the rickety little Varney planes of the time. Each
day I knocked at the doors of motion-picture studios, talked
with assistant directors, argued with private secretaries. The
routine seldom varied. Everyone was sympathetic, but the peo-

ple I wanted to see were always "in conference," and the movie stars so essential to the success of our show were even more elusive.

With the help of George Bancroft and Wally Beery, a series of parties for motion-picture executives were staged at the Roosevelt Hotel.

Through Harry Brand of United Artists, I met Mary Pickford, who graciously accepted for both herself and Douglas Fairbanks. I spent an evening escorting the lovely Claudette Colbert through San Francisco's Chinatown, and she responded with a "maybe." Through a friend, Roscoe Turner, the celebrated stunt flier, I managed to lunch with Maureen O'Sullivan and Virginia Bruce, *but* they wouldn't say yes, they wouldn't say no.

My best bet was Sid Grauman of the Chinese Theatre, a former San Franciscan. I asked Sid to be top man in escorting the group of movie stars to his "old home town." He was interested but a bit coy and wanted time to think it over. Then one day, with time running out and very little accomplished, I happened to be on the same plane with the Governor, James Rolph, Jr., an old friend.

For two hours I cried on his shoulder, brought him up to date on my adventures in movieland and told him that he was the one person in all California who could help us deliver a pack of movie stars in his home town on July 28. He told me to write my own ticket.

From the Governor's suite at the Biltmore Hotel I contacted Miss Louella Parsons, the movie columnist. The Governor arranged an appointment and soon I was on my way to Miss Parsons' home. Over a cup of tea she listened to my story, promised to help and, before I departed, secured the acceptance of Bebe Daniels and Ben Lyon over the telephone.

I rushed out to Grauman's Chinese Theatre and handed Sid a list of those who had already accepted. He agreed to make the trip but refused to take charge. I had some twenty well-known names, but my problem actually was to get them aboard the train, and to do that I needed Grauman's help. My next move was a mean trick to play on Sid, but it turned out all right in the end.

After hurriedly taking a plane home, I placed the following half-page advertisement in the newspapers:

SAN FRANCISCO'S OWN SID GRAUMAN IS BRINGING A TRAIN-LOAD OF MOVIE STARS FOR THE HOLLYWOOD ELECTRICAL PAGEANT.

Supplementing the announcement were pictures of a score of stars who had agreed to come. I flew back to Hollywood and laid copies on Grauman's desk. Sid took one look and began tearing at his bushy hair.

"You've put me in a terrible predicament," he groaned. "You've ruined me. How can I make good on that?"

Two minutes later he had Joe Schenck, president of United Artists, on the telephone.

"You've got to help me, Joe," he shouted. "They've put me on the spot." Then, to his secretary, "Miss Skall, get me Eddie Robinson, get Vic McLaglen, get Polly Moran. I'm in a terrible hole."

Perhaps Sid Grauman was really worried, or maybe he was just putting on an act, but during the next twenty-four hours I worried enough for the two of us. I had tied up practically every drawing room, compartment and bedroom on the Lark and wondered how much of the space would be occupied. I phoned Miss Skall during the afternoon to ask how things were going and if Mr. Grauman was still mad at me. She remarked that all movie people were temperamental but that Mr. Grauman had lined up even more stars and was sure most of them would show up. And show up they did.

When Sid finished counting noses, his party included Joseph

Schenck, Douglas Fairbanks, Ben Lyon, Bebe Daniels, Richard
Bennett, Tom Mix, Mae Clarke, Boris Karloff, Mary Carlisle,
Hedda Hopper, George Raft, Roscoe Ates, Dorothy Jordan,
Jean Hersholt, Anita Page, Lew Cody, Buster Keaton, Estelle
Taylor, Polly Moran, Joe E. Brown, Joan Marsh, Lyle Talbot,
Harold Lloyd, Edward G. Robinson, George Bancroft, Wal-
lace Beery and Howard M. Strickling, Louis B. Mayer's per-
sonal representative.

There was an elaborate banquet at the Palace Hotel with
Governor Rolph as host. Then a line of electrically decorated
cars, each carrying its motion-picture celebrity, followed by
floats of breath-taking beauty, threaded its way through turbulent rivers of humanity that overflowed the sidewalks while
lines of police stood helplessly by, unable to do more than observe the spectacle.

Wrote Wooster Taylor in the San Francisco *Examiner* of July
29: "Dazzled, awestruck, spellbound, the greatest crowd in
the history of San Francisco witnessed last night the Shriners'
crown jewel of pageantry—the Hollywood Electrical Parade.
Guided by flaming torches that marked a magic square, hundreds of thousands converged upon the Civic Center. The
towering grandstands black with people absorbed thousands
more. San Francisco records no such spectacle as this in the
past."

Excerpt number one from the official convention report:
"The sale of grandstand tickets was $128,713."

Excerpt number two: "The entire cost of producing the
Electric Pageant was approximately $1,000 less than the budget
allowed."

We shipped the spectacular floats to Los Angeles, where a
few weeks later, before 100,000 people in the coliseum, Miss
Marion Davies used them as the principal feature of an Electrical Pageant for the Motion-Picture Relief Fund. On that
same occasion one of our illustrious citizens, Mr. Franklin D.

Roosevelt, then campaigning for the Presidency, was the guest of honor.

Reporting at Los Angeles in time for the opening ceremonies of the Olympic Games on July 30, 1932, I worked with the chairman, Frank Blankley of Chicago, and the head coach, Bob Kiphuth of Yale, preparing the American swimming team for the international events in the Olympic pool, and also served as a judge of finish in Track and Field competition in the coliseum.

On the evening of August 13, with the Olympic Games finished except for the closing ceremonies, the athletes representing England, Canada, Australia, New Zealand, India and South Africa, together with the American contingent, which included A.A.U. and Olympic officials, entrained for San Francisco, where the British Empire-United States Games, fifth of a series which began in London in 1920, would be held in Kezar Stadium the following afternoon.

Before an audience of twenty-five thousand people the games opened with ceremonies featuring the massed athletes of the English-speaking nations, flanked by Army troops from the Presidio and sailors from visiting naval vessels. Of thirteen competitive events America won eight and the British won five. At an elaborate banquet to team members and officials given that night in the Olympic Club at Lakeside, the usual toasts were proposed to the President of the United States and to His Majesty King George the Fifth, by Avery Brundage, president of the Amateur Athletic Association. Appropriate souvenirs were presented to members of both teams by Mayor Rossi in behalf of the city of San Francisco, with a response from Lord David Burghley, representing Britain, and Morgan Taylor, representing the United States. Profits from this event, totaling nearly five thousand dollars, were turned over to the A.A.U., rather than to the American Olympic Committee.

A month later when I handed over the affairs of the A.A.U. to my successor, it was like shedding a great burden. Four years had been a long, long time. Following the Olympic fund-raising campaign, Pacific A.A.U. championships, final Boxing and Track and Field Trials, convention committees, the motion-picture extravaganza, the Tenth Olympiad in Los Angeles, and the British-American show in San Francisco, the job of promoting East-West games seemed simple and easy by comparison.

The next several months brought important changes in company personnel and operating policy that would greatly affect my future, so it is well to mention here that despite the time and effort devoted to civic affairs and East-West games, in particular, these outside interests were never allowed to interfere with business routine.

Since the big merger in December of 1930 the General Office Equipment Corporation and the Underwood Typewriter Company had continued to operate each under its original management. Consequently, when on March 15, 1933, all properties and personnel were combined, I was highly gratified to be placed in charge of consolidated operations in Northern California.

Only five months later, Mr. F. F. Wright, who sixteen years before had given me my first opportunity as a salesman, was called to New York to become general sales manager and I was appointed Pacific district manager in full charge of an area beginning east of El Paso, Texas, at the Mexican border, north along the Dakota line to the Canadian border and west to the Pacific. Responsibility included supervision of all personnel, inventories, collections and other phases of Underwood's vast operations in the far West.

* 34 *

THE YEAR 1935 found me swathed in Oriental robes as Illustrious Potentate of Islam Temple of the Shrine, whose roster carried the names of ten thousand citizens of our community. The twelve months' term of office would embrace a calendar crammed with activity ranging from the sublime to the ridiculous.

He who accepts leadership in a fraternal organization such as the Ancient Arabic Order of Nobles of the Mystic Shrine must also accept the consequences, good or bad, and my lot during the ensuing year would be neither better nor worse than that of my predecessor in office or the victim next in line.

There would be receptions, cocktail parties and bingo games; grand balls that would tax the capacity of the largest meeting places; theater parties beginning at midnight and ending with breakfast on the hoof.

The good ship *Lurline* would strain at her seams while ferrying a cargo of happy fez wearers to the hospitable Isles of Hawaii, and from there the S.S. *President Taft* would take over for a recruiting pilgrimage to China, Japan and the Philippines. And on a blustery day in late November, Islam's Potentate and two score of fez-wearing adventurers would find themselves marooned on Santa Cruz Island off the barren shores of Santa Barbara while wire services hummed with the distressing news, and the U.S. Coast Guard rendered gallant service to save hardy mariners from a fate "worse than death," all liquid refreshments having been consumed hours ago.

After finishing that hectic term of office there was every reason to believe that 1936 would prove uneventful by contrast, but it was not to be. Since taking over his important duties in New York some two years before, Fred Wright had done a marvelous job of knitting together the various elements of the three merged companies. In the process, however, his health had become impaired to such an extent that recovery would depend upon a prolonged stay in a less rigorous climate; so early in the year I suggested that he resume his former position as Pacific district manager, while I would revert to my former status.

He took the suggestion under consideration and on the advice of medical advisors, who knew his true condition, agreed to return to California. At the same time, however, company officials decreed that I should become western district manager with headquarters in Chicago. Western was the company's most important district and the best paying job outside of New York.

I accepted the promotion with mixed feelings; happy that my friend could spend his remaining time in California's sunshine; sorrowful and depressed because for me it would mean pulling up roots that had grown strong over a quarter of a century and leaving the one city in all the world I loved the most and had sworn never to desert. There was a civic banquet; speeches in which many kind words were said; press notices were reminiscent of an obituary. It seemed utterly fantastic that I should be leaving a community to which I had dedicated so much of my past life. Since a July day in 1902 I had known "The City" at its fascinating best—and worst; had walked its streets jobless and hungry; had watched while it shook and crumpled and then purged itself with fire and flame.

With pick and shovel and swinging sledge I had worked on many of its landmarks—a Church of God, a famous club, an institution devoted to the upbuilding of youth, and on a plot of land opposite the monument of Robert Louis Stevenson in

Portsmouth Square, the Hall of Justice, a solid edifice of steel and stone where men in iron cages sometimes wonder about "Liberty and Justice for All."

There was just one bit of comfort in my gloomy plans for the future: an understanding with my fellow East-West trustees that I should continue to direct the charity game by remote control from my Chicago headquarters, commuting to San Francisco as frequently as might be necessary. This plan carried the full approval of Underwood Company officials. Thus on a June day in 1936 I found myself transplanted bag and baggage to the shores of Lake Michigan. My new duties involved the reorganization of company activities in key cities throughout a dozen states.

The Midwest will long remember that summer as a hectic period of severe drought, dust storms, dying livestock and ruined crops, as bankrupt farmers and Joad families by the score deserted the barren dust bowl in search of greener fields elsewhere. The business trend was downward; most of our own branch offices were overmanned, and operating expense was high in proportion to sales. I was soon in the midst of an economy drive that carried me on a sort of continuous merry-go-round via Indianapolis, St. Louis, Kansas City, Omaha, Minneapolis, Milwaukee and Chicago, trimming personnel, eliminating this, reducing that, until operating units were finally whittled down to proper size. It was not a pleasant task.

In the late fall word came that Fred Wright had suffered a relapse. I took a plane to San Francisco and found him hospitalized and failing rapidly. After remaining with him several days I reported back to my job, but in a few weeks I was suddenly summoned to New York. There I was informed by company officials that Fred's passing was only a matter of days, perhaps hours. Asked my attitude concerning a return to the Pacific District, I insisted that it was not only my right in the event of a change but Fred's expressed wish that I do so.

After a conference with the vice-president, L. C. Stowell, it was agreed that I should return. When the president, Philip D. Wagoner, concurred, I immediately took a plane to the Coast to be with my friend as long as possible.

Other farewells had been tearfully spoken and only his dear wife Rose and I remained in the room. Kept alive by stimulants, too weak even to lift a thin hand in greeting, Fred looked searchingly at me and in a voice barely above a whisper asked who would take over the Pacific District. When I begged him not to discuss business, he said, "That is my only unfinished business; I have had plenty of time to put my personal affairs in order. Now, I must know who will take over out here." When I told him of the company's decision he said, "I'm glad; with that settled, I want my son Fred Wright, Jr., to enter the company's service and carry on my name." He mentioned three long-time associates in the company and asked that I watch over their future welfare. Then after a brief farewell, he said, "Now, I should like to be alone with Rose."

Our small group hovered miserably in an anteroom until the end came a few hours later. A truly fine man had departed this life. His work was done. Nearly twenty years have passed, yet the memory of him is as vivid as if he had left us only yesterday. Since his departure his son Fred Wright, Jr., has passed on, as have two of the three whose names he whispered in that last short interview. Of four, only one remains.

Back at my old desk in the Underwood Building a few weeks later, I picked up the broken threads of a short six months before, when I had left for the East with little thought of a permanent return. The next football classic was only three weeks away; that meant fast action to complete all arrangements including housing and training of the two squads, even then leaving their schools for the Coast.

Looking back on that last half of 1936 when so much happened in so short a time, I often wonder how I managed to attend to the numberless duties in preparation for the next football game and at the same time do a job in the Western District. Yet the record will show that whereas sales were below quota and expense unduly high when I took Western on July 1, by December 31 I had qualified for a bonus, which meant that sales had been brought above par and operating expense held within bounds.

Thirty consecutive East-West games have been played at this writing. Each has produced its share of drama and colorful thrills, and each has made its contribution to the cause of helpless crippled children. For sheer work and worry, however, I give you the seventeenth annual game, played in New Orleans, on January 3, 1942, as a transplanted war orphan.

Until the first week in December of 1941 plans had worked out even smoother than in past years. Team rosters just released included far more name players than ever before. For instance, *Collier's* magazine, just on the newsstands, featured their annual All-American Eleven, selected by Grantland Rice, as follows: Ernie Blandin of Tulane; Endicott Peabody of Harvard; Bernie Crimmins of Notre Dame; John Rokisky of Duquesne; Bob Reinhard of California; Frankie Albert of Stanford; Malcolm Kutner of Texas; Bill Dudley, U. of Virginia; Bruce Smith of Minnesota; Bob Westfall of Michigan; and Vince Banonis of Detroit U. Of the eleven thus honored, ten had accepted invitations to play in the East-West game. Kezar Stadium was practically sold out and receipts exceeding $100,-000 were in the bank.

Then suddenly on December 7 came the news from Pearl Harbor. The order to cancel the East-West game came first from Governor Olson's office in Sacramento on December 13. Next from Pasadena came a phone call saying the Rose Bowl game between Oregon State College and Duke University had been ordered canceled.

It took me less than two minutes to complete a telephone connection with John L. De Witt, General of the Western Defense Command, state my name and business, and ask the direct question, "General, will it do any good to appear before you in person in the hope of changing your mind?" The reply was strictly to the point, "Come if you like, Mr. Coffman, but do not expect a change of mind." The interview was over.

Sunday, December 14, just one week after the Japanese attack, was a busy day. First, I located Andy Kerr and learned that he was already in touch with A. N. Goldberg, president of the New Orleans Mid-Winter Sports Association. Next, Bernie Bierman contacted Dr. Rufus Harris, president of Tulane, concerning the use of the stadium.

In the hours that followed I received several invitations offering the use of stadiums in Denver, Atlanta, Soldier Field in Chicago and the Universities of Texas, Kansas and Oklahoma. Then the New Orleans group extended an invitation to play the game in Tulane Stadium on Saturday, January 3, two days after the Sugar Bowl game between Fordham and Missouri. I accepted the offer.

At midnight I was awakened by a telephone call from New York City. The speaker advised that a meeting of newspapermen and others had been in progress for several hours and that I was now to receive an invitation to hold the game in the Yankee Stadium with a guarantee against any possible loss. Another party came on the line, identified himself as Mr. Hertz of the automotive industry, explained that he had sponsored many events for charity and offered to underwrite the East-West game.

He proposed to house, feed and train both teams on his own estate in Westchester County; he agreed to pay all bills previously incurred, plus all expense of staging the game in Yankee Stadium; and he further agreed to turn over all net profit to the Shriners Hospital. Upon acceptance of his offer he would immediately send me a certified check for $10,000 payable to the hospital, to be retained regardless of the financial outcome of the game.

It was a magnanimous offer without any strings or conditions, but in five minutes I had talked him out of it as a bad risk. I pointed out that our forty-six players were the most publicized stars of the current season, and because of that fact, probably the most temperamental. After playing a hard schedule under difficult weather conditions, they had accepted invitations to spend nearly three weeks in California, topped off by visits to Hollywood studios. I reminded him that New York's rigid climate in midwinter would prove a poor substitute for such an excursion. I ventured the opinion that playing the game in the Yankee Stadium would bring withdrawals of key players and necessitate numerous substitutions. Public interest would decline in proportion to the loss of star players and result in a financial debacle for the sponsor and loss of prestige in future East-West games. On the other hand, a switch to New Orleans with its milder climate, its many tourist attractions and a chance to watch the Fordham-Missouri game would, no doubt, hold the entire roster in line. Mr. Hertz was quick to see the point, thanked me for my frankness and hung up the receiver, probably much relieved in getting out from under.

I arranged with our coaches to have all West players report direct to the southern city, then sent the ticket manager, L. B. Samuel, and the publicity man, Chris Lykke, ahead by train, while I enplaned to Chicago to head off the East team, then assembling at Northwestern University. Andy Kerr had proceeded direct to New Orleans to arrange for training quarters, so Bernie and I rounded up the East squad and headed south.

Under a special arrangement with the banks of Northern California, nearly $100,000 was being turned back to disappointed

ticket holders in San Francisco while Lou Samuel, Chris Lykke
and I tackled the heartbreaking task of doing a job all over
again, with only fifteen days to go.

Number one headache was the ticket situation. No one had
thought to tell us that printing a set of tickets for Tulane Stadium took weeks, or that the printing job was done in far-off
Little Rock, Arkansas, where our frantic call for tickets, tickets
went unheard and unheeded. The Sugar Bowl people gave us
every possible co-operation, and the press outdid themselves
in publicizing our game, but when thousands of rabid football
fans converged on our Maison Blanche ticket headquarters, no
tickets were available, so the crowds left without buying, promising to come back tomorrow—and after that another tomorrow.
And when tomorrow and the tickets did come, just seven days
before the game, along came the rains as well.

While Samuel struggled with his problem of how to sell tickets without having any to sell, and Chris Lykke settled down to
do an entire reconstruction job on the program—editorial and
advertising alike—our small headquarters suite in the Roosevelt
Hotel fairly hummed with activity from early morning until
near midnight when we put out the DO NOT DISTURB sign,
closed the blinds and hit the wet pavement for a rendezvous at
the St. Charles, or the Old Absinthe House, or a reasonable
facsimile thereof.

When some newspaperman asked if we planned to put on
our usual display of pageantry, we said "Why not?" We called
in leaders of high schools, colleges, Shrine Temples and other
fraternal organizations, showed them our Kezar blueprints,
and on January 3 actually put on a knockout display of color,
music, pomp and ceremony.

On New Year's Day, while a jam-packed stadium watched
Fordham defeat Missouri by a score of 2 to 0, the heavens
opened wide in a series of cloudbursts, leaving in their wake
just about the wettest gathering of football fans in history. One

could almost hear seventy thousand collective voices moaning, "If I ever get out of this fishpond without drowning, it'll be a lesson to me." There went our last chance for a big gate on Saturday, two days hence.

Next morning, however, the sun shone brightly and thousands rushed to purchase tickets for the East-West game, but unfortunately, one dry day was not enough. That night I stayed up doing the hot spots to kill time, too excited over the possibility of a dry day on the morrow to go to my hotel room and relax in sleep. Then, when daylight came, it began raining once again. At nine in the morning it was still raining as a group of newspapermen gathered in my room suggesting that the game be postponed until the next day, Sunday. I stepped into the next room to ask the opinion of Bernie Bierman and found him on the telephone receiving orders to report to the Marine Base at Quantico, Virginia, the next day. Then I realized that many of our players had received similar instructions, so postponement was out of the question.

I picked up a San Francisco newspaper. Some writer in my home town had written a glowing article predicting a complete sellout of the East-West game. I closed my eyes and saw a wet, dismal stadium with only a handful of people in the stands. Suddenly I hot-footed it over to Sugar Bowl headquarters. At my request they agreed to put a half-dozen girls on the telephone to call all military encampments within seventy-five miles, inviting troops as guests of the East-West game. Soon the big trucks were rolling in loaded with troops. By game time Tulane Stadium was more than half filled, even though the rain was still falling.

The event was preceded by pageantry featuring at least one thousand marching persons. The game itself, played on a muddy turf with rain falling intermittently, was acclaimed by newspapermen as one of the greatest football games seen in years.

American in the Rough

The crowd of nearly thirty-five thousand saw two evenly matched elevens battle brilliantly to a 6 to 6 tie. East scored on a 23-yard pass from Bill Dudley of Virginia to Geyer of Colgate in the third quarter. Then the West came from behind to score on a 12-yard pass from Jack Jacobs of Oklahoma to Bob Robertson of U.S.C. in the fourth period.

The kick for the one point that might have won the game was made by Stanford's Frankie Albert, but was blocked by Ralph Fife of Pitt. Jacobs and Robertson of the West put on a brilliant passing attack time after time but failed to score again. Westfall of Michigan, Geyer of Colgate, and Rokisky of Duquesne led the East's running attack, aiding greatly in building up a total of 141 yards on the ground to the West's 16 yards, while West's passing attack gained 113 yards against East's 49. Those comparative figures merely tell the story of how the East managed to balance its superiority on ground plays against the apparent superiority of the West's passing attack. Said William Keefe in the New Orleans *Times-Picayune:* "San Francisco and the Shriners of the West Coast have seen brighter days and bigger crowds, but they never saw a better football game than was played Saturday afternoon between the East and West All-Stars." Said Bill Cunningham of Boston, "I will never cover a Bowl game on New Year's Day again without thinking about a better game being played in San Francisco."

The seventeenth annual East-West game played in "foreign territory" did more to put the classic on the gridiron map nationally than all of the games played heretofore. Congregated in Tulane's newly renovated press box were writers who had covered all other Bowl games on New Year's Day, and each was loud in his praise of the East-West game.

When all financial returns were in, including receipts and disbursements in New Orleans, expense of the canceled game in San Francisco and refunds to ticket holders in California, there was left a net profit of $6,366 of which $3,000 was given the Shreveport unit of the Shriners Hospital for Crippled Children.

With the passing years the fame of the East-West game has grown enormously while charity's portion of the proceeds has more than kept pace.

The net proceeds of the thirtieth-anniversary game played on January 1, 1955, were $240,337, bringing the grand total from the thirty-year series to $2,350,635.

Though now in its thirty-first year, the classic is still conducted as a strictly amateur event, conforming to all rules of the National Collegiate Athletic Association and the Amateur Athletic Union. As in the original game, there are no paid promoters. Players, coaches and game officials alike still continue to give their services without fee or compensation of any kind. Truly, in the East-West game the satisfaction of giving is its own reward.

* 35 *

BY THE END of 1947 I had served Underwood Corporation for thirty years, twenty-two of which had been shared with the East-West game, on company time, using company offices and facilities.

As the enterprise grew in size and importance, making increased demands on my time, Underwood's intricate operations in the West had likewise expanded rapidly, with added lines and greatly increased personnel, all of which involved more travel and concentrated effort on my part.

As the pressure increased, with the game taking more and more of my time, I placed my growing problem in the lap of company officials in New York. They complimented me on Pacific District operations, offered no objection to the time given my outside interests and urged me to continue without change.

This I did for two more years, but with the playing of the twenty-fifth anniversary game on December 31, 1949, I chose to relinquish my major duties with Underwood, while accepting the company's proposal to continue as a special representative of the president, L. C. Stowell, and the chairman of the board, Philip D. Wagoner, a position I still hold.

July 20, 1952, marked the fiftieth anniversary of my arrival in San Francisco, hungry, unwashed, penniless, friendless. The years between have treated me kindly, but there are memories, some as vivid as yesterday, others as elusive as tomorrow.

Memories of times and places and things; memories of silver leaves and African lilies; of massive Table Mountain standing guard over the Cape of Good Hope, pointing the way to the Indies.

Memories of Hamburg's Kleinermarinastrasse; of London's Billingsgate and Fishmonger's Hall; of Santa Rosalia; of Tony, Frenchy and little British Johnny; of Dublin and Maggie McGee; of Queenstown for orders, and coals from Newcastle.

The never-to-be-forgotten memory of a beautiful ship moving silently through tropic seas, every rag of canvas billowing before gentle trade winds, the mermaid that is her figurehead pointing to the Southern Cross, slowly taking shape over the far horizon.

Memories of screaming winds, feathering snow and the lonesome prairie; of sheep—endless lines of sheep rounding the jagged edge of a canyon; of other slow-moving lines—lines of ragged, unkempt, hungry, lonesome men, shuffling toward the Bowery Mission and a bountiful Christmas dinner.

And most vivid of all, a memory never to be erased, the most terrifying yet the most magnificent sight ever to behold: the burning, the almost complete destruction of a city, the city that was San Francisco in April of 1906.

Memories of a new and more beautiful city, rising phoenix-

like from its own ashes, to stand proudly today as it stood in
Bret Harte's day:

> Serene, indifferent to fate,
> Thou sittest at the Western Gate.
> Upon thy heights so lately won,
> Still slant the banners of the sun;
> Thou seest the white seas strike their tents,
> O warder of two continents;
> And, scornful of the peace that flies,
> Thy angry winds and sullen skies,
> Thou drawest all things small or great,
> To thee beside the Golden Gate.

Memories all; and a salute to some guys and gals who, in one
way or another, crossed my path in the shadowy realms of
yesterday.

To Ernie Smith and Emory Bronte, who said good-by and
landed in a tree on Molokai; to a gallant gal, Amelia Earhart,
who said good-by and landed who knows where; to friend
Ruth Elder, who made happy landings; and to Lincoln Ellsworth and his bride, with whom I shared cold roast pork and
apple sauce in a Nebraska farm house at dawn after a plane
mishap. Gallant fliers all!

To Bobby Montgomery and young Doug Fairbanks, who
once led me a merry, dark-to-dawn chase; and to Polly Moran,
who was a pal when I needed one; to Vic McLaglen and big
brother Cyril, and Wally Ford, who'll know what I mean, and
to my old sailor pal, George Bancroft, and our departed friend
Wally Beery.

To good old Jimmy Walker, who excitedly referred to me as
a "lousy son of a female dog" when I initiated him into the
mysteries of a highly explosive electric chair; and to still another Jimmy, Sunny Jim Rolph, who, when he departed this
scene, took much of old San Francisco with him.

To Hughey McKevitt and Jack Spaulding and Walter Eckersall and Damon Runyon and Sid Grauman and Tex Rickard and Big Bill Naughton and Harry B. Smith and Granny Rice and Colonel Russ Newland—salutations all, though you have already answered the final call.

And now, if, as legend has it, old sailors just sail away to Fiddlers Green, perhaps the spirit of this Old Salt will join up with the Flying Dutchman and his ghostly crew, who, according to maritime lore, are doomed to sail far southern seas endlessly and restlessly, their toes dipping into the spume that dashes against the tip of Old Cape Stiff and the perpendicular sides of Diego Ramírez.

Until then, the body substance lingers on a mile-high acre of rock surrounded by the blue waters of a calm Sierra lake.

A tiny isle, a frail canoe,
A cup of grog, a book to read
And a touch of Heaven too.

INDEX

Index

Index

Index

De Witt, Gen. John L., 288
Diamond Palace (San Francisco), 221
Diego Ramírez Islands, 90, 146, 170, 296
Diggins, Dr. 215, 216, 221
Dilweg, Lavern, 266, 267
Dinan, Police Chief Jerry, 217
Dippel, Johann, 206
Dix, Gov. John, 41
Dixon (Calif.), 64
Dockstader, Lew, 232
Dogs, Isle of, 114
Dolan, Arthur, 252
Doll, Don, 262
Dora, "Madame," 42
Dorffner, Olga, 253
Douglass, Capt. (*formerly* mate), 129, 131, 141, 149, 162, 222
Dover, Strait of, 113, 122, 131
Downs, Al, 251
Downs, The, 113
Doyers Street (New York), 29, 42, 43
Drake University (football team), 262, 266
Dublin, 117, 125, 294
Dublin Bay, 125
Duckworth, El, 98
Dudley, Bill, 261, 287, 292
Dugan, Mike, 174, 175
Duke Street (Liverpool), 126
Duke University (football team), 261, 287
Dump, The (New York), 44
Dungeness, 113
Dupont Street (San Francisco), 204, 207
Duquesne University (football team), 287, 292
Durack, Fanny, 256
Durrant, Theodore, 249
Dutch Treat Club (New York), 189, 197

Eagle Dance Hall (Aberdeen, Wash.), 182, 229
Eames, Emma, 206
Earhart, Amelia, 295
Earl Street (San Francisco), 164, 198, 217, 226
East River (New York), 29
East Side, lower, 32, 34, 39, 43, 44-5
East Street (San Francisco), 164, 198
East-West (All-Star Shrine) Football Games, ix, 261, 263, 264, 265, 266, 267, 268, 270, 271, 273, 274, 282, 285, 287, 288, 289, 291, 292, 293
Easter Island, 195
Eckersall, Walter, 267, 296
Eddy Street (San Francisco), 66, 204
Edgren, Bob, 275
Edwards, Tom, 266
El Paso, 282
Elbe, river, 132

Elder, Ruth, 295
Elizabeth Street (New York), 38
Elks, 262
Elliott, Ole, 231
Elliott Fisher Company, 254, 274
Ellsworth, Lincoln, 295
Emanuel Baptist Church (San Francisco), 249
Empire Nickelodeon (San Francisco), 203
Englehart, Charlie, 42, 43, 45, 46
English Channel, *see* Channel, English
Erb, Charlie, 263, 265
Erickson, E. S., 184n., 228
Ethel Zane (schooner), 234
Eureka (Calif.), 224, 234n.
Eureka (Nev.), 230
Ewing Field (San Francisco), 261
Examiner, San Francisco, 280
Examiner-Call-Chronicle, San Francisco, 211
Excelsior Hotel (San Francisco), 226, 227

Fairbanks, Jr., Douglas, 295
Fairbanks, Sr., Douglas, 278, 280
Falkland Islands, 97, 98, 144, 172
Falmouth (England), 103, 104, 107, 112, 131
Fanny Dutard (schooner), 164
"Fare-ye-well" (song), 139
Farwick, Gus, 266
Fat Dougherty's (San Francisco), 204, 229
"Fatal Rose of the Red, The" (song), 47
Fath, Gustav, 190, 197
Fears, Tom, 262
Fereday (New Orleans swimmer), 251
Ferry Building (San Francisco), 63, 198, 210
Fiddlers Green, 296
Fiesta (San Francisco), 203
Fife, Ralph, 292
Fiji Islands, 180, 195
Fillmore Street (San Francisco), 236
Fish Street Hill (London), 115
Fisher, George, 266
Fisherman's Wharf (San Francisco), 218
Fishguard (Wales), 107
Fishmonger's Hall (London), 294
Fitafita Barracks (Pago Pago), 196
Fitz (shipmate), 78, 110, 111, 112, 117, 118, 119, 121
Fitzsimmons, Bob, 44
Flattery, Cape, 183, 224
Fleabag (New York), 44
Florida, University of (football team), 266
Flushing (The Netherlands), 117, 122
Flying Dutchman, 296
Ford, Wally, 295

300

Index

Fordham University (football team), 288, 289, 290
Forester (schooner), 188
Fortman, Daniel, 261
Fourteenth Street (New York), 24
Fourteenth Street (San Francisco), 236
Fourteenth Street Theater (New York), 24, 27
Fourth Avenue (New York), 25
Fox (Motion Picture Co.), 277
Fra Diavolo, 45
Francis, Addie M., 41
Frayne, Pat, 267
Fremstad, Anna, 206
French, Hon. Leon, 275
French Quarter (San Francisco), 213
Friedman, Chief Yeoman, 215
Fry, Wes, 266
Funston, Gen. Frederick, 210, 219, 233
Furuseth, Andrew, 183, 198-99

Galiffa, Arnold, 261
Galligan, Claire, 253
Gans-Nelson World Championship (Goldfield, Nev.), 232
Garbisch, Ed, 261, 266
Gardner, Frank, 229
Gare du Nord (Brussels), 120, 122
Garrett, Bobby, 262
Gaskins, John, 15
Gaskins, (Aunt) Lina, 13, 15, 17, 27, 57, 74, 160, 224
General Frisbie (vessel), 212, 213, 223
General Office Equipment Corporation, 274, 282
Gentleman Jim Corbett, 43-4
George V, King, 281
George C. Tilyou's Steeplechase Park (Coney Island), 45
George Street (Sydney), 178
Georgia Institute of Technology (football team), 266
Geyer, Bill, 292
Gibson, "Uncle Joe," 6
Girard, Earl ("Jug"), 262
Glasgow, 104
Glassgow, Willis, 262, 272
Gleeson, Edgar T. ("Scoop"), 256, 267
Globe Museum and Theatorium (New York), 29
Clyde, J. H., 64
Goat Island (San Francisco), 227
Gohl, Billy, 182, 183, 184n., 190-91
Goldberg, A. N., 288
Golden, Frank, 231, 234
Golden Gate, 74, 75, 76, 104, 223, 224, 235, 242, 295
Goldfield (Nev.), ix, 229, 230-34
Good Hope, Cape of, 113, 294
"Good-by" (song), 139

Goodrich, Edna, 232
Goodwin, Bud, 251
Goodwin, Nat, 232, 233
Goodwin, Ralph C., 246
Grace Dollar (vessel), 235
Grafton Street (Dublin), 125
Graham, Judge Thomas, 217
Granby, Alex, 206, 207, 208, 223
Grand Hotel (Cape Town), 173
Grand Street (New York), 26
Grande Place (Brussels), 120
Grauman, Sid, 278, 279, 296
Grays Harbor (Wash.), 164, 165, 166, 181, 186, 191, 227
Great Ormes Head, 131
Greenock, 72, 110
Greenwich, 114
Greenwood (S.C.), 16
Grey, Lady Jane, 115
Gribble, Arthur, 72, 73, 74, 76, 81, 85, 86, 89, 93, 94, 99, 107, 110, 137
Gris-Nez, Cape, 134
Groote Schuur, 174
Guaymas, 129, 155, 184, 186
Guinness's brewery (Dublin), 125

Hadberg, Charles, 184n.
Hall of Justice (San Francisco), 218, 239, 285
Hamburg, 117, 127, 129, 130, 132, 133, 134, 164, 294
Hanley, Dick, 271, 272
Harbor Hospital (San Francisco), 210, 214
Harmon, Tom, 261
Harries, Julian D., 270
Harris, Dr. Rufus, 288
Harrisburg, 254, 256
Hart, Leon, 261
Harvard University (football team), 261, 287
Hatch Steamship Company, 216
Hatfield, George J., 277
Hayward, Harry, 267
Hawaiian Islands, 178, 251, 283. *See also* Honolulu and Molokai
Havman, Jessie, 204
Hebner (Illinois swimmer), 247, 251
Hedges brothers (Freddy and Alvin), 229, 231
Henderson's beer garden (Coney Island), 45, 46
Herald-Examiner, Chicago, 267
Hermitage (Goldfield, Nev.), 230
Hersholt, Jean, 280
Hertz, Mr. (automotive industrialist), 288, 289
Herzog, Dr., 215
Hester Street (New York), 25, 36
Hewitt, William (Bill), 261

Index

Hickey, J. R., 263
Hickey, Vern, 265
Hickman, Herman, 261
Higgins, Gov. Frank, 41
Hind, Rolph and Company, 189
Hinkle, Clark, 261
Hinkley and Pinkley alleys (San Francisco), 204, 207
Hippodrome (San Francisco), 67, 204
Hodges Ferry (Va.), 8, 9, 15
Hoernschmeyer, Robert ("Hunchy"), 261
Hole in the Wall (Sydney), 178
Hollingbery, Orin E. ("Babe"), 263, 265, 268, 271
Hollywood, 277, 289
Hollywood Electrical Motion Picture Pageant, 276, 280
Honeyman, Mr. (Nebraskan farmer), 48, 50, 51, 53, 54
Hong Kong, 72, 74, 119
Honolulu, 197, 244, 253. See also Hawaiian Islands
Hopper, Hedda, 280
Hoquiam, 186, 188
Horn, The (cape), ix, 72, 75, 84, 92, 96, 98, 101, 107, 113, 116n., 118, 127, 130, 133, 135, 138, 145, 146, 148, 165, 170-71, 193, 296
Horrell, Edwin L. ("Babe"), 261, 265
House of All Nations (San Francisco), 68
House of Detention (New York), 39-40
Houston, 40, 42
Houston Street (New York), 25, 28, 29, 30, 43
Howard Street (San Francisco), 63, 70, 211, 223
Huber's Museum (New York), 24, 25
Hughes, Ed. R., 267
Hui Nalu Club (Honolulu), 244
Hung Far Low's (New York), 42, 43
Hunt, Joel, 271
Hunter, river (Australia), 178
Huntersville (Va.), 13
Hutchinson, Harold, 266
Hutson, Charles, 275

Idaho, University of (football team), 265
Idora Park (Oakland), 256
Illinois, University of (football team), 261, 272
Illinois Athletic Club (Chicago), 246, 251
Imlay, Tut, 265, 267
Indiana University (football team), 261, 263, 265, 266, 267
Indianapolis, 285
Industrial Workers of the World (IWW), 233
Ingram, Bill ("Navy Bill"), 261, 263, 265, 266, 267, 268, 269, 270
Innescara, 108

International Seaman's Federation, 198
Iowa, 47
Iowa, University of (football team), 262, 266, 272
Irish Fuseliers, 125
Iroquois Theater disaster (Chicago), 160
Isbell, Cecil, 261
Islais Creek (San Francisco), 212
Islam Temple, Shriners, 196, 197, 263, 276, 283
Isle of Dogs, 114
IWW, 233

J. H. Barrow (schooner), 111, 112, 117, 125, 127
Jacks, Noel C., 239, 240
Jackson, John A., "professor," 239
Jackson Street (San Francisco), 63, 68
Jacobs, Jack, 262, 292
James, Jessie and Frank, 7, 25, 191
Janowicz, Victor, 262
Japan, 283
Jessup, Edgar, 274
Joesting, Herb, 262, 271
Johnson, Lincoln V., 242-43, 251
Jones, Charles T., 39, 40, 41, 42
Jones, Edgar, 266
Jordan, Dorothy, 280
Juan de Fuca Strait, 224
Juan Fernández (island), 88
Jumbo (Goldfield, Nev.), 232
"Just Break the News to Mother" (song), 47

Kaffirs, 173
Kahanamoku, Duke, 243, 244, 246, 247, 251
Kanakas, 195, 196
Kansas, University of (football team), 262, 288
Kansas City, 285
Karloff, Boris, 280
Kazmaier, Richard (Dick), 261
Kearney Street (San Francisco), 63, 68, 204, 210
Keaton, Buster, 280
Keefe, William, 292
Kelley, Lawrence (Larry), 261
Kelly, Bill, 269
Kelly, Red, 229
Kendal, Tom, 231
Kennedy, Bob, 262
Kerr, Andy, 271, 272, 288, 289
Kezar Municipal Stadium (San Francisco), 268, 271, 281, 287
Kienley, Andie C., 263
Kilby, Mat, 12
Killarney (vessel), 109
Killman, Capt. ("Crazy") D. J., 224, 225, 226

302

Index

Index

Margate, 113
Marie Antoinette, 115
Marines, U.S., 210
Marino Hospital (San Francisco), 235
Marion (U.S. naval training ship), 214
Market Street (San Francisco), 64, 203, 205, 208, 210, 213, 214
Marks, Larry, 266, 267
Marquette University (football team), 266
Marsh, Joan, 280
Martin, Dr. Harry, 275
Martin, river (Ireland), 108
Martineau, Earl, 266
Marylebone Road (London), 115
Mashona (South African tribe), 173
Masters, Mates and Pilots Association, 190
Matabele (South African tribe), 173
Matson, Ollie, 262
Matthews, Rags, 271
Mautz, Bobby, 265
Mayer, Louis B., 277, 280
Meiggs Wharf (San Francisco), 75, 218, 222
Melbourne, 178
Merritt, Dr. Emma L., 244, 246, 247, 249, 250, 253
Merritt, Dr. George, 249
Merriwell, Frank, 7
Mersey, river, 131
Metro-Goldwyn-Mayer, 277
Michigan, Lake, 285
Michigan, University of (football team), 261, 266, 287
Michigan State College (football team), 262
Midway (San Francisco), 67, 204
Midway Plaisance (San Francisco), 203
Mike Lyons (New York), 43
Mike Saulter's (New York), 43, 44
Milford Haven, 111, 113, 115
Millie R. Bohannan (schooner), 21, 76
Mills Hotel (New York), 28, 32
Milwaukee, 285
Mine Owners Association, 233
Miner's Theater (New York), 29, 30
Minna Street (San Francisco), 206
Minneapolis, 285
Minnesota, University of (football team), 262, 266, 271, 272, 287
Mint (Goldfield, Nev.), 231
Mission Rock (San Francisco), 223
Mission Street (San Francisco), 206, 208, 213
Missouri, University of (football team), 288, 289, 290
Mix, Tom, 280
Mizen Head, 125
Mohawk (Goldfield, Nev.), 231, 232, 233

Molokai (Hawaiian Islands), 295
Monadnock Building (San Francisco), 254
Monadnock Hotel (San Francisco), 210
Moncrief, Monte, 262
Montana (San Francisco), 229
Montana State College (football team), 269
Montgomery, Robert, 295
Montgomery Street (San Francisco), 203, 204
Moore, Charles C., 251
Mopeha, island, 193, 195, 197
Moran, Polly, 279, 280, 295
Morse, Brick, 267
Morse, Franklin B., 267
Morse, Ray ("Butch"), 262
Morton Street (*later* Maiden Lane; San Francisco), 204
"Moth and the Flame, The" (song), 47
Mother Hall's (Newcastle, Australia), 179
Motion Picture Producers Association, 277
Motion-Picture Relief Fund, 280
Mott (swimmer), 247
Mott Street (New York), 29, 42
Moulin Rouge (Brussels), 120
Mulberry Street (New York), 39
Muldoon, Capt. Timothy, 112, 113, 116, 117, 119, 122, 125, 126
Muller, Harold ("Brick"), 261, 263, 265, 267
Municipal Lodging House *or* "City Dump" (New York), 33, 36, 42
Murphy, Eddie, 267
Murphy, Frank, 276, 277
Murrow, Ed, 190

Nagurski, Bronko, 262, 272
Nansemond County (Va.), 4, 5
Napoleon, 151
National Collegiate Athletic Association, 293
National Guard, U.S., 210
National Shrine Convention (San Francisco), 276
Naughton, "Big Bill," 296
Naval Academy, U.S., 269
Navy, U.S. (football team), 261, 269
Nebraska, 47-56, 295
Nebraska, University of (football team), 262, 266, 271
Needles, Jimmie, 265
Neilson, Capt., 159, 162, 163
Nevada, 57-58
Nevada, University of (football team), 265
Nevada ghost towns, 230
New Amsterdam Island, 177

Index

New Bowery (New York), 25, 44
New Orleans, 25, 287, 288, 289, 292
New Orleans Mid-Winter Sports Association, 288
New Orleans *Times-Picayune*, 292
New Rochelle, 253
New York (City), ix, 23-46, 63, 67, 138, 189, 282, 284, 285-86, 288, 289, 293. *See also separate entries on streets, theaters, saloons, and other sites.*
New York Athletic Club, 251
New Zealand, 195
Newcastle (Australia), 175, 176, 178, 179, 180, 294
Newland, Col. Russ, 296
Newman, "Cowboy," 229
Newport News, 15
Nickey (San Francisco entertainer), 67
Niobrara, river (Nebr.), 48
Nisbet, Archie, 265
Nixon, George, 231, 234
Nob Hill (San Francisco), 205-06, 213, 221
Noe Street (San Francisco), 222
Nome (Alaska), 231
Norfolk (Va.), 9, 14, 27
Norman, Nellie, 179
North Atlantic, 103
North Beach (San Francisco), 213, 218
North Carolina, University of (football team), 262
North Foreland, 113
North River (New York), 28
North Sea, 117, 131, 133, 134
Northern (saloon, Goldfield, Nev.), 231, 233
Northwestern University (football team), 261, 271, 289
Notre Dame, University of (football team), 261-62, 271, 272, 287
Nowack, Butch, 261
Nymphia (San Francisco), 68

"O, the anchor is weighed and the sails are set" ("Away-Rio"), 138, 139
O. K. (San Francisco), 228
Oakland, 209, 220, 256
Oakland Creeks, 203
Oakland *Tribune*, 211
Oberon Music Hall (San Francisco), 66
O'Brien, Jack, 228
O'Connell's Bridge (Dublin), 125
O'Connell's Hotel (Sydney), 179
Oddie, Tasker L., 231
O'Farrell Street (San Francisco), 66, 204
Ogden (Utah), 58
Ohio State University (football team), 262
Oklahoma, University of (football team), 262, 288

Olcott, Chauncey, 24
Old Absinthe House (New Orleans), 290
Old Cape Stiff, *see* Horn, Cape
Old Homestead, The, 24
Old Horseshoe (Reno), 58
Old Mother Smerden's (Liverpool), 128
Old Poodle Dog (San Francisco), 203, 204
Old South, 8
Old Tivoli Theater (San Francisco), 203
Olson, Gov. (Calif.), 287
Olympiad, Tenth (Los Angeles), 251, 276, 277, 281, 282
Olympic Boxing and Track and Field trials, 276, 282
Olympic Club (Lakeside), 242, 243, 265, 268, 274, 281
Olympic Club building (San Francisco), 238, 239, 242
Olympic Club's Athletic Committee, 263
Olympic Games, *see* Olympiad, Tenth
Omaha, 47, 285
On Leon Tong (New York), 43
O'Neill, James, 24
Opera House (San Francisco), 206
Oregon, University of (football team), 262, 265
Oregon State College (football team), 262, 265, 287
Oriental (Goldfield, Nev.), 231
Oriental Palace (Brussels), 120
Orpheum (San Francisco), 66, 203
Orsi, John, 261
O'Sullivan, Maureen, 278

Pacific, College of the (football team), 262
Pacific A.A.U., *see* Amateur Athletic Union, Pacific
Pacific Coast Conference (East-West game), 263
Pacific Grove (Calif.), 275
Pacific Street (San Francisco), 63, 64, 68, 204, 210, 227, 228, 234
Page, Anita, 280
Pago Pago, 195, 196
Palace (Goldfield, Nev.), 231
Palace Club (Reno), 58, 229
Palace Hotel (San Francisco), 206, 280
Palm Grill (Goldfield, Nev.), 231, 233, 234
Panama Canal, 171
Pan-American Exposition (Buffalo), 46
Panama Pacific International Exposition, 251
Papeete, 195, 196
Paradise Street (Liverpool), 126
Parente's (San Francisco), 204, 229
Park Commission, San Francisco, 252
Park Lane (Liverpool), 126

Index

Parker, Clarence ("Ace"), 261
Parker, James (Jim), 47, 48, 66
Parsons, Louella, 278
Pasadena, 269, 287
Pastor, Tony (New York), 24
Patrick, Albert T., 40, 41
Patrick, Jack, 265
Pawnee Bill's Wild West Show, 175
Peabody, Endicott ("Chub"), 261, 287
Peachtree Street (Atlanta), 19
Pearl Harbor, 287
Pelham Club (New York), 43
Pell Street (New York), 29, 42, 43
Pennsylvania, University of (football team), 262
People's Theater, The (New York), 29
Personne, rue d'Une (Brussels), 121
Peru, 136
Peter Iredale (vessel), 118
Peters, Frosty, 272
Petersen, Capt., 192
Philadelphia, 21-23, 76, 253
Philippines, 283
Phillies (baseball team), 23
Phillips, chief engineer, 239
Phoenix (Goldfield, Nev.), 231
Phoenix Park (Dublin), 125
Pickford, Mary, 278
Pig Point (Va.), 8, 12
Pihos, Peter, 261
Pikes Peak (Colo.), 56
Pingel, John, 262
Pinkley Alley (San Francisco), *see* Hinkley and Pinkley alleys
Pittman, Key, 231, 234
Pittsburgh, University of (football team), 266, 292
Pittsburgh Pirates (baseball team), 23
Place Verte (Antwerp), 119
Plate, river (Río de la Plata), 99, 103
Plaza de Toros (Guaymas), 184
Plaza Hotel (San Francisco), 210
Plymouth (England), 113
Pomeroy, Walter, 242
Pool, Hampton, 262
Port Costa, 72, 74
Port Elizabeth, 176
Portland (Ore.), 118, 236, 251
Portsmouth (Va.), 3, 5, 9, 13, 14, 20, 21, 27
Portsmouth Rifles (regiment), 9
Portsmouth Square (San Francisco), 218, 285
Potter, Bill, 78, 83
Powell, H., 266
Powell Street (San Francisco), 66, 204
President Taft (vessel), 283
Presnell, Glen, 271
Presidio (San Francisco), 210, 281
Princess Docks (Liverpool), 129

Princeton University (football team), 261
Puget Sound, 224
Pup (San Francisco), 204
Purcell, Lew, 68, 204
Purdue University (football team), 261

Quai Van Dyck (Antwerp), 117
Quantico, 291
Queen's Surf (Honolulu), 197
Queenstown (Ireland), 72, 103, 106, 107, 294

R. C. Slade (schooner), 165, 189, 190, 192, 197
Raft, George, 280
Raithel (Illinois swimmer), 247, 251
Randels, Ray, 271
Rawhide (Nev.), 230, 233
Rawlins, William J., 244
Ray, Carl, 262
Reagan, Frank, 262
Red Top (Goldfield, Nev.), 232
Redondo Beach Natatorium, 243
Reese, Gil, 266
Reinhard, Bob, 287
Reno, ix, 57, 58, 229, 266
Resleure (San Francisco swimmer), 251
"Reuben-Ranzo" (song), 139
Rhodes, Cecil, 174
Rialto (New York), 24
Rice, George Graham, 233
Rice, Grantland, 287, 296
Rice, William Marsh, 40, 41, 42
Richards, Ray, 262
Rickard, Tex, 231, 232, 233, 296
Riegels, Roy, 261
Riley, Mike, 229
Rincon Hall (San Francisco), 205
Río de la Plata (river Plate), 99, 103
Rivington Street (New York), 35
Roanoke (vessel), 234, 234n.
Robertson, Bob, 292
Robinson, Edgar G. (Eddie), 279
Robinson Crusoe, 88
Rockford (Ill.), 274
Rokeby (Nev.), 57, 58
Rokisky, John, 287, 292
Rolph, Jr., Gov. James, 275, 278, 280
Rolph, Mayor "Sunny" Jim, 189, 266, 295
Rolph Street (San Francisco), 245, 257
Rondebosch, 174
Roosevelt, Franklin D., 280-81
Roosevelt, Theodore, 44, 233
Roosevelt Hotel (Hollywood), 278
Roosevelt Hotel (New Orleans), 290
Rose Bowl (Pasadena), 269, 287
Roseville (Calif.), 59
Ross, Norman, 25
Rossi, Mayor, 281
Rote, Kyle, 262

306

Index

Index

Index

ABOUT THE AUTHOR

1900–1902: *Hobo.*
Bowery bum.
Singing waiter.
Sheepherder.

1902–1910: *Shanghaied onto sailing ship; three times around the Horn and once around the world as able seaman and mate.*

1906: *San Francisco earthquake survivor.*

1910: *Day laborer.*

1911–1914: *Y.M.C.A. swimming instructor.*

1914–1917: *Manager, Sutro Baths, San Francisco.*

1917–1922: *Salesman.*

1922–1933: *Regional sales manager.*

1925–1955: *Managing Director, Shrine East-West football game.*

1928–1932: *President, Pacific Association of Amateur Athletic Union of the U.S.A.*

1932: *Assistant Manager of the U. S. Olympic swimming team.*

1933–1949: *Pacific District Manager, Underwood Corporation.*

1935: *Potentate of Islam Shrine Temple, San Francisco.*

1942–1955: *Board of Governors, Shriners Hospitals for Crippled Children.*

1946: *Voted Football's Man of the Year by the Football Writers of America.*

1950–1955: *Special executive representing the officers of the Underwood Corporation.*

1950: *President, San Francisco Park Commission.*

1955: *Director, San Francisco Maritime Commission.*